بسم الله الرحمن الرحيم

Man's Natural Disposition

(FIṬRAH)

Man's Natural Disposition
(FIṬRAH)

Murtaḍa Muṭahharī

Translated by
Mansoor Limba

British Library Cataloguing-in-Publication Data
A catalogue record for this book is available from the British Library.

Ordering Information:
Quantity sales. Special discounts are available on quantity purchases by corporations, associations, and others. For details, contact the distributor at the address below.

Shia Books Australia
www.shiabooks.com.au
info@shiabooks.com.au

ISBN 978-1-922583-20-8

First Edition 2013
Second Edition 2021

Contents

Transliteration IX
Foreword XI
Translator's Foreword 1
About the Author 4
Preface 8
Chapter 1: The Meaning of *Fiṭrah* 10
Natural Disposition *(Fiṭrah)* and Upbringing *(Tarbiyah)* 11
The Word *Fiṭrah* 14
Ibn Athīr's Words 16
Ibn 'Abbās' Words 20
The Late Shaykh 'Abbās al-Qummī's Statement 21
Fiṭrah, Ṣibghah and *Ḥanīf* 22
The Meaning of *Ḥanīf* 25
Ṭabī'ah, Gharīzah and *Fiṭrah* 27
1. *Ṭabī'ah* 27
2. *Gharīzah* 29
3. *Fiṭrah* 31
Does Human Being Have Dispositions *(Fiṭriyyāt)*? 31
Chapter 2: Man's Dispositions 36
Is Having Conscience a Proof of Innateness? 38
Human Being as the Most Unknown Creature 40
Man's Dispositions in the Context of Knowledge and Knowing 42
Plato's View 43
Muslim Philosophers' View 44

Qur'anic View 46
The Deniers' View and its Repercussion 49
Dispositions in the Context of Wants and Desires 54
Chapter 3: Sacred Inclinations 59
Human Being's Superiorities 62
Emotional Dispositions 65
1. Truth-Seeking 65
2. Inclination Toward Good and Virtue 70
3. Inclination Toward Beauty and Aesthetic Value 71
4. Inclination Toward Creativity and Innovation 73
5. Love and Worship 75
Chapter 4: Love and Worship as Proof of Human Inclinations 79
Theories on the Nature of Love 80
The Lover's Annihilation in the Beloved 85
Wiliam James' Statement 88
Russell's Statement 89
Justification for the Abovementioned Five Subjects 89
Justification Based Upon Negation of Emotional Inclinations 90
Audacious and Non-Audacious Sensualists 93
Nietzsche's Statement 94
A Tradition Concerning the Human Being's Creation 96
The Parable of Rūmī 98
Chapter 5: Spiritual Love: Marxism and the Permanence of Human Values 101
Another Analysis of the Nature of Spiritual Love 102
Love According to the Mystics 108
Are Human Values Changing? 110
Dr. Hashtrūdī and its Refutation 113
Chapter 6: The Evolution of Human Originality 119
A Comparison Between Nietzsche's and Marxists' Views 120
The Meaning of Evolution of Human Originality 122
Types of Evolution of Human Society 123
1. Evolution in Man's Relationship with Nature 123
2. Evolution in Collective's Structural Relationship 124
3. Evolution in Humanness 126

Natural Disposition and the Evolution of Human Society in Humanness ... 129
Marxism and the Evolution of Human Society in Humanness ... 130
Existentialism and Human Originality ... 131
Human Essences as Intrinsic ... 138
Chapter 7: The Foundation and Origin of Religion ... 140
Losing the Self Means Forgetting the Self ... 142
Rūmī's Statement ... 144
Origin of Religion According to Feuerbach ... 147
Refuting Feuerbach's Theory ... 149
Religion as a Product of Ignorance According to Auguste Comte and Spencer ... 151
Religion as Originated from Weakness and Fear According to Russell ... 155
Criticism and Analysis ... 157
The Qur'an and the Question of Knowing God ... 159
Chapter 8: Love and Worship ... 167
Another Review of the Issue of Love ... 167
Real Worship ... 172
The Parable of Sa'dī ... 175
The Story of Zulaykhā ... 179
Chapter 9: The Innate Nature of Religion ... 181
Marxism and the Origin of Religion ... 182
Refuting the Marxist Theory ... 184
Is Religion a Product of Ignorance? ... 188
Will Durant's Statement ... 190
Chapter 10: An Examination and Refutation of Durkheim's Theory ... 195
Nominal and Real Compositions ... 195
What Kind of Composition is the Human Society? ... 197
The Origin of Religion According to Durkheim ... 199
Refuting Durkheim's Theory ... 204
Human Being as Having a Multilayered 'Self' ... 206
The Qur'anic View ... 207
Summary ... 208
Chapter 11: The Qur'anic View on the Origin Of Religion ... 213

Transliteration

Symbol	Transliteration	Symbol	Transliteration
ء	’	أ	a
ب	b	ت	t
ث	th	ج	j
ح	ḥ	خ	kh
د	d	ذ	dh
ر	r	ز	z
س	s	ش	sh
ص	ṣ	ض	ḍ
ط	ṭ	ظ	ẓ
ع	‘	غ	gh
ف	f	ق	q
ك	k	ل	l
م	m	ن	n
ه	h	و	w
ي	y	ة	ah
Long Vowels		Short Vowels	
آ	a	ـَ	a
اي	ī	ـِ	i
او	ū	ـُ	u
Persian Letters			
Symbol	**Transliteration**	**Symbol**	**Transliteration**
پ	p	چ	ch
ژ	zh	گ	g

At the end of Farsi words, 'eh', '-e', and '-ye' have been used.

Foreword

Considering necessity of preparing appropriate Islamic texts in English for the modern world and aiming at satisfying that need, Al-Mustafa International Research Institute (M.I.R.I.) decided to establish "Islam and West Research Centre" in 2009. This centre has accomplished that duty in the best way by producing, translating, and reprinting tens of such appropriate texts. The present book is among works translated and published by Islam and West Research Centre.

Man's Natural Disposition is a translation of the Persian book *Fiṭra* which consists of 10-session lecture series given by the great Muslim thinker and reformer Āyatullāh Murtaḍā Muṭahharī in 1976-77.

Some of the topics discussed in this book are as follows: *fiṭra* and upbringing, man's dispositions, love and worship as proof of sacred inclinations, spiritual love, and Qur'anic view on the origin of religion.

We hope that this book would be an invaluable contribution to the Islamic thought and of great benefit for all readers in general and people of research in particular.

Al-Mustafa International Research Institute (M.I.R.I.)

Translator's Foreword

The present volume is an English rendition of the 274-page Persian book *Fiṭrat* by the great Muslim thinker and reformer, Āyatullāh al-Shahīd Murtaḍā Muṭahharī, 16th printing (Tehran: Ṣadrā Publications, Mehr 1385 S.A.H (circa February 2006)).

I was first acquainted with the book when I was translating in 2013 the first volume of Dr. 'Alī Rabbānī Gulpāygānī's *Discursive Theology* (Makati City, Philippines: Al-Mustafa International College, 2013), which quotes it at some length in Lesson 3 (Natural Disposition *(Fiṭrah)* and Knowing God), pages 31-43.

Unless otherwise stated, the translation of Qur'anic passages is adapted from Sayyid 'Alī Qulī Qarā'ī's *The Qur'an with a Phrase-by-Phrase English Translation* (London: Islamic College for Advanced Studies, 2004). The translation of quotations from *Nahj al-Balāghah* is based on that of Syed 'Ali Raza (Qum: Foundation of Islamic Cultural Propagation in the World, 1995). For the poetic quotations from Sa'dī's *Gulistān*, *Būstān*, Rūmī's *Mathnāwī-ye Ma'nawī*, and the *Dīwān* of Ḥāfiẓ, the translations of Edward Rehatsek [*Gulistān or Rose Garden of Sa'dī* (Tehran: Peyk-e Farhang, 1998)], Henry Wilberforce Clarke [*The Būstān of Sa'dī* (Tehran: Peyk-e Farhang, 2004)] and Reynold A. Nicholson, *The Mathnawī of Jalālu'ddīn Rūmī* (Tehran: Soad

Publisher, 2002), and Henry Wilberforce Clarke [*The Dīwān of Ḥāfiẓ* (Tehran: Aban Book, 2005)], respectively, are hereby adapted.

In a number of places, words or expressions marked by brackets were added to the text either to fill a gap or to render the meaning clearer.

Footnotes with the sign "[Trans.]" are not those of the author, and thus, not in the original Persian text, but provided by the translator to facilitate better understanding for the English readers. Footnotes in brackets are those of Āyatullāh Murtaḍā Muṭahharī's Works Supervisory Council or the publisher.

It needs mentioning that this project could not have been realized had it not been for the full support and trust given by Ḥujjat al-Islām wa'l-Muslimīn Dr. Mohsen Miri, Head of "Islam and West Research Centre" in Al-Mustafa International Research Institute Institute (M.I.R.I.), for giving me an ample time to render the last stroke of my pen. Utmost gratitude also goes to Professor Hamidreza Ayatollahy, former Director of the Tehran-based Institute of Humanities and Cultural Studies (IHCS), for facilitating the signing of the translation contract.

I am also indebted to Mohammad Meftah of the Qum-based International Institute of Islamic Studies for his most helpful translation consultancy, to Salahaddin Limba for proofreading the initial manuscript and to the editor, Amir Dastmalchian, who went through the manuscript most meticulously. Yet, any error that may be detected in the text is mine.

Mansoor L. Limba
January 31, 2015
Rabī' al-Thānī 10, 1436 (A.H.)

About the Author

Professor Āyatullāh Murtaḍā Muṭahharī (1298-1358 S.A.H) was born to a family of clergymen on Bahman 13, 1298 S.A.H [February 3, 1920] in the village of Farīmān near Mashhad. At the age of 12, he went to Mashhad where he learned the basics of Islamic sciences and then moved to Qum where he attended the sessions of the great authorities of the theological center.

From 1319 S.A.H [1940] Muṭahharī attended the sessions held by Imām Khomeinī and other famous teachers of the time. Moreover, he himself gave lectures in subjects like Arabic literature, logic, *kalām* (scholasticism), jurisprudence (*fiqh*), and philosophy.

In 1331 S.A.H (1952) Muṭahharī moved to Tehran and in 1334 S.A.H (1955) he was invited to teach Islamic sciences at the Faculty of Islamic Sciences, Tehran University. He was arrested at midnight on Khordād 15, 1342 S.A.H (1963) and remained in prison for 43 days. After Imām Khomeinī's migration to Paris in France, Muṭahharī went to meet him, and the Imām assigned him the responsibility of organizing the Revolutionary Council.

On the night of Ordībehesht 11, 1358 S.A.H (May 1, 1979) Muṭahharī was martyred by one of the agents of the terrorist Furqān group. He wrote more than 50 books and tens of articles, and delivered scores of speeches.

A cursory examination of the 22-volume *Ṣaḥīfeh-ye Imām*[1]—the largest ever compiled anthology of Imām Khomeinī's speeches, messages, interviews, religious decrees, permissions, and letters—reveals that the martyred Professor Muṭahharī undoubtedly occupied a distinct station in the sight of the Great Leader of the Islamic Revolution and the Idol-Breaker of the 20th Century.

Imām Khomeinī's communications with Āyatullāh Muṭahharī in the form of religious permissions (*ijāzāt*) and personal letters as well as descriptions of him in the Imām's letters, speeches, messages, statements, interviews, autobiography, and memorial note during and after Muṭahharī's lifetime as indicated in the encyclopedic authentic reference source suggest that the former considered the latter a trustworthy representative, compassionate teacher, erudite scholar, competent jurist, eloquent speaker, combatant *'ālim*, and an epitome of martyrdom in the way of truth and freedom of thought.

These benevolent views regarding him are consistent in an encyclopedic reference source of Imām Khomeinī's works—from the first volume of the anthology in which Professor Muṭahharī is indicated having been granted authority (*ijāzah*) on Dhu'l-Ḥijjah 24, 1388 S.A.H (March 13, 1969) by the Imām in the financial and religious law affairs, up to the 21st volume (volume 22 being the indexes of the whole voluminous treatise) wherein he—in the Imām's message dated Shahrīvar 14, 1367 S.A.H (September 5, 1988) addressed to the Muslim nation of Pakistan and the *'ulamā'* of Islam on the occasion of the martyrdom of Sayyid 'Ārif Ḥusayn Ḥusaynī—is mentioned as having been among "the freedom loving *'ulamā'* of

1. *Ṣaḥīfeh-ye Imām: An Anthology of Imām Khomeinī's Speeches, Messages, Interviews, Religious Decrees, Permissions, and Letters*, volumes 1-22 (Tehran: The Institute for Compilation and Publication of Imām Khomeinī's Works, 2007). [Trans.]

the Islamic world subjected to conspiracy and terrorism".

To the Imām, Shahīd Muṭahharī was more than a student, representative, associate, confidant, friend, or son. Indeed, it can be said that to him, Muṭahharī could not be confined to a single dimension as he embodied a totality of aspects. Muṭahharī is Muṭahharī.

***

A PhD holder in International Relations (University of Tehran) who also earned units in MA Islamic Studies, Mansoor L. Limba, the translator, has tens of written and translation works to his credit on such subjects as international politics, history, political philosophy, jurisprudence (*fiqh*), scholastic theology (*'ilm al-kalām*), Qur'anic sciences, *ḥadīth*, ethics, and mysticism.

Limba's English rendition of the Persian book *Shī'eh Pasukh Mīdahad* (*The Shī'ah Rebuts*) by Dr. Sayyid Riḍā Ḥusaynī Nasab (Tehran: Ahl al-Bayt (A.S.)[1] World Assembly, 2007) was recognized as best translation of the year in the Shaykh al-Ṭūsī International Festival (Qum, 2008) while his paper "*Mahdawiyyah* as Final Vocabulary: A Postmodernist Reading of Islamic Iran's Foreign Policy Principles" was awarded "best paper" at the 5th International Conference on the Doctrine of *Mahdawiyyah* (Tehran, 2009).

The present volume is the fourth work by Āyatullāh Muṭahharī that the translator has translated into English, the others being the books *Iḥyā-ye Tafakkur-e Islām* (*The Revival of Islamic Thought*) (Tehran: Ahl al-Bayt (A.S.) World Assembly, *forthcoming*), *Naẓariyyeh-ye Shinākht* (*The Theory of Knowledge: An Islamic Perspective*) and *Ta'līm wa Tarbiyat dar Islām* (*Training and

1. The abbreviation, "'*a*" stands for the Arabic invocative phrase, *'alayhi's-salām, 'alayhim'us-salām,* or *'alayhā's-salām* (may peace be upon him/them/her), which is mentioned after the names of the prophets, angels, Imāms from the Prophet's progeny, and saints *(A.S.)*. [Trans.]

Education in Islam) (Tehran: Institute of Humanities and Cultural Studies and Ahl al-Bayt (A.S.) University, 2012). He is currently translating the author's *Falsafeh-ye Akhlāq* (*Philosophy of Ethics*) (London: MIU Press, *forthcoming*).

Preface

Fiṭrah is the theme of a 10-session lecture series given by the martyred thinker Professor Murtaḍā Muṭahharī in 1355-56 S.A.H (circa 1976-77) in the presence of teachers of Nīkān School in Tehran, and apparently due to his engagement in the Islamic movement and his increasing social involvements, it was not continued.

The issue of *fiṭrah* – which in the words of the professor is a primary issue *(umm al-masā'il)* in Islamic studies – had been discussed by him on four occasions from various perspectives. One [such occasion] was with the Islamic Association of Physicians; another was in the Islamic seminary of Qum (which has more Qur'anic dimension and whose audio cassette recording was no longer extant but the notes taken by his students do still exist); the third [occasion] was in Nīkān School and the fourth was in a series of meetings in Tehran known as Yazdīs' Meeting. By the way, the martyred professor's lecture notes on this topic do exist as well.

Initially, we intended to present all the above-mentioned discussions in a single volume, but since the content and style of each discussion differ with each other while having certain commonalities, we deemed it better to choose the most favourable of the four occasions to be printed, and include the other three occasions as well as the author's lecture notes in the publication of [Shahīd Muṭahharī's] Collection of Works.

Much earlier and in the initial years of the victory of the Islamic

Revolution – when the publication of the martyred professor's works had no such desirable arrangement – a book with the same title and marred with many typographical mistakes was published under the name of the martyred professor by one of the Islamic associations. Of course, after the expression of opinion of the Supervisory Council, its publication was suspended.

It is hoped that this work of the martyred professor, as with other works of the martyred erudite thinker, could help us in understanding further the valuable Islamic science which is the foundation of the sacred Islamic Revolution. As such, through necessary enlightenment, we could step further toward the lofty goals of Islam on its correct path. By doing so, apart from discharging a religious responsibility, we could be able to convey to the whole world the message of oppression of the martyrdom of that bright star in the sky of knowledge and action, and earn the pleasure of his soul and that of our late great leader, Imām Khomeinī (may Allah be pleased with him) who emphasized time and again the need to study the professor's works and who considered him part of his body.

Supervisory Council of Āyatullāh Murtaḍā Muṭahharī's Works

Mordād 1369 S.A.H (circa July-August 1990)

Chapter 1: The Meaning of *Fiṭrah*

The subject of the discussion is *fiṭrah*. The topic of *fiṭrah*, on one hand, is a philosophical discussion...[1] The important topics of philosophy are these three, viz. God, the universe, and man. This topic is a discussion related to "man" and it can be said that from one perspective and from one dimension, it is related to man and God. One of its primary concerns is man and the other is God. In Islamic sources, that is the Qur'an and the *Sunnah*, the essence of *fiṭrah* has been much emphasized, and in this session I shall touch on some of them which I have taken notes of before. That the Qur'an acknowledges the human being having *fiṭrah* (natural disposition) is a kind of unique perspective on the human being.

What kind of word is *fiṭrah*, and prior to [the revelation of] the Qur'an, was there anyone who had used it in relation to the human being, or is it among the things which the Qur'an has used for the first time in relation to the human being? Apparently, this word had no precedence prior to the Qur'an and it has been used by the Qur'an for the first time in relation to the human being. I shall present later its Qur'anic references.

At the outset, we must first try to know what kind of word *fiṭrah* is, and we must acquire its exact root-word.

---

1. [Interruption in the audio cassette recording.]

Another concern which we must touch on here is this – is the human being in general has a series of *fiṭrahs*– which we will define – or not and does he lacks any sort of *fiṭrah*?[1]

Our third discussion is about the nature of religion. Is religion innate [in human nature] or not? The Qur'an has explicitly mentioned that religion is indeed innate [in human nature]. We must have an academic discussion on man and religion and let us try to find out if religion is basically innate [in human nature] or not.

Natural Disposition *(Fiṭrah)* and Upbringing *(Tarbiyah)*

Of course, this issue has many ramifications in various fields; one of which is the discussion on training and education which is a broad discussion. If the human being has a series of *fiṭrahs*, it follows then that his training must definitely be done by taking into consideration this set of *fiṭrahs*. The root of the word *tarbiyah* – if ever it is used consciously or unconsciously – is also grounded on this, because *tarbiyah* means to bring up and to train, and this based upon the acknowledgment of a set of talents – and in today's parlance, a set of characteristics – in the human being.

Tarbiyah (training) is different from *ṣan'ah* (craftsmanship) for in *ṣan'ah*, the reckoning is that of building [or making something]. That is, a person has a purpose in mind. Then he uses a set of materials in order to realize his objective in mind while not paying attention to each of these materials – whether it maximizes its potentials or not with this function that it performs; [it makes no difference for the craftsman] if a material maximizes its potentials or not. 'My' purpose must be realized.

1. We do not consider other [Persian] words such as *sarshat* and the like as its synonyms because we have not yet completely defined the word *fiṭrah*.

The objective of a carpenter, an architect, or a builder whose work is a sort of construction must be provided for. It is not important for him if he enhances the essence or nature a certain amount of lumber, steel, cement, and the like, thereby maximizing its potentials or not. In fact, sometimes it is necessary for him to minimize the potentials of a material so as to use if for his own purpose.

While having his own purpose or objective in mind as well as particular interest, however, the work of a gardener is based upon the enhancement of the flower or plant's nature. That is, he takes into consideration the flower or plant's nature. He knows the way to its growth and perfection as provided by nature, and nurtures it along the same natural, and in a sense intrinsic, way and makes use of it.

I have mentioned this example before. There is a time when a person regards a sheep as something for itself and there is also a time when he considers the same as something for a human being. If we want to consider a sheep according to its own interest, is it to its own interest to be caponized? Not at all. By caponizing it, first of all we devalue it and [secondly] we make it imperfect. That is, we take out from it one of the essential tools which nature provides for it and which must be there and makes it perfect, and we regard it as something for ourselves. We do not care if the sheep is perfect or imperfect; [we say,] "I want to fatten it and get more meat out of it; as such, I have to caponize it so that it will no longer look for a female sheep and concentrate only in chewing; it would eat more, become more fat and have more meat so that when I slaughter this sheep, it could give us more meat."

The same is true in the human beings. A person can be moulded in two ways:

1. To build him in the way same things are built or constructed.

That is, the builder only takes into consideration his own objective. He moulds a person in such a way that would advance his own objective. He wants to attain his objective either through the imperfection of what he moulds, or the opposite.

2. Those who believe in the primacy of the collective – and this primacy of the collective ends up in the primacy of a particular class which is the same ruling class – want to mould human beings in such a way that could serve better the interest of the ruling class, or in their own words, in a way that would be beneficial to the society. We will discuss this point in the future – is there any contradiction between individual and collective perfection, or none? Are we compelled in many instances to render an individual imperfect so as to pave way to the society's perfection, or there is no such thing? They say that the society is in need of such and such individuals. What type of individuals? For example, they say that the society is in need of absolutely disciplined soldiers who unconditionally obey the order from higher authority and who do not think of anything else other than the order of their commander. Now, if a person wants to have the primacy of freewill and intellect in the sense that he must have independence in terms of reasoning and thinking, and to think why he is doing a certain thing, or to have a set of human emotions, then he could not be of any use in this function [of being a totally soldier], and in their own words, "He is of no use for the society." In their opinion, the individuals who are useful for the society are those who devoid of intellection and emotion. If they give him a bomb and tell him to go and drop it in a city, he would not think about the sin or offence that the people committed, if ever they did; he would no longer think who will be killed – male or female, old, young or child. He should neither think [of these things] nor have an iota of emotion. Just as they caponize the sheep so as for it to get fatter and produce more meat, they rub an

individual of his or her human emotions and feelings, thereby rendering him or her like a preying animal (*istisbā'*)[1] which is totally bereft of any independence or autonomy to think [for its own safety]. It is only then that a person would be totally useful for them.

This, however, is not based upon *tarbiyah* in its real sense. *Tarbiyah* signifies nurturing of the real potentials of a person. If he has rational or intellectual potentiality and he has the ability to question matters, these must be nurtured, instead of eradicating these potentials. If ever he has a human affection (like compassion), this must be nurtured. Of course, these must be moderated.

My intention is to explore the compatibility between the issue of *fiṭrah* and that of *tarbiyah*, which we will discuss separately.

One of the important issues in today's philosophy of man and sociology is the issue of "evolution of history". If we believe in the human being as having *fiṭrah*, we must justify the "evolution of history" in a particular way, and if we do not subscribe to *fiṭrah* – as many of today's schools of thought totally negates *fiṭrah* for the human being – we must justify the "evolution of history" in a different way. These are discussions which I concisely pointed out.

The Word *Fiṭrah*

Now, we shall begin with the first issue. What kind of word is the word *fiṭrah* as it appears in the Qur'an?

﴿ فِطْرَةَ اللَّهِ الَّتِي فَطَرَ النَّاسَ عَلَيْهَا لَا تَبْدِيلَ لِخَلْقِ اللَّهِ ﴾

...the origination of Allah according to which He

1. The Persian word *istisbā'* is used to refer to a preying animal (such as rabbit) which upon facing a predator (such as a lion) tends to lose its composure – to realize that it is facing a predator and to find a way to escape and save its life – and to remain standing as the predator approaches and sometimes even to approach its predator. It signifies self-defeatism, lack of self-confidence and loss of willpower. [Trans.]

originated mankind. (30:30)

The root-word *faṭara* (فطر) is repeatedly mentioned in the Qur'an:

﴿ فَطَرَهُنَّ ﴾

...originated them. (21:56)

﴿ فَاطِرِ السَّمَاوَاتِ وَالأَرْضِ ﴾

...the originator of the heavens and the earth. (6:14, and five other verses)

﴿ إِذَا السَّمَاءُ انْفَطَرَتْ ﴾

When the sky is rent apart. (82:1)

﴿ مُنْفَطِرٌ بِهِ ﴾

...wherein will be rent apart. (73:18)

In all instances, origination (*ibdāʿ*) and creation (*khalq*) are embedded in the meaning of the word. In a sense, *ibdāʿ* means creation without any precedence. The word *fiṭrah* with this form (*ṣīghah*) – that is, upon the rhythm of *fiʿlah* – only appears in one verse and it refers to the human being and religion by saying that the religion is "the origination of Allah" *(fiṭrat Allāh):*

﴿ فَأَقِمْ وَجْهَكَ لِلدِّينِ حَنِيفًا فِطْرَةَ اللهِ الَّتِي فَطَرَ النَّاسَ عَلَيْهَا لاَ تَبْدِيلَ لِخَلْقِ اللهِ ﴾

So set your heart on the religion as a people of pure faith, the origination of Allah according to which He originated mankind. There is no altering Allah's creation. (30:30)

We shall later present at some length the exegesis of this verse.

Those who are familiar with the Arabic language know that the rhythm (*wazn*) *fi'lah* signifies a type or kind. *Jalsah* means sitting while *jilsah* means a particular kind of sitting.

جَلَسْتُ جِلْسَةَ زَيْدٍ،

"I sat the way Zayd sat."

Ibn Mālik says in *Alfiyyah*,[1] thus:

وَفَعْلَةٌ لِمَرَّةٍ كَجَلْسَة   وَفِعْلَةٌ لِهَيْئَةٍ كَجِلْسَة[2]

As we have said, in the Qur'an the word *fiṭrah* appears in relation to the human being and his relationship with religion:

﴿ فِطْرَةَ اللهِ الَّتِي فَطَرَ النَّاسَ عَلَيْهَا ﴾

That is, in the same particular type of origination that we have given to the human being; in other words, the human being is created in a unique way. This term that they describe today as "man's characteristics" – if we believe in the human being as having a set of characteristics in the essence of creation – suggests to mean *fiṭrah*. Man's *fiṭrah* means the characteristics which exist in the essence of man's creation or origination.

Ibn Athīr's Words

One of the authoritative books which have been written on *ḥadīth* terminology is a book entitled *Al-Nihāyah* by Ibn Athīr – who is somehow famous and since we want to cite evidence from

---

1. *Al-Khulāṣat al-Alfiyyah*, better known shortly as *Alfiyyah*, is a rhymed book of Arabic grammar written by Ibn Mālik (Abū 'Abd Allāh Jamāl al-Dīn Muḥammad ibn Mālik) in the 13th century. Having at least 43 commentaries written about it, this work is one of the two major foundations of a beginner's education in Arab societies until the 20 th century. [Trans.]
2. 'Abd al-Laṭīf ibn Muḥammad al-Khaṭīb, *Matn Alfiyyat Ibn Mālik* (Kuwait: Maktabat Dār al-'Arūbah Li'n-Nashr wa't-Tawzī', 2006), 33 - *Abniyat al-Maṣādir*, line 455. [Trans.]

authoritative sources, we quote from this book[1] – just as *Al-Mufradāt*[2] by Rāghib al-Iṣfahānī is a very fine treatise on the terminology of the Qur'an. Rāghib closely scrutinized the etymology of Qur'anic terms while Ibn Athīr did the same for *ḥadīth* terminologies.

In *Al-Nihāyah*, Ibn Athīr appropriately quotes this famous tradition:

كُلُّ مَوْلُودٍ يُولَدُ عَلَى ٱلْفِطْرَةِ...

"Everyone born is born in [the state of] *fiṭrah*..."[3]

That is, every person born is born in the Islamic state of *fiṭrah* but his parents (external factors) make him deviant by making him a Jew, a Christian, or a Magian. We shall discuss this tradition later. As he quotes this tradition, he defines the word *fiṭrah*, thus:

أَلْفِطْرُ: أَلْإِبْتِدَاءُ وَالْإِخْتِرَاعُ.

"*Fiṭr*: initiation and creation."

That is, initial creation. What is meant by "initial creation" – which is also occasionally called *ibdā'* – is non-imitational creation. God's handiwork is *fiṭr*; it is *ikhtirā'* (invention or creation) but that of a human being is usually *taqlīd* (imitation). Even in a human

1. There were three brothers who were all known as Ibn Athīr, each of whom was a prominent Muslim scholar. They were 'Izz al-Dīn, Majd al-Dīn and Ḍiyā' al-Dīn. *Kāmil al-Tawārīkh* and *Usd al-Ghābah* are written by 'Izz al-Dīn while *Jāmi' al-Uṣūl* which is a book on *ḥadīth* and *Al-Nihāyah* which is one of the fine and rigorous books which explain *ḥadīth* terminology are authored by Majd al-Dīn.
2. *Al-Mufradāt*, or *Al-Mufradāt fī Gharīb al-Qur'ān* in full, is a dictionary of Qur'anic terms by the Muslim scholar Rāghib al-Iṣfahānī (Abū'l-Qāsim al-Ḥusayn ibn Mufaḍḍal ibn Muḥammad), which is widely considered prominent among works of Qur'an-related Arabic lexicography. [Trans.]
3. *Ṣaḥīḥ al-Bukhārī*, "Kitāb al-Janā'iz," sections (*abwāb*) 80, 93.

invention, there are elements of imitation. What does it mean?

Human handiworks are an imitation of nature. In other words, earlier there is something which exists in nature and the human being takes it as the model and designs something on the basis of it, builds something, or carves something. Occasionally, a person invents or innovates also and has the ability to invent and innovate, but basic foundations of any human invention or innovation is the nature itself. That is, he copies it from nature. (In Islamic sciences – in *Nahj al-Balāghah*[1] and the like – this point has been much highlighted and definitely such is the case.) [But] God's handiwork is not copied from any other's handiwork, for whatever exists is His handiwork and there is nothing which precedes His handiwork.

As such, the word *fiṭr* is equivalent to initiation and invention; that is, an action which is not imitated from something else.

Ibn Athīr then says, thus:

> وَٱلْفِطْرَةُ ٱلْحَالَةُ مِنْهُ كَالْجِسْلَةِ وَٱلرِّكْبَةِ.
>
> "And *fiṭrah* means a [unique] state [or type] of it (creation) such in the case of [the words] *jislah* (a particular way of sitting) and *rikbah* (a particular way of standing)."[2]

---

1. *Nahj al-Balāghah* (The Peak of Eloquence) is a collection of speeches, sayings and letters of the Commander of the Faithful, Imām 'Alī ibn Abī Ṭālib *(A.S.)* compiled by Sharīf al-Raḍī Muḥammad ibn al-Ḥusayn (d. 406 AH/1016). Its contents concern the three essential topics of God, man and the universe, and include comments on scientific, literary, social, ethical, and political issues. With the exception of the words of the Glorious Qur'an and of the Holy Prophet (S), no words of man can equal it in eloquence. So far, over a hundred commentaries have been written on the *Nahj al-Balāghah*, indicating the importance of this treatise to scholars and learned men of research and investigation. For further information, visit: http://www.al-islam.org/nahjul. [Trans.]
2. I mention these in particular so that when we define it (*fiṭrah*) it later, you would know that the said definition is based upon literal meaning of the word.

وَٱلْمَعْنَىٰ أَنَّهُ يُولَدُ عَلَىٰ نَوعٍ مِنَ ٱلْجِبِلَّةِ وَٱلطَّبْعِ ٱلْمُتَهَيِّئِ لِقَبُولِ ٱلدِّينَ فَلَوْتُرِكَ عَلَيْهَا لاسْتَمَرَّ عَلَىٰ لُزُومِهَا.

That is, the human being has been created with the particular kind of nature, disposition and essence in that he is perceptive to the acceptance of religion unless external and compulsive factors stand along his way.

Ibn Athīr then says that the word *fiṭrah* repeatedly appears in the corpus of *ḥadīth*. For instance, it is thus stated in a tradition from the Holy Prophet (S),[1] which Ibn Athir did not quote earlier:

عَلَىٰ غَيْرِ فِطْرَةِ مُحَمَّدٍ.

In other words,

عَلَىٰ غَيْرِ دِينِ مُحَمَّدٍ.

That is, here instead of the word *dīn* (religion) what appears is the word *fiṭrah*. Imām ʻAlī (A.S.) is also reported to have said:

وَجَبَّارُ ٱلْقُلُوبِ عَلَىٰ فِطَرَاتِهَا.[2]

God, the Exalted, who has created the hearts, is the *jabbār*[3] of the hearts on the basis of their dispositions. Here, *fiṭrah* takes plural form – *fiṭarāt*. What we can observe here is that what is considered intrinsic to the human being from the Islamic viewpoint is not only

Prominent grammarians used to describe it as correct literal meaning.

1. The abbreviation, "ṣ", stands for the Arabic invocative phrase, *ṣallallāhu ʻalayhi wa ālihī wa sallam* (may God's blessings and peace be upon him and his progeny), which is mentioned after the name of the Holy Prophet Muḥammad (S). [Trans.]
2. [There is a similar saying mentioned in *Najh al-Balāghah*:
وَجَابِرُ ٱلْقُلُوبِ عَلَىٰ فِطَرَاتِهَا.]
3. That is, the Compensator or Creator.

one; in fact, the human being has *fiṭrahs*. Ibn Athīr thus says:

عَلَىٰ فِطَرَاتِهَا أى عَلَىٰ خِلقِهَا.[1]

Ibn 'Abbās' Words

There is a remarkable tradition reported from Ibn 'Abbās, and I cite the same tradition to prove that the word *fiṭrah* is one of the words which were introduced by the Qur'an for the first time. Ibn 'Abbās who was a cousin of the Prophet (S) and a learned man of Quraysh – and he was not a Bedouin Arab whom we can accuse of not knowing the Arabic language – says, "I understood the meaning of the word *fiṭrah* which is mentioned in the Qur'an when I met a Bedouin man which used the word in a certain case. When he used the word in that case, the meaning of the verse became clear to me. He says,

مَا كُنْتُ أَدْرِي مَا فَاطِرُ ٱلسَّمَاوَاتِ وَٱلْأَرْضِ حَتَّىٰ إِحْتَكَمَ إِلَيَّ أَعْرَابِيَّانِ فِي بِئرٍ.

> "I did not correctly understand the word *fāṭir* which is mentioned in the Qur'an until when two Bedouins came as they quarrelled over a pit of water. One of them said:
>
> أَنَا فَطَرْتُهَا.

"He wanted to say, 'The well is mine.' He meant that 'I was the first to dig it.' (As you know, when a well is dug [after sometime] water gushes forth beneath; thus, it would be dug twice and water would gush forth ever lower.) He wanted to say, 'I was its owner during its primary stage.'" That is, it was me who dug the well for the first time. Ibn 'Abbās says, "I learned from there the meaning of the word *fiṭrah* in the Qur'an – an absolutely primary creation in the human being which has no precedence even in other living beings.

In other instances where the word *fiṭrah* has been used in Arabic

---

1. Ibn Athīr, *Al-Nihāyah*, vol. 3, 457.

language, the meaning of being first-time and unprecedented is embedded. For example, the Arabs say:

فَطَرَ نَابُ ٱلْبَعِيرِ فَطْرًا إِذَا شَقَّ ٱللَّحْمَ وَطَلَعَ.

When the first tooth of a camel appears and chews a meat for the first time, this first appearance is called *faṭara*. Also, the first amount of milk that comes out of an animal's mammary gland – provided that it is the first taken – is called *fuṭr*.

Rāghib al-Iṣfahānī has also scrutinized this word to the same extent Ibn Athīr did in *Al-Nihāyah*, and since it is more or less a repetition, we shall no longer deal with it.

The Late Shaykh 'Abbās Al-Qummī's Statement

In his book *Safīnat al-Baḥār*,[1] the late Shaykh 'Abbās al-Qummī – may Allah be pleased with him – quotes Muṭarrizī,[2] who is another Arabic grammarian, saying that *fiṭrah* signifies creation (*khilqah*). He then quotes this tradition from *Ghawālī al-Li'ālī*:[3]

كُلُّ مَوْلُودٍ يُولَدُ عَلَى ٱلْفِطْرَةِ...

"Everyone born is born in [the state of] *fiṭrah*..."[4]

1. The most important book of the late Shaykh 'Abbās al-Qummī, *Safīnat al-Baḥār* deals with traditions. He has identified the traditions in 'Allāmah Majlisī's *Biḥār al-Anwār* with terminologies. In fact, it is an index to the traditions in *Biḥār al-Anwār*. In the said book, he has somehow imitated Ibn Athīr's *Al-Nihāyah*, with the difference that while Ibn Athīr concentrates on the terminologies, he pays much attention to the traditions.
2. Burhān al-Dīn Abū 'l-Fatḥ al-Muṭarrizī (1144-1213): a philologist, jurist and man of letters (*adīb*) whose compendium of Arabic grammar is widely circulated. [Trans.]
3. It refers to *Ghawālī al-Li'ālī 'l-'Azīzīyah fī'l-Ḥadīth al-Dīniyyah* by Shaykh Muḥammad ibn 'Alī ibn Ibrāhīm (ibn Abī Jumhūr) al-Aḥsā'ī (d. after 878 AH/1479). [Trans.]
4. *Ṣaḥīḥ al-Bukhārī*, "Kitāb al-Janā'iz," sections (*abwāb*) 80, 93.

And then he quotes a tradition from Imām al-Ṣādiq (A.S.) in which the word *fuṭrah* is used although it is different from the *fiṭrah* we refer to. Abū Baṣīr says, "One day we visited Imām al-Ṣādiq (A.S.). Camel's meat was and we ate. After sometime, milk was offered from which the Imām (A.S.) took and drank and then he told me, 'You also drink,' and I did so and I ask, "What is it? (I observed that it gave a particular taste.)" The Imām (A.S.) replied,

إِنَّهَا ٱلْفُطْرَةُ.

> "It is *fuṭrah* (mould of fresh milk at the time of milking)."[1]

As such, the word gives again the same meaning of being primary or fresh (*ibtidā'iyyah*).

Fiṭrah, Ṣibghah and Ḥanīf

There are three words in the Qur'an which, in view of the meaning or implication the Qur'an provides for "religion" (*dīn*) – ﴿ فِطْرَةَ اللَّهِ الَّتِي فَطَرَ النَّاسَ عَلَيْهَا ﴾ – have been used to refer to a single meaning. In other words, they are three difference concepts that give a single meaning. One is this word *fiṭrah*, the other one is the word *ṣibghah*, and the third one is the word *ḥanīf*. That is, regarding "religion", it is referred to as *fiṭrat Allāh*, *ṣibghat Allāh* and *li'd-dīni ḥanīfan*. Now, we shall deal a bit with *ṣibghah* and *ḥanīf*.

It is thus stated in the Qur'an:

﴿ صِبْغَةَ اللَّهِ وَمَنْ أَحْسَنُ مِنَ اللَّهِ صِبْغَةً ﴾

> The baptism of Allah, and who baptizes better than Allah? (2:138)

---

1. In my opinion, this is what is called *jīk* in Khurāsān and *āghūz* in some other places, which refers to the same preliminary milk which comes from an animal that gives birth anew.

This word is also with the rhythm of *fi'lah*. *Ṣibghah* has the same root-word with such words as *ṣibgh* and *ṣabbāgh*. *Ṣibgh* literally means to colour or dye. *Ṣabbāgh* means dyer or tinter while *ṣibgh* is a type of colouring or dyeing. *Ṣibghat Allāh* means a type of colour that God applies in the core of creation; that is, the Divine colour. Regarding religion, it is stated that religion is "the colour of God"; it is the colour with which the Hands of the Real colours the human being in the core of creation and origination. Exegetes of the Qur'an (*mufassirūn*), including Rāghib al-Iṣfahānī, have said that this expression in the Qur'an signifies baptism which the Christians used to do.[1] Christians believed in baptism and they still practice it. When they want to Christianize a person – even an infant who is born with a Christian parenthood – they baptize him and this is a means of admitting him into Christianity. This giving a bath is a sort of initiation and adoption into Christianity. The Qur'an states that the colour is that which God applies in the essence of creation.

It is thus stated in a verse:

﴿ مَا كَانَ إِبْرَاهِيمُ يَهُودِيًّا وَلَا نَصْرَانِيًّا وَلَكِنْ كَانَ حَنِيفًا مُسْلِمًا وَمَا كَانَ مِنَ الْمُشْرِكِينَ ﴾

> Abraham was neither a Jew nor a Christian. Rather he was a ḥanīf (monotheist), a muslim. (3:67)

The Qur'an states that the human being has a natural disposition (*fiṭrah*) which is religious in nature, and the religion is Islam, which in turn, is the true religion from Prophet Ādam (Adam) up to the Seal of the Prophets (*khātam al-nabiyyīn*).[2] The Qur'an does not

---

1. It is said that since a person is immersed in water, it is called baptism (*ta'mīd*). There are claims that this water had a particular colour (such as yellow).
2. It is asked whether the *sharī'ahs* (Divine laws) were also intrinsic *(fiṭrī)* or not. We shall later clarify what it means when we say that the religion is intrinsic. Are its principles of belief intrinsic? Are its laws and orders intrinsic as well? These are details which we must deal with later on.

subscribe to "religions" but rather to "the religion". As such, the word *dīn* (religion) is never pluralized in the Qur'an or *ḥadīth* because the religion is intrinsic in nature; it is the way; it is the truth which is embedded in human nature. The human beings have not been created in different ways, and all commandments and orders of all the prophets who were sent are based upon the revival, awakening and nourishment of the intrinsic feeling. What they have presented are the very things demanded by the same human nature. Human nature does not have a variegated demand. As such, the Qur'an states that what Prophet Nūḥ (Noah) (A.S.) had is the religion whose name is "Islam" and what Prophet Ibrāhīm (Abraham) (A.S.) is the religion whose name is "Islam" and what Prophet Mūsā (Moses) (A.S.) had is the religion which name is "Islam". The names (for the religion) which come afterward are deviation from the original religion (*dīn*) and the original natural disposition (*fiṭrah*); hence, the Qur'an states, "Abraham was neither a Jew nor a Christian. Rather he was a *ḥanīf* (monotheist), a *muslim*." It does not want to say that Prophet Ibrāhīm (A.S.) was like any of the Muslims at the time of the Prophet; that is, he was a member of the community (*ummah*) of the Last Prophet (S). It states that Judaism is a digression from the original Islam; Christianity is also a deviation from the genuine Islam; Islam is nothing but one and only. In the said noble verse – which I quoted – it is asked, "What is the effect of these baptisms?! What is the effect of these immersions in water?! Can a person become someone else merely by means of baptism?!" True baptism is that which is embedded in human nature. It is as if the Qur'an wants to say that what our Prophet conveys is the same original Islam and the same natural disposition (*fiṭrah*). Natural disposition means the colour which God has intrinsically endowed in the human soul.

Rāghib al-Iṣfahānī says:

صِبْغَةُ اللهِ إِشَارَةٌ إِلَىٰ مَا أَوْجَدَهُ اللهُ تَعَالَىٰ فِي ٱلنَّاسِ مِنَ ٱلْعَقْلِ ٱلْمُتَمَيِّزِ بِهِ عَنِ ٱلْبَهَائِمِ

> كَالْفِطْرَةِ. وَكَانَتِ ٱلنَّصَارىٰ إِذَا وُلِدَ لَهُمْ وَلَدٌ غَمَسُوهُ فِي ٱلْيَوْمِ ٱلسَّابِعِ فِي مَاءٍ عَمُودِيَّةٍ مَسِيحِيها. يَزْعَمُونَ أَنَّ ذٰلِكَ صِبْغَةٌ. فَقَالَ تَعَالىٰ لَهُ ذٰلِكَ: ﴿ صِبْغَةَ اللهِ وَمَنْ أَحْسَنُ مِنَ اللهِ صِبْغَةً ﴾
>
> "*Ṣibghat Allāh* refers to what Allah, the Exalted, has created in man from the intellect which distinguishes him from beasts, as the *fiṭrah* also does. And when someone was born among the Christians, they baptized him on the seventh day to become a Christian. They thought that such was baptism. As such, the Exalted said in this regard, The baptism of Allah, and who baptizes better than Allah?" (2:138)

It is thus stated in a tradition:

... أَلدِّينُ ٱلْحَنِيفُ وَٱلْفِطْرَةُ وَصِبْغَةُ اللهِ وَٱلتَّعْرِيفُ فِي ٱلْمِيثَاقِ.[1]

That is, the *ḥanīf* or *fiṭrī* religion, or *ṣibghat Allāh* is that which God informed man of in the covenant (*mīthāq*) – that is, the covenant between God and the human souls. It refers to the subject which is called *'ālam al-dharr*. Definitely, the issue of *'ālam al-dharr* must be discussed here. What is its meaning and implication? Had really the human beings been in this material world or world of nature in the form of small organisms and later on transformed [into this form that they have now]? Does it (*'ālam al-dharr*) have a more subtle meaning – as indeed it has?

The Meaning of *Ḥanīf*

Zurārah asked Imām al-Bāqir (A.S.), "What does it mean by *ḥunāfā'a lillāh*? What is *ḥanīfiyyah*?" The Imām (A.S.) said,

1. *Biḥār al-Anwār* (new edition), vol. 3, section (*bāb*) 11, 276, as quoted in *Ma'ānī al-Akhbār*.

"*Ḥanīfiyyah* means *fiṭrah.*" He then referred to something natural and intrinsic.

In his previous book *Al-Tawḥīd*, Shaykh al-Ṣadūq says that Zurārah asked Imām al-Bāqir (A.S.) about *ḥunafā'a lillāhi ghayra mushrikīna bih* and then about *ḥanīfiyyah.* The Imām (A.S.) thus replied:

هِيَ ٱلْفِطْرَةُ ٱلَّتِي فَطَرَ ٱلنَّاسَ عَلَيْهَا لاَ تَبْدِيلَ لِخَلْقِ اللهِ.

> "It is the *fiṭrah* (origination) with which He originated mankind. There is no change in Allah's creation."

The Imām (A.S.) also said:

فَطَرَهُمْ اللهُ عَلىٰ ٱلْمَعْرِفَةِ.

> "Allah originated them on [His] gnosis (*ma'rifah*)."

Then the Imām (A.S.) referred to the account of *'ālam al-dharr* and said, "The Prophet (S) also said:

كُلُّ مَوْلُودٍ يُولَدُ عَلىٰ ٱلْفِطْرَةِ يَعْنِي عَلىٰ ٱلْمَعْرِفَةِ بِأَنَّ اللهَ عَزَّ وَجَلَّ خَالِقُهُ.

> "Everyone born is born in [the state of] *fiṭrah*; that is, in the gnosis with which Allah, the Almighty, created him."

In another tradition, Imām al-Bāqir (A.S.) said:

عُرْوَةُ اللهِ ٱلْوُثْقىٰ أَلتَّوْحِيدُ وَٱلصِّبْغَةُ ٱلْإِسْلَامُ.

> "Allah's firmest handle are monotheism (*tawḥīd*) and the baptism of Islam (*ṣibghat al-islām*)."

Under the entry of the root-word *ḥ-n-f* (حنف), Ibn Athīr gave the same meaning which is indicated in our traditions. That is, *ḥunafā'* means that God has created the human beings free from sins:

خَلَقْتُ عِبَادِي حُنَفَاءَ أَيْ طَاهِرِي الْأَعْضَاءِ مِنَ ٱلْمَعَاصِي وَقِيلَ أَرَادَ أَنَّهُ خَلَقَهُمْ
حُنَفَاءَ مُؤْمِنِينَ لَمَّا أَخَذَ عَلَيهِمُ ٱلْمِيثَاقَ أَلَسْتُ بِرَبِّكُمْ قَالُوا بَلىٰ، فَلاَ يوجَدُ أَحَدٌ إِلَّا
وَهُوَ مُقِرٌّ بِأَنَّ لَهُ رَبًّا وَإِنْ أَشْرَكَ بِهِ وَٱخْتَلَفُوا فِيهِ. وَٱلْحُنَفَاءُ جَمْعُ حَنِيفٍ وَهُوَ ٱلْمَائِلُ إِلىٰ

ٱلْإِسْلَامِ ٱلثَّابِتُ عَلَيهِ وَٱلْحَنِيفُ عِنْدَ ٱلْعَرَبِ مَنْ كَانَ عَليٰ دِينِ إِبْرَاهِيمَ (عَلَيهِ ٱلسَّلَام)
وَأَصْلُ ٱلْحَنَفِ أَلْمَيلُ.

In sum, he wants to convey that *ḥanīfiyyah* means desire or inclination toward the truth.

If we want to define the word *ḥanīf*, therefore, its definition is as follows: truth-centeredness, truth-orientedness or God-centeredness. There is *ḥanīfiyyah* in the human being's natural disposition. That is, there is truth-orientedness and God-centeredness in his natural disposition. Up to this point, the discussion revolves around the word *fiṭrah* with the aim of extracting its roots in the verses of the Qur'an and traditions (*aḥādīth*) and concisely knowing that *fiṭrah* has a root in the traditions and Qur'anic verses and it is one of the fundamentals. As such, it was necessary to elaborate of this.

Ṭabī'Ah, Gharīzah and Fiṭrah

1. *Ṭabī'ah*

Now, we shall talk about human dispositions (*fiṭriyyāt*). (For the meantime, we shall refrain from engaging in religious or Qur'anic discussion.) Does the human being have *fiṭriyyāt* or not? Basically, what is the meaning of *fiṭriyyāt*?

We have three terminologies which should ideally be differentiated and distinguished from one another. One terminology is *ṭabī'ah*. Usually, the word *ṭabī'ah* or *ṭab'* is used in relation to inanimate objects. Of course, it is also used in relation to living things. What I want to say is that this word is particularly used in relation to inanimate objects. For example, we say that the *ṭab'* (nature) of the water is such and such. Whenever we have to express a salient feature of this inanimate object called 'water', we say that the *ṭab'* of water is such and such. We also say that the *ṭabī'ah* (nature) of oxygen is such that it is combustible; the nature of hydrogen and nitrogen is such and such. We believe in the essential features of things according to the various characteristics that they have. We call 'nature' the name of the essential feature [of an inanimate object]. This stems from a philosophical way of thinking which exists in all human beings. In other words, the human being thinks in such a way that two things similar in all aspects cannot have different characteristics. If the characteristics are different, there is also a reason for these two things to be different and distinct from each other. As the human being observed that things are the same in some aspects and that although certain things are all material and physical, they have diverse characteristics – for example,[1] he could observe that water is material and physical; so is the earth; yet, each of them has a particular set of characteristics which cannot be found in the other – he has option [but to conclude in such a way] that there is a power or energy or element in one physical entity which is the cause of a certain peculiarity, and there is another element in another physical entity which is the cause of another characteristic. And that element which is the cause of a particular characteristic is called 'nature' (*ṭabī'ah*). Nowadays, we also use this word in the same cases. For example, we say that the nature of cherry is such and such, and the nature of so-and-so tree is that it endures in cold weather and cannot survive in warm weather, and the nature of another tree is that it can thrive in tropical region and not in other regions.

Of course, we also use the word 'nature' in other than the

1. Since this way of thinking has been there even before, I shall also mention a classical example.

inanimate objects – that is, living things such as human beings, animals and plants – but in those aspects which are common with the inanimate objects, for the living things have those characteristics that the inanimate objects have, but they have certain other characteristics that inanimate objects do not have.

2. *Gharīzah*

Our second terminology is *gharīzah* (instinct) which is more frequently applied to the animals and rarely used in relation to the human beings, but in relation to the inanimate objects and plants, it is not used at all. The essence of instinct is still not clear; that is, no one can still properly explain what instinct in animals is. Yet, we know for a fact that animals[1] have inward distinctive characteristics which serve as the guide to their lives, and there is a semi-conscious state in animals which shows them the right way of doing things. And this state is not acquired or learned; it is natural and non-acquisitive. For example, even the kid of a superior animal – immediately after birth and prior to acquiring any learning or experience – does a set of actions which is essential for it to survive. Contrary to an infant which must be fed with milk immediately after birth (although an infant somehow twists its lips and seems very weak to be able to look for something), as soon as an animal kid (such as a pony) is born, it immediately strives by itself to stand up. It would fall down many times but it will finally succeed to stand up and without any guidance from its mother, it will immediately look for its mother's mammary glands. It is obvious that it looks for its mother's mammary glands, and within one or two minutes, it will find its mother's mammary glands and begin to suck milk. What is this state of the pony of standing up immediately after

1. There is more instinct in inferior or lower animals (such as insects) than in superior animals.

being born and looking for its mother's mammary glands and could be able to look for it quickly? It is said that this is animal instinct. The animals' instincts are so diverse. For instance, the ants have a unique instinct in gathering food:

مور گرد آورد به تابستان   تا فراغت بود زمستانش

Ant gathers [food] in summer
So as to relax in winter

This animal has an amazing ability and even in accumulating its own food supply, it does extraordinary works which is not known[1] what its basis or root is. It is said that the ant knows if the wheat it gathers is intact and can still grow later and will be of no use to it. As such, it splits the wheat so that it could no longer grow. And there are other amazing things which this animal does. What do we call these things? We say that these are 'instincts'. Instinct is something which is semi-conscious. It can be said that it is conscious; it can also be said that it is not conscious. It is a state which is very ambiguous.

همچو میل کودکان با مادران   سرّ میل خود نداند در لبان

Just as the child's inclination is toward the mother,
Secret does not incline toward frankincense.

On one hand, since inclination or desire is a conscious state, inclination or desire is a psychological state in that the human being has a kind of intuitive consciousness toward 'inclination' or 'desire' itself. Yet, it does not have the least consciousness of it. In other words, it has intuitive consciousness of the 'desire' but it has no

1. It is not known in the sense that there are many views in this regard.

knowledge anymore of its knowledge. It does not know the secret behind its own consciousness. It is only that this desire spontaneously and unclearly appears in it but it pays no attention to this desire. It is conscious of this desire but pays no attention to it, for paying attention is different from consciousness and presence of a thing.

Regarding animals, the word *gharīzah* is used. I have not seen so far any instance wherein the word *fiṭrah* is used – whether in religious or non-religious parlance. Now, even if a person uses it in that context, he commits no sin but I cannot remember an instance regarding animals in which the word *fiṭrah* were used instead of the word *gharīzah*.

3. *Fiṭrah*

We use the word *fiṭrah* in relation to the human beings. Like *ṭabī'ah* and *gharīzah*, *fiṭrah* is something innate (*takwīni*). In other words, it is an integral part of human nature. (When we say *takwīnī*, we want to point out that it is not something acquired or learned (*iktisābī*).) It is something more conscious than *gharīzah*. A person can be able to know that he knows what he knows. That is, the human being has a set of dispositions (*fiṭriyyāt*) and he knows that he has such dispositions.

Does Human Being Have Dispositions (*Fiṭriyyāt*)?

Another difference between *fitriyyāt* and *gharīzah* is that *gharīzah* is within the confines of material issues in an animal's life while the human being's *fiṭriyyāt* are related to the issues which we call human issues (meta-animal issues). In reality, therefore, [the discussion on] *fiṭrah* is this: Are all these issues which are put forth as specifically human issues – that is, meta-animal issues – and not raised in relation to animals, acquired later and do not have any root in human constitution? Or, are these issues all rooted in human constitution and disposition? For example, there is an issue called 'love for truth' which is a separate subject by itself. What I mean by 'love for truth' is this [state] in which a person wants know and discover the reality of the unknown things around her. First of all, does the human being really love the truth or not? One may possibly deny this and say that the human being does not love the truth at all, and if ever he loves it, he does it for his own interests. This in itself is a discussion in the realm of science (because science aims to discover the truth for the human being). Does the human being believe in the intrinsic value of science, or does he believe only in its utilitarian value? There is no doubt that science is a tool of the human beings. As the saying goes, "Knowledge is power." Science gives power to the human being and once it is given, it will serve as a tool for him to have a more comfortable life. There is, however, another issue: Does science have an intrinsic value for the human being, or not? If we believe that science has an intrinsic value for the human being at the present in the sense that today's human being loves the truth, [this question is posed:] Does this love for the truth suggest social necessities for the human being, or is it an integral part of the human constitution and that the human being is created having love for the truth?

Another example is 'moral goodness'. So far today we have concepts and meanings in our midst which we call 'moral goodness'. In other words, ethically we call them 'humane' and 'morally good' and their opposite is what we call 'morally evil'. For instance, what does gratitude mean? That is, if a person did something good to another person, that person should do the same to him and be grateful to him. Its opposite is ingratitude. In other words, gratitude means 'to reciprocate goodness with goodness'. This is an ethical issue. Today, finally, we have acknowledged this:

﴿ هَلْ جَزَاءُ الْإِحْسَانِ إِلَّا الْإِحْسَانُ ﴾

Is the requital of goodness anything but goodness? (55:40)

This verse which is in the form of a question wants to solicit the answer from the human *fiṭrah*. It is something intrinsic [that the requital of goodness is nothing but goodness. It asks,] can the requital of goodness be other than goodness itself? The human being says, "No. The requital or recompense of goodness is goodness."

From where did the human being get this ruling? Is it something inculcated and that social necessities have imposed it upon the human being? (Naturally, in this case, if the social conditions change, this ruling will also change and cease to exist, and this is exactly the concept of ethical relativism.) Or, is it something embedded in the human constitution?

The issue of religion and worship itself is one of them. Is this feeling which, today, exists in human beings as religious feeling in whatever form, something that emanates from the human constitution? Is it a demand in the nature and inner being of a person, or is it something which is a product of a set of other factors (factors which we shall briefly talk about later on).

We shall present, therefore, the discussion on human dispositions (*fiṭriyyāt*) in this way: They have been a set of issues which are called 'humanity' today. There is no school of thought which denies this set of 'human values' in today's jargon.[1]

One day a human being looks for his own gain or profit. This is apparently something logical because according to the dictate of his

1. This discussion on 'value' is one of those interesting topics which we will deal should time permits us.

instinct, he wants to survive and continue to live and naturally he is inclined to anything which could help him to survive. And it is logical and natural that a human being is looking for gain.

There are other things which cannot be reconciled with profit. In other words, the issue is not that of profit and it cannot be harmonized with the logic of profit. The Westerners have erroneously called it 'value'. In essence, this naming emanates from a set of errors.[1] What are these things which are called 'human values' today? Are they rooted in the human nature and constitution? If it is so, what is this root and for what purpose? This in itself is a very important issue, for if there is something in the human constitution, that thing will tell something about other issues and realities.

No doubt, Islamic teachings are based upon the acceptance of a set of dispositions; that is, all those things which, today, are called human issues and meta-animal, and we call them 'human values'. From the Islamic point of view, they are rooted in the human nature and constitution. We will say, thereafter, that the primacy of human being and real humanity of human being depend on the acknowledgment of dispositions (*fiṭriyyāt*). It is nonsense to say that we should not believe in human being as having dispositions; that is, we should not believe in their root in the human constitution and we should talk about humanism and the primacy of human being.

Our next discussion, therefore, is about these human values and

---

1. They have used the word 'value' because in reality, they wanted to say that these are not 'real' because he gives credit to it according to contract. In reality, something to which we give value according to contract is nothing. For example, we give value to a one thousand *tūmān* bill according to contract. If we give this bill (as payment), we can be able to get a ton of wheat. If this contract and credit is nullified, this bill will have no difference with a sheet of paper, no matter how we call the former.

the meaning of their being intrinsic, and we will then make conclusion from these, and then examine these values which we consider human dispositions. Afterward, we will see what reason for their being intrinsic we can deduce from Islamic sources. Can we bring forth any proof from the Qur'an and [other] Islamic sources that moral goodness is a set of things which is embedded in human nature? Can we extract a set of human dispositions on moral issues from the following holy verse?

﴿ وَنَفْسٍ وَمَا سَوَّاهَا ★ فَأَلْهَمَهَا فُجُورَهَا وَتَقْوَاهَا ﴾

> By the soul and Him who fashioned it, and inspired it with [discernment between] its virtues and vices. (91:7-8)

We can deduce something from this verse?

﴿ هَلْ جَزَاءُ الإِحْسَانِ إِلا الإِحْسَانُ ﴾

> Is the requital of goodness anything but goodness? (55:40)

Usually, instead of the Qur'an asking question, it demands an answer from the natural disposition (*fiṭrah*) of people. It wants to say that there are things which are embedded in the natural constitution of people, and everyone knows it. In future sessions, we will answer some of the questions in the course of discussion.

Chapter 2: Man's Dispositions

At the outset, we shall reply to two of the questions being raised and then we will deal with our subject. One question is that are the issues which the Noble Qur'an express through the general human medium intrinsic (*fiṭrī*) or not? For example the Qur'an says,

﴿ وَيَقُولُ الْإِنْسَانُ أَئِذَا مَا مِتُّ لَسَوْفَ أُخْرَجُ حَيًّا ﴾

> Man says, 'Shall I, when I have died, be brought forth alive?' (19:66)

Cannot be inferred here that the belief in the Resurrection is not intrinsic?

Generally speaking, this is a good question; that is, it is a question which must be probed and seen if the set of what the Qur'an narrates through the general human medium is related to a series of things intrinsic in man or not. At any rate, generally, this question can be discussed and deliberated, and the whole set of verses relevant to it must be collected. But what can be said in relation to the verse, "Man says, 'Shall I, when I have died, be brought forth alive?'" is that first of all, it must be determined if this "Man says" refers to the human being in general or to a particular person. Now, I cannot exactly remember but most probably the context of the revelation pertains to a particular event.[1] A certain person has said so. It is as if with surprise and denial, the Qur'an says "You see, this person says so." If it is so, then it is not a statement of man in general but that of a particular person.

Secondly, as to the question whether belief in the Resurrection is intrinsic or not depends on how we conceive of the belief in the Resurrection. At times we conceive of it in the same way it is conceived in most of the verses. The meaning and understanding which the Qur'an gives to the Resurrection is to return to God:

﴿ إِنَّا لِلَّهِ وَإِنَّا إِلَيْهِ رَاجِعُونَ ﴾

> Indeed we belong to Allah, and to Him do we indeed return. (2:156)

If this is the intended meaning and concept, then the answer is, "Yes, belief in the Resurrection is intrinsic."

In most cases, however, this matter is discussed inaccurately by not providing its real meaning and concept. For some individuals, it seems that just as a craftsman makes something, dismantles it and then remakes it anew, [God does the same]. [According to the abovementioned verse], someone who says so imagines in that way, and not in the way which is consistent with the real meaning of Resurrection. He has heard that during the Resurrection, the people will become alive again, but this revival from death is regarded by them as a sort of return to this world – as most of the people do imagine – and not returning to God. If our conception of the Resurrection is such that it is a kind of coming back to this world, then it is most certain that belief in the Resurrection is not intrinsic.

---

1. [The author of *Majma' al-Bayān* writes, "The said verse has been revealed in reference to Ubayy ibn Khalaf al-Jumaḥī and according to another opinion, it refers to Walīd ibn Mughīrah.]

If our conception of the Resurrection, however, is that its reality and essence is returning to God, then it is something which is connected to the relationship between man and God; then it is something intrinsic, as we shall discuss it as its opportune time.

Is Having Conscience a Proof of Innateness?

The other question which is raised is this:

> "In proving the existence of *fiṭrah* in man, shall we be contented that we can discern human dispositions (*fiṭriyyāt*) in ourselves, or is there another reasoning? For, in the first case, *gharā'iz* (instincts), *hawas* (desires) and *fiṭriyyāt* are interchangeable, and to rely on technical or lexical differences is not not enough. In short, what is the more accurate demarcation between *fiṭrah* (disposition) and *gharīzah* (instinct)? And are these demarcations conventional (*qarārdādī*) or real (*wāqi'ī*) (such as the division between what is conscious and what is unconscious)?"

In reality, these are two questions juxtaposed with one another. They ask, "In proving the innateness of a thing shall we be contented in saying that we can discern it in ourselves?" The answer is that first of all, we have not yet embarked on proving the innateness of a thing or the signs of its innateness, and about which we can talk afterward. Secondly, granted that it is such, it is not something surprising that a certain thing is intrinsic or innate for us and our reason for its being innate or intrinsic is that we can discern its innateness in our own selves. It is similar to the case when we have a series of primary premises (*badīhiyyāt-e awwaliyyeh*). For example, we say that "The whole is bigger than its parts and it is impossible for its part to be equal in size or bigger than the whole" is self-evident (*badīhī*). Then someone would say,

"What is the basis of its being self-evident? It is self-evident by itself but is its being self-evident speculative (*naẓarī*) or self-evident? We also say that it is self-evident that it is self-evident. If we assume that [its being self-evident] is not self-evident but rather speculative, then we must provide a proof to substantiate it. How about this proof of ours? It is self-evident or speculative? If we assume that our proof is speculative, it follows then that it requires another proof to substantiate it. Now, how about the proof of the proof? Is it speculative or self-evident? If in the end, we arrive at something self-evident whose being self-evident does not necessitate any proof, it can therefore be correct. But we never arrive at such a 'self-evident', it follows then that we do not have anything self-evident, nor do we have anything speculative. In other words, once we do not have anything self-evident, we cannot bring forth any reasoning because [in this case] our argument is [based upon] something speculative – that is, something unknown (*majhūl*). If we want to prove something unknown from something speculative (that is, from another unknown), it is like adding zero to zero which has no effect.

There is no surprise, therefore, that someone would say, "We have a series of intrinsic things and we can recognize their being intrinsic in our own selves and we are not in need of any proof. In succeeding sections we shall elaborate on this subject.

In continuation of the question, they say: "In this case, there is no more difference among *gharīzah* (instinct), *hawas* (desire) and the like."

Incidentally, the subject we have discussed is a lexical discussion; that is, the question is this: in which case is this word *fiṭrah* which is used in the Qur'an and then in the jargon of the scholars (*'ulamā'*) used? We have no issue with someone who calls all these intrinsic things 'instinct'. Is the term 'instinct' with which we label those things a settled issue? The discussion on the nature of that 'instinct' and it is something intrinsic. Now, you want to call it 'instinct' or 'disposition'. We are not concerned with the terminology[1] whether or not there is any difference between the words *fiṭrah* and *gharīzah*. The bone of contention is this: is that which is called 'humanity' or 'humanness' (*insāniyyah*) and recognized to be the human criteria acquired (*iktisābī*) or not? Are those criteria infused into man from outside, or do they emanate from the human essence? This is our point of discussion. When we say that these criteria are intrinsic, it means that they originate from the human essence and that man is a being on the depth of whose existence the seed of these criteria is implanted and does exist. Now, you want to name them 'instinct'; then do so. This will become a lexical discussion. We just want to point out that in usual cases the word 'instinct' is not applied in such things. Also, let anyone who wants to use the word 'instinct' use it. Usually, 'disposition' (*fiṭrah*) is not used in relation to the animals. [But] let anyone who wants to apply the word 'disposition' [to the animals] apply it. As such, the discussion is not lexical.

Since it is said, however, that that which is in man is conscious and that which is in animal is unconscious, there is no discussion that there is also such difference. Hence, for us this must not be a cause of criticism, question or issue for us. Now, let us continue with our discussion.

Human Being as the Most Unknown Creature

Of all the creatures in the universe, none is in need of knowing as

---

1. Of course, "We are not concerned" in the sense that we want to point out that the term has no effect on our claim, but we are also concerned with terminology.

much as the human being is. We said that the subjects which are discussed in philosophy – that is, all schools of philosophy in the world deal with them – are God, the universe and man. Now, some schools of philosophy have dealt more with issues pertaining to God. Others have explored more about the universe while a third group concentrates more on the human being.

Of all the parts of the universe, what distinction the human being has because of which we say, "Man and the universe"? Is the human being not an integral part of the universe? Yes, the human being is an integral part of the universe but this part is different from all other parts – or, let us say that he has certain intricacy – for which compared to all other parts of the universe, he is more in need of interpretation and justification. A metal is also an integral part. Iron, steel, gold, silver, and plant are also parts of the universe, but they are not much in need of interpretation and justification in that there must be a need for a set of assumptions, theories and schemes in order to know or identify them. As such, now, it is claimed that the human being is the most unknown creature in the universe. There is a book by Alexis Carrel[1] entitled *Man, The Unknown* (*L'Homme, cet inconnu*) (1935). It is a good title. It is surprising that although man himself is the agent in knowing other things and he has known much more things far from him and at times it is claimed that there is nothing unknown about them, regarding the closest beings to him – who is the very agent of knowing things, that is, man – has many unknown aspects.

One of the unknowns regarding man is the very issue of human

---

1. Alexis Carrel (1873-1944): a French surgeon and biologist awarded the Nobel Prize in Physiology or Medicine in 1912 for pioneering vascular suturing techniques, who, in his *Man, The Unknown* (1935), claimed the existence of a "hereditary biological aristocracy," arguing that 'deviant' human types should be suppressed using techniques similar to those later employed by the Nazis. [Trans.]

dispositions (*fiṭriyyāt*)[1] which are of two kinds; one is in the context of knowing, understanding and discernment, and the other is in the context of wants and desires.

Man's Dispositions in the Context of Knowledge and Knowing

In the context of knowing and discernment, the question is: Does the human being possess a set of intrinsic pieces of knowledge – that is, pieces of knowledge which are not acquired – or not? Now, we have thousands of conceptions *(taṣawwur)* and affirmations *(taṣdīq)* in our minds,[2] most of which are certainly acquired (*iktisābī*) pieces of knowledge.

From this verse of the Qur'an which is in blessed *Sūrat al-Naḥl*,

﴿ وَاللهُ أَخْرَجَكُم مِّن بُطُونِ أُمَّهَاتِكُمْ لاَ تَعْلَمُونَ شَيْئًا وَجَعَلَ لَكُمُ السَّمْعَ وَالأَبْصَارَ وَالأَفْئِدَةَ لَعَلَّكُمْ تَشْكُرُونَ ﴾

> Allah has brought you forth from the bellies of your mothers while you did not know anything. He made for you hearing, eyesight and hearts so that you may give thanks. (16:78)

Some have attempted to justify that all pieces of knowledge of man are acquired or learned, and there is no such thing as intrinsic pieces of knowledge. The apparent meaning of the verse is that when God has brought you forth from the bellies of your mothers, you did not know anything. That is, your *tabula rasa* is clean and pure, and nothing is drawn or written in it. Eyes and ears were given to you – which are obviously an example of senses which are not

---

1. As some psychologists do, one may use the word *gharā'iz* (instincts).
2. For a concise discussion on the difference between *taṣawwur* and *taṣdīq*, see chapter 2 of *Al-Manṭiq* by ʿAllāmah Muḥammad Riḍā al-Muẓaffar (1904-64). [Trans.]

limited to eyesight and hearing – and heart was given to you which was meant for thinking; that is, in your *tabula rasa* nothing was ever written. It is through the pen of the senses and through the strokes of the heart and mind that certain things could be inscribed in this empty canvas. This is one view.

Plato's View

There is another view which is that of Plato,[1] and it is the exact opposite of the first. Plato says that when the human being comes to this world, he knows everything. There is nothing which he does not know. Prior to the body, the human soul has existed in another realm. According to him, that realm is the realm of archetypes (*muthul*) and the human soul in the realm of archetypes – which in his belief is the reality of the beings in this world – can perceive ideas and discern the realities of things. Then, as the soul is transferred to the body, there arises a sort of veil between him and what he knows and it is like any [ordinary] person who knows certain things but he temporarily forgets them. According to Plato, anyone who comes to this world knows all branches of knowledge (such as mathematics). What then is the function of teaching and learning? He maintains that teaching and learning are reminding and calling to mind. The teacher is a reminder; that is, he reminds the learner what he inwardly knows and the learner, in turn, will remember those things known to him before. It is for this reason that "teaching" in the Platonic school is mere reminding and nothing else. This is the second view which is the exact opposite of the first view.

1. Plato (428/427-348/347 BCE): a Classical Greek philosopher, mathematician, writer of philosophical dialogues, and founder of the Academy in Athens, the first institution of higher learning in the Western world. Along with his mentor, Socrates, and his student, Aristotle, Plato helped to lay the foundations of natural philosophy, science, and Western philosophy. [Trans.]

Muslim Philosophers' View

The third view is that the human being intrinsically knows certain things which are, of course, few. The roots of human thinking which are the common roots of thinking of all human beings are intrinsic while the branches and derivative elements of thinking are acquired. Those who say, however, that the roots of thinking are intrinsic say so not in the Platonic sense that the human soul has learned them in the other world and has forgotten the same here [in this world]. It rather means that in this world, the human being will be acquainted with them but in learning them, he is not in need of a teacher, syllogism-formulation, analogy, experimentation, and the like. The human being's mental constitution is such that mere presentation of things is already enough for him to perceive them. There is no need for argumentation or reasoning. It is not that the human being has known them before. This is another view which is usually held by Muslim philosophers. Aristotle has also subscribed to this view – with difference in some aspects.

Among the modern philosophers, this difference of opinion also exists. Of course, perhaps one does not believe in the Platonic view in the modern era, but even in the modern era, some philosophers regard some pieces of knowledge as intrinsic and *a priori* (*qablī*) for the human being while other pieces of knowledge are *posteriori* (*ba'dī*) and empirical. The champion of this view is a great famous philosopher in the world in the modern centuries; That is Kant[1] who believes in a set of *a priori* knowledge which are not acquired through experience and the senses; that is, they are pieces of knowledge which, according to him, are a requisite of mental

1. Immanuel Kant (1724-1804): the German philosopher regarded by many as the most influential thinker of modern times. Describing in the *Metaphysics of Ethics* (1797) his ethical system which is anchored in a notion that the reason is the final authority for morality, actions of any sort, Kant believed, must be undertaken from a sense of duty dictated by reason, and no action performed for expediency or solely in obedience to law or custom can be regarded as moral. [Trans.]

constitution.

This idea exists among the German philosophers, but most of the British philosophers who are mostly sensualists (such as John Locke and David Hume) hold the exact opposite view. They opine that no knowledge in the human being's *tabula rasa* and all things are learned by him from the outside world and all things are learned or acquired.

The point I have raised – which we have also mentioned in *Uṣūl-e Falsafeh [wa Rawish-e Realism] (The Principles of Philosophy [and the Method of Realism])*[1] – is so subtle. Muslim philosophers believe that the primary principles of human thinking are not learned and discursive and are not in need of reasoning. At the same time, however, these principles are not considered innate by them while Plato or Kant considers them innate. Muslim philosophers say that at the moment that a person is born she does not know even those principles of thinking, but the primary principles of thinking which are later discovered are not found through experience. They cannot be acquired through argumentation nor can be learned through a teacher. Rather, just as the human being conceives two sides of propositions (subject and predicate), the mental structure is such that immediately and quintessentially gives judgment on the relationship between the subject and the predicate. For example, if we say, "The whole is bigger than its part," Plato would say that just like other things, this has been known to the soul from the beginning. Kant would say, "The fact that we say that the whole is bigger than its part shows that there is a set of innate mental elements which interfere in the mental structure. Some of them are taken from outside while other [elements] originated from the mind itself." Muslim philosophers would say, "When a baby is born in this

1. It refers to 'Allāmah Sayyid Muḥammad Ḥusayn al-Ṭabaṭabā'ī's work in collaboration with his student Āyatullah Muṭahharī who provided footnotes and explanations easily comprehensible to the common people. The work was designed to present Islamic philosophy as a superior alternative to Marxism. [Trans.]

world, she does not know anything. She does not know even the abovementioned proposition because she has no conception of 'whole'. Neither has she any conception of 'part'. But as soon as she acquires conception of 'whole' and 'part' and these two are placed side by side before her, without having any need for proof, teacher and experience, she would immediately give judgment that 'The whole is bigger than its part.'"

We have seen, therefore, that there are differences of opinion on the issue of perceptions so much so that this question arises: Do we have an intrinsic perception in the Platonic sense or according to the Muslim philosophers, or not? Up to this extent is the scope of our discussion and talk.

Qur'anic View

Meanwhile, let us see the view of the Qur'an. On one hand, we have seen that the Qur'an says,

> ﴿ وَاللهُ أَخْرَجَكُم مِّن بُطُونِ أُمَّهَاتِكُمْ لاَ تَعْلَمُونَ شَيْئًا وَجَعَلَ لَكُمُ الْسَّمْعَ وَالأَبْصَارَ وَالأَفْئِدَةَ لَعَلَّكُمْ تَشْكُرُونَ ﴾
>
> Allah has brought you forth from the bellies of your mothers while you did not know anything. He made for you hearing, eyesight and hearts so that you may give thanks. (16:78)

That is, when a newborn comes to this world his *tabula rasa* is clean and devoid of anything. At the same time, however, the Qur'an presents some issues in such a way that it can be inferred that [those issues] do not necessitate reasoning. One example is the way the very issue of *tawḥīd* (Divine unity) is presented in the Qur'an and how verses can be reconciled with one another. The issue of *tawḥīd* in the Qur'an – whose relevant verses we will recite afterward – is an intrinsic matter. As such, how to reconcile this "you did not know anything" and the fact that you know God in an intrinsic and inward manner? No, they are reconcilable.

Again, one of the salient features of the Qur'an is that it talks about "reminding" (*tadhakkur*). It is very surprising! While the Platonic view is so strongly rejected in the Qur'an, we can observe it addressing the Prophet (S), thus:

﴿ فَذَكِّرْ إِنَّمَا أَنتَ مُذَكِّرٌ * لَّسْتَ عَلَيْهِم بِمُصَيْطِرٍ ﴾

> So admonish – for you are only an admonisher, and not a taskmaster over them. (88:21-22)

(Verses of admonishing (*āyāt al-dhikr*) are not just one or two verses.) Even the Qur'an itself has been called *dhikr* (remembrance). The Noble Messenger (S) himself is also described as a reminder (*dhikr*):

﴿ قَدْ أَنْزَلَ اللّٰهُ إِلَيْكُمْ ذِكْرًا رَسُولًا ﴾

> Allah has already sent down to you a reminder, an apostle. (65:10-11)

As such, [these verses] show that at the same time, the Qur'an affirms certain things for which admonition and reminding are enough and they do not necessitate reasoning. For example, it gives a rhetoric question[1] in this verse:

---

1. In the parlance of the method of teaching, this is called "Socrates' method". It is said that in his method of teaching, he used to adopt the same style. Whenever he wanted to prove something to a person, he would start from the most self-evident things and pose as a question, "Isn't it so?" Since it was so self-evident, that person would answer the way Socrates would expect. As the mind of the person began to open, Socrates would pose the next most self-evident question. Again, he would answer the way Socrates would expect. Socrates would continue doing so until such time that the said person would realize that he had accepted Socrates' claim without him imposing it. In other

﴿ هَلْ يَسْتَوِی الَّذِينَ يَعْلَمُونَ وَ الَّذِينَ لا يَعْلَمُونَ ﴾

Are those who know equal to those who do not know? (39:9)

In this approach of the Qur'an – which is one of the distinct approaches in the Qur'an – it brings forth an issue in the form of question. As it wants to enjoin faith and good deeds, the Qur'an says,

﴿ أَمْ نَجْعَلُ الَّذِينَ آمَنُوا وَعَمِلُوا الصَّالِحَاتِ كَالْمُفْسِدِينَ فِي الْأَرْضِ أَمْ نَجْعَلُ الْمُتَّقِينَ كَالْفُجَّارِ ﴾

Shall We treat those who have faith and do righteous deeds like those who cause corruption on the earth? Shall We treat the God-wary like the vicious? (38:28)

That is to say, "We ask a question and you yourselves should provide the answer. Following this type of verses, it says:

---

words, Socrates would take out answers from the person himself. As he was a man of technique and smart psychologist who knew very well the way of thinking of a person, he would start from a set of introductory questions without making any declarative sentence. He would let a person open his mind by himself.

Socrates' mother was a midwife. He himself said, "Like my mother, I perform midwifery work." The midwife does not deliver the baby. It is the mother's nature to deliver the baby. The midwife's function is only to guide the expectant mother on how to sit down and how to make a move. She helps her deliver the baby. It is not the midwife's task to take out the baby from the womb by her own hands. It is wrong. The midwife should be patient waiting for the moment when the baby could be spontaneously delivered. Socrates used to say, "My job is the same as that of the midwife." That is to say, "I do something so that mind would give birth to an idea just as the mother gives birth to a child. I only help the minds to give birth to new ideas."

﴿ إِنَّمَا يَتَذَكَّرُ أُولُو الأَلْبَابِ ﴾

Only those who possess intellect take admonition. (39:9)

As such, the dispositions (*fiṭriyyāt*) which the Qur'an subscribes to are not those of the Platonic type such that prior to his birth a child is aware of those dispositions, being endowed with them when he was born. It is rather in the sense that the talents are in every person in the sense that as the child reaches the stage when he can be able to conceive (*taṣawwur*) them, affirmation (*taṣdīq*) of them shall be intrinsic for him. It follows, therefore, that the verse, 'Allah has brought you forth from the bellies of your mothers while you did not know anything. He made for you hearing, eyesight and hearts so that you may give thanks'(16:78) has no conflict with the fact that belief in the Divine unity (*tawḥīd*) is intrinsic as well as the fact that the Qur'an mentions many things as a sort of reminder or admonition (*tadhakkur*). It is because to be intrinsic (*fiṭrī*) means that it does not necessitate learning and reasoning and not in the sense that prior to birth, one knew them, for in that case, the said two verses become contradictory. This is in the parlance of intellectual dispositions.

The Deniers' View and its Repercussion

Those who totally reject dispositions (*fiṭriyyāt*) say that the human intellection does not have a set of fixed principles which requires functioning of the intellect (*'aql*) – and not requiring organization of the intellect as Kant says.

Regarding the principles of thinking, for example, they say, among other things, that "Contradiction – that is, the combination of two opposites – impossible." That is, it is impossible for one thing to be really and actually such and not such in itself, in the sense that it is impossible for an idea or view in itself to be compatible with the reality and not compatible at the same time.[1] Or, they say, "Two

1. Of course, regarding this issue there are many ideas in the philosophy of Hegel

objects equal to a third object are all equal to one another;" "The whole is bigger than its part;" "Preponderance without a preponderant is impossible;" and the like. "Preponderance without a preponderant is impossible" means that if there are two opposite possibilities with respect to a thing and these two possibilities have equal chances, for this thing to opt to any of the possibilities requires an external factor. If there is no interference of an external factor, for one possibility to have greater chances of happening is impossible.

To cite an example, let us say that assuming there is a standing weighing scale which is so accurate and sensitive.[1] If there is no interference of any factor – now, this factor may be a wind movement, a weight which is placed on any of the pans of scale, a touch or strike on any of the pans, a magnetic force, the will of a person having an extraordinary willpower which can make an alteration in nature, and the like[2] – and at the same time, this pan goes up and down, the intellect dictates that this is something impossible.

There are also other similar examples. For instance, it is impossible for an object to occupy two spaces at the same time, and naturally, it is also true with respect to its opposite. That is, it is also impossible for two things to occupy a single space at the same time.

These are things for which proof cannot be brought forth but it is not because they are unknowns which we are not sure if they really exist or not.

For certain things, no proof can be put forward and we do not

---

and later on in Marxism which are totally outside the subject of discussion. If we deal with them, the discussions will become much longer.

1. Now, do not say that in nature, there is no such weighing scale which is so sensitive for after all, it is a human product. Let us assume, for instance, it is micro-gram sensitive. We mean sensitive up to that level.

2. For example, something is to be taken from any of them, or one will get old, or something will be removed from anyone of them. All of them are factors. Do not be mistaken.

know if they are really such or not. For instance, regarding the dimensions of the universe – whether they are finite or infinite – someone may possibly say, "I do not know if they are finite or infinite because one cannot brought forth any proof for it. Or, a popular example is as follows: If someone would say that all things are relatively becoming bigger, someone else would say in reply, "If I were really getting bigger, how comes that before I was 170 centimetres long and as I measure my height now, I am not 180 centimetres long, for instance?" The first person would say, "Meter has also become bigger relative to you." This claim [that all things are relatively becoming bigger] cannot be refuted by any proof.

So is the case if someone puts forth the opposite proposition; that is, to claim all things relatively become smaller. This also can neither be negated nor affirmed. And this will remain something unknown for the human being.

Meanwhile, this claim that "This object occupies two spaces at the same time" is something for which no amount of proof can be presented. It is not because it remains something unknown but rather it is something which is definitely false; that is, it is impossible.

Those who believe in the innate principles of thinking have no option but to regard these original principles of thinking as inalterable, infallible and impeccable. They say that these principles are correct here in our location and even if we are placed in a different condition and circumstances (say, for example, in another planet), the case is the same.

There are other issues. Although it is not self-evident and only almost self-evident, yet it is of the same case; for instance, 2 x 2 = 4. In this world 2 x 2 = 4 and in the hereafter 2 multiplied by 2 is also 4. In this period 2 x 2 = 4 and during the time when the planet earth was still blazing, 2 multiplied by 2 has been equal to 4. Even if millions of years will pass afterward, 2 multiplied by 2 will remain 4.

If we subscribe to such innate principles for thinking, we can also give importance to the secondary elements or branches for they are also founded on the same principles.

Now, one may also possibly say that even these principles are acquired in the sense that one factor has made us [believe in these principles as self-evident] and the said factor's state dictates that we must think in that way. We are like a mirror which is placed in front of faces. Since we are presently placed in front of those faces and we have been always placed in front those faces and now we can see them, [we think in that way]. If they will be removed in our front and something else is placed, what we will see is something else. Now, we say that the whole is bigger than its part. It is these conditions of the environment which have dictated us to think that way. If the environment is changed, it is possible that we will think in the opposite way and we will then say that the part is bigger than the whole. (At present, I only want to state the conclusion.) Once we deny the innate principles of thinking, no understanding and no knowledge will remain valuable. Mathematics as a whole is based upon a set of acceptable principles. According to their viewpoint, these acceptable principles have no credibility, and for instance, [they say that] these [principles] are related to a specific structure of our mind. If we program our mind in a different way, therefore, we will also say something else. [These principles] are related to the fact that we live on the planet earth. If we live in the planet mercury, we will think in a different way. Naturally, according to this viewpoint, no philosophy has any credibility. As such, we arrive at this conclusion so far. For the meantime, I do not want to prove this conclusion.

Those who deny the primary principles of thinking cannot

definitely have a worldview; they cannot have a philosophy which logically rules that we have knowledge of the universe and it is such.

By chance it is like that. That is, they themselves are not aware of it. Their story is like that of a person who sits on top of a tree, cutting with a saw the branch where he sits, and he himself is not aware that this act will be the cause of his falling down [from the tree].

Materialistic philosophies have no option but to be absolute sensualists (*ḥissi-ye maḥḍ*), and if they are absolute sensualists, they have no option but to regard all ideas as products of specific external factors, and therefore, they do not believe in indisputable, definite and error-free primary principles of thinking. In other words, all views and implications that we express are based upon these baseless foundations. Hence, this philosophy itself which are based upon these foundations is not also credible, and no philosophy (as you say) is credible, and the outcome of these expressions is the philosophy of doubt, negation of knowledge and denial of philosophy, and not inclination toward a particular ism; perhaps, whatever I know are all products and outcomes of certain conditions of the environment.

So, up to here is our discussion about dispositions (*fiṭriyyāt*) in the context of knowledge and understanding. The conclusion we have so far is that after mentioning the dispositions and choosing a view that "The principles of thinking is intrinsic" and explaining that this "intrinsic" (*fiṭrī*) that we say is different from what Kant or Plato has meant (that is, connate) and by "intrinsic" we do not mean connate or congenital, we arrive at the conclusion that the only way of giving value to human knowledge, human thinking and human philosophy is to accept the innateness of the primary principles of thinking. Other than this, we have nothing left except absolute doubt. As such, the philosophies which do not subscribe to the innateness of the primary principles of thinking and they (proponents of those philosophies) also want to claim that "We believe in a particular philosophy – for example, dialectical materialism – and the universe is nothing but matter, [they must be told that] this in itself is also a way of thinking which has no credibility, apart from the fact that one could also raise objections to its contents, because this foundation upon which you establish it (philosophy such as dialectical materialism) is not a foundation. In other words, you are like the one who was sitting on a branch of tree and cut it. You cut or are cutting the branch on which you sat or are sitting. You can no longer stay there and you have already fallen from there.

Dispositions in the Context of Wants and Desires

The second part is dispositions in the context of wants and desires. Does not the human being have a set of dispositions in the context of his wants and desires, or not? The first part is knowledge and understanding, whereas this is wants and desires. At the outset, I shall divide this section into two. (I am not also particular with terminology whether here the [proper] term is instinct (*gharīzah*), disposition (*fiṭrah*), or something else.) Intrinsic or instinctive desires of human being are of two kinds – physical and psychological. Physical desire means the demand which is totally associated with the body, such as instinct to be hungry or eating, desire for food, looking for food following hunger. This is something which is so physical and material, but it is instinctive; that is, it is related to the bodily structure of the human being and every animal. After the human being felt the need for what the ancients called "substitute for what is worn out" (*badali mā yataḥallal*) – food is digested and there is a need for another set of food – a set of secretions can be felt in his stomach. Thereafter, these will be reflected in the mind in the form of a feeling, even if a person such as a small child is totally unaware of his stomach. Then, in order to put an end to this feeling, he begins to eat. And after eating he will no longer have that feeling; in fact, he would even abhor food. The same is true with sexual instinct. So long as the sexual instinct is related to lust[1] and so long as it is related to the body hormones and secretions of the glands, there is no doubt that it is a matter of instinct – whether you call it "intrinsic" or not. That is, it is something which is not acquired or learned, and it is related to the human constitution. In the same manner, sleep – regardless of its nature, whether it is weariness of the cells, poisoning of the cells due to extreme amount of work, or consumption of energy which must be consumed by the body – after all, is related the physical constitution of the human being. They are usually called "instinctive matters".

At present, we are not concerned with these physical instinctive or intrinsic matters. They are beyond the scope of our discussion. There is a set of instincts or dispositions in the context of wants and desires which are even called "psychological matters" in psychology and the pleasure which stems from them is called "psychological pleasure", such as desire to have a child. Desire to have a child is different from sexual instinct as the latter is related to the satisfaction of sexual desire. In addition, everyone wants to have a child, and the pleasure which a person experiences for having a child is something which is unlike these pleasures; in other words, it is not physical pleasure and it is not associated to any bodily limb. For the meantime, let us set aside the difference which psychologists set between psychological pleasure and physical pleasure. It is beyond the scope of our discussion.

Aspiring for superiority, craving for supremacy and power-

1. This is because there is a dispute as to whether love and lust are one and the same, or not. Even in the relationship of two individuals, is love a kind of lust or not? For the meantime, we will not complicate [the discussion].

seeking are also a psychological thirst for man. No matter how much power a person acquires, still he will desire for more power and this is something which knows no bound. Sa'dī[1] says,

نیم‌نانی گر خورد مرد خدای بذل درویشان کند نیم دگر
هفت اقلیم ار بگیرد پادشاه همچنان در بند اقلیمی دگر

When a pious man eats half a loaf of bread
He bestows the other half upon the dervishes.
If a king were to conquer the seven climates
He would still in the same way covet another.[2]

Once a person succumbs to power-seeking, aspiring for superiority and expansion of dominion, this path knows no end. Even if the entire world is under his power and sovereignty and if there are human beings and civilizations in another planet, he will contemplate on going there and invading it. [The same is true with] the quest for truth, fact-finding, question of science, knowledge, discovery of realities, arts, aesthetics, creativity, craftsmanship, invention, innovation, and on top of them, what we call "love and

---

1. Shaykh Muṣlīḥ al-Dīn Sa'dī (1184-1283) was one of the greatest Persian poets. Born in Shīrāz, he studied Sufi mysticism at the Nizāmiyyah madrasah at Baghdad, with Shaykh 'Abd al-Qādir al-Jīlānī and with Shahāb al-Dīn Suhrawardī. He made the pilgrimage to Mecca many times and traveled to Central Asia, India, the Seljuq territories in Anatolia, Syria, Egypt, Arabia, Yemen, Abyssinia, and Morocco. His best known works are *Būstān* [Garden] and *Gulistān* [Rose-Garden], also known as *Sa'dī-Nāmeh*. The former is a collection of poems on ethical subjects while the latter is a collection of moral stories in prose. He also wrote a number of odes, and collections of poems known as *Pleasantries, Jests* and *Obscenities*. His influence on Persian, Turkish and Indian literatures has been very considerable, and his works were often translated into European languages from the 17 th century onward. [Trans.]
2. *Gulistān*, chap. 1 (The Manners of Kings), story 3.

worship". In essence, worship is that which springs from the arena of love. As to the kinds of worship which are [expressed] through craving [for some gain] or fear [of something more powerful], we know that from the viewpoint of Islam it does not have much value. In other words, their value is preliminary and with the purpose one would proceed to the higher level [of worship]. It is like someone who sends off a child to the school through threat or allurement, but it is not because going to school is indeed something that can be bought and sold, and that a reward must be given to him. It is really not so. It has an essential value but since he is just a child and he cannot still comprehend its value, he must be sent to the school by attracting him with a chick-pea of raisins or buying him a bike.

These are a set of wants and desires which we will discuss again as to whether they are intrinsic or not. By denying intrinsic facts in the context of knowledge and understanding, we reached a critical point – the critical point of absolute doubt, the kind of doubt which will totally drag us toward philosophism, negation of knowledge, and denial of real understanding. Now, let us see if we have intrinsic desires or none. We will also discuss it this way. Before proving that we have intrinsic desires or otherwise, we would like to see if, granting that we have such desires, to which point we will reach and what will be holding in our hands, and if we do not have such desires, what will be left with us? Just as in the context of knowledge and understanding, some individuals denied the primary principles of thinking while clinging to the secondary principles for no reason, does it mean that here, by denying these dispositions and fundamental realities, we will also meet the likes of those individuals who, as we can observe, have uprooted the foundation and sat on the branch, clinging to it while not knowing that they themselves have cut off the root? Then, we will proceed to the next level which is of proving.

Now, one may possibly say that I do not believe in dispositions in the context of knowledge and that I am that philosophist and absolute doubter, and he might also say that I do not accept dispositions as true in the framework of desires and that I do not believe in humanity at all. In other words, he might say, "You are using what the logicians call 'dialectics' (*jadal*)." That is to say, "You use the things which they (opposite camp) accept against them themselves. We do not accept at all that which they accept. Can you independently prove these things to us, or not?" Let me answer, "Yes, we can prove them, so that we can proceed to other subjects."

Chapter 3: Sacred Inclinations

There are two questions here. Since both questions are part of our discussions, for the moment we have no option but to spend our time answering them. I like so much to briefly state that there are such questions. One is actually about the meaning of innateness of the search for God. By the way, a subject is cited from the book entitled *Khudā az Dīdgāh-e Qur'ān* (*God from the Viewpoint of the Qur'an*),[1] stating that human beings were looking for the cause of phenomena that they used to observe, and every cause that they would discover they would, in turn, for look for its cause. This state of affairs has finally led human being to the point where after this series of causes, it must end in something. This is because if every phenomenon is supposed to be the effect of another phenomenon which is like the first phenomenon, this so-called - thinking will lead to an endless cycle [of cause and effect]. As such, their thinking will end at most to the point that there must be a central point which is the Cause of causes and all causes must originate from It. This is cited from it (the abovementioned book) and then it is thus written:

> "We have seen here, therefore, that external phenomena drive human beings to look for the Primary Cause. If we say that the search for God and as you say – in volume

1. [Written by Shāhīd Dr. Āyatullāh Sayyid Muḥammad Beheshtī.]

> five of *The Principles of Philosophy [and the Method of Realism]* – the discussion about God is innate, then how can we justify the involvement of external phenomena in urging the human being to talk about God? In other words, do we not personally acknowledge that external phenomena make the human being aware of the discussion about God and not a factor in man's being?"

I think if you read well *The Principles of Philosophy [and the Method of Realism]*, the answer to this question is there. As I general remember, we have said something about the means of general causation; that is, the human being rises up to search for God. It is for this reason that the "principle of causation" is embedded in his spirit; that is, it is looking for the causes, and this search for the causes, in turn, makes him reach the Cause of causes. It is the same point which is the "factor" in man's being. In other words, if only this motive to discover the causes and to reach the Origin the causes were not present in the human being, he would have just indifferently passed by these phenomena that he would observe. The point is that when a person sees an external phenomenon, what is that which persuades him to look for its cause? The external phenomenon which presents itself to the human being also presents itself to the animal. That is, that which can be seen by human being can also be seen by animals, but the thing which after seeing this external phenomenon urges him to look for its causes is that feeling in man that every phenomenon necessitates a cause and naturally, if the said cause is also a phenomenon like the first phenomenon and is in need of a cause [to exist], then this idea comes to the mind: Do all causes originate from a single Source and that Source is a cause which is not a phenomenon? And this is the meaning of being innate or intrinsic (*fiṭrī*). This innateness is not contradictory with this point and even affirms it. Now, let us set aside its details until we discuss them later.

The second question pertains to the signs of innateness. We have also said before that this is a discussion which we will have in the future – what are the signs of innateness of a character? How could we know that such-and-such trait or such-and-such character of a person is something innate in the human being, or just an effect of a set of external factors – whether they are social or individual factors?

Let us continue the discussion. We have said that what is certain and leaves no room for any doubt or dispute is that the human being has certain distinctions with all creatures that we know.[1] One is that he is the being that can perceive the external world. In other words, he thinks about the external world. To put it differently, he is a being that thinks, and in today's jargon, he is the being that is conscious. He is conscious of himself as well as of the world. Given this character of his, he has a set of understandings of the external world, which we call "perceptions" (*adrāk*), and what an elegant word has been chosen since then! This is because *adrāk* means to understand and reach. Philosophers have also clung to the lexical root of this word. In Arabic language, if a person is looking for something and founds it, it is said, "*Adrakahu*" (He found it). For example, if a person is pursuing someone escaping and catches him in the end, it is said, "*Adrakahu*" (He found him).

The human being's understanding of the external world is a kind of connection and link between the human being and the external world. It is said that so long as man is ignorant, there is a veil or barrier between him and the world. The more he is knowledgeable with the world, the more he will "reach" the world; it is a kind of

1. We do not want to negate all other distinctions or differences.

reaching or arrival at a point.

There is no doubt that in this regard, the human being can be compared neither to the inanimate objects, plants nor animals. The animals have a kind of vague awareness of the external world, and it is certain that such awareness is not at par with that of the human being. The least is that the animals do not think, because thinking means that a being acquires a new asset through acquired assets it has. That is, he discovers whatever he does not know through that which he knows. When you sit, you think of something. Whenever you have a problem, you take a seat, think and then find a solution for it. What kind of action is this "thinking"? This is an action which transforms an unknown to an effect by means of a sort of setting connections among known things. That is, you will discover a new solution, which is exactly like reproduction in the material or physical world in which two beings – male and female – shall be married and through their marital union new birth comes into being. When a person thinks of combining those assets together, he sets a linkage for combining them, and as a result, new idea and new solution will be found by him. The animals do not possess these [qualities]. The animals can only feel; the same superficial observation. For instance, they can also see the colours that we see. They can also feel the heat that we feel. There is nothing more than this. But to think is one of the distinctive characteristics of the human being.

Human Being's Superiorities

The second issue related to the human being's advantage over non-humans is a set of specific inclinations in him which, on one hand, can be called "sacred inclinations" and be treated, on the other hand, as inclinations which are not based upon self-centeredness. That is, the human being has a set of inclinations which are beyond "self-centeredness". What is "self-centeredness"? It refers to inclinations which in the end points to the individual. This also exists among animals. It is also common among human beings. Animal has also inclination toward nourishment, but this inclination toward nourishment is an inclination toward one's self. That is, it has inclination to acquire food for itself. Of course, human being has also a set of inclinations on the basis of self-centeredness, but apart from being human, he is also an animal. In fact, he is an animal first before being a human. These kinds of inclination also exist in human being.

Now, the issue is that the human being has another set of inclinations. First of all, these inclinations are not based upon self-centeredness, and secondly, in his conscience he believes in a kind of sanctity for these inclinations. That is, he believes in them as high or holy, and he will regard anyone having such inclinations as nobler or holier person. Animal's inclinations are either self-centred such as inclination toward sleep, food and the like, or if ever they are "others-centred" they are limited to survival of the same species; that is, limited to reproduction – and they are limited to instinct. (Once again, we are the point of defining "instinct".) In other words, they are confined to a conscious, voluntary and selective action. This is very obvious and tangible. Let us consider, for example, a horse. As it gives birth to its pony – or the more its birth gets nearer – it has a strong attachment to its pony which God knows. Once the pony is there and you ride on the horse, this animal does not want to move. It is worried about its pony. It always faces its pony, and if we keep it away from the pony, it would follow it. This continues until the time that the pony grows up. As the pony grows, the horse's attachment to it becomes lesser. Then, as it turns into a fully grown horse, [this attachment ceases to exist]. A horse which is, for example, seven years old and a pony which is, for example, two years old,[1] it is expected that it will be pleased to look at its pony whereas it has no more attachment to its young one, and if it will be approached, it will kick and leave it alone. Why? It is because this instinct (of attachment) is only limited to the protection of the young one so as to ensure the continuity of the generation, and there is nothing more than this. As the pony is fully grown like its own mother, it is just like any other horse of the mother.

Also, the action of the animals which live collectively is not a selective (*intikhābī*) action but rather appointed (*intiṣābī*). That is, it is such by nature as they are appointed for that action and they perform their actions as something forced; that is, they have no option but to perform them inevitably. For instance, bees or some ants (such as termites) are social animals. The deer are also social animals to some extent. But their actions are also a sort of instinctive actions. In other words, they are a kind of spontaneous and semi-conscious actions and not selective. Instead, they are determined by nature from the very beginning and these animals cannot go against the way they are. These are animal's inclinations.

The human being, however, has inclinations which, first of all, cannot be justified by self-centeredness – and if there is any such justification, it is something objectionable and disputable – and secondly, they are selective and conscious [inclinations], and at any rate, they are the things which are recognized as the criteria and standard of humanity. If ever all schools of thought in the world talk about "humanity," "humanity" refers to the same inclinations and things. That is, other than them there is nothing else. Nowadays, all schools of thought in the world including divine, materialistic and sceptic – and whatever you would like to say – finally talk about

1. I do not know how the horses and men were during the time of Firdawsī so much so that it is said, "Three five (fifteen) years of horse and three ten (thirty) years of man." Men with thirty years of age are already old and horses with fifteen years of age are already dead!

issues related to the human being, and these issues are issues which are considered beyond the animal level. At the outset, we must present these issues, and then we will see if they are intrinsic for the human being or not. If they are not intrinsic, what conclusion we should draw, and they are intrinsic, how we should make the conclusion, and thereafter we will proceed by looking for the proof of their being intrinsic or otherwise.

Emotional Dispositions

1. Truth-Seeking

These inclinations – which we have said are sometimes called "sacred" – are generally five, or at least for the meantime, we will identify five of them. One of them is the subject of "truth" (*ḥaqīqah*). We can also call the subject of "truth" as the subject of "knowledge" or the subject of "knowing the reality of the universe". It means that there is such inclination in the human being – inclination to discover the realities of whatever exists; perception of the truths of things "as they are"; that is, the human being wants to know the world, the universe, [and] the things as they are. The following is one of the supplications attributed to the Noble Messenger (S):

أَللَّهُمَّ أَرِنِي ٱلْأَشْيَاءَ كَمَا هِيَ.

"O Allah, let me know the things as they are."[1]

Basically, this is the very purpose of what is called "wisdom" (*ḥikmah*) and philosophy. In essence, if ever a person who pursues philosophy, it is because he wants to understand the truth and the realities of things. We may also label this feeling as "philosophical feeling". You may call it "truth-seeking". You may call it "subject of truth," "philosophical subject" or "subject of knowledge". There is a statement – I have seen that the foremost person to have used this

1. *Ghawālī al-Li'ālī*, vol. 4, 132.

term was Abū ʿAlī Sīnā[1] and I do not know if was anyone prior to him who has used it and later on Shaykh al-Ishrāq[2] and others – regarding the purpose or objective of philosophy, or a definition of philosophy according to its purpose or outcome. It says,

صَيْرُورَةُ ٱلْإِنْسَانِ عَالَماً عَقْلِيًّا مُضَاهِياً لِلْعَالَمِ ٱلْعَيْنِيِّ.

That is to say that the outcome of being a philosopher is the human being must be the rational world just like the actual world. That is, he should understand this actual world as it is. Then he himself must be a world, but the world out there is the actual world. It must be the same world, but this one is the rational form of that world. This question of truth or truth-seeking, according to the philosophers, is the same theoretical perfection of man, and he inherently and intrinsically wants to attain theoretical perfection; that is, he would understand the truths of the world. There is such

---

1. Abū ʿAlī al-Ḥusayn ibn ʿAbd Allāh ibn Sīnā Balkhī, known as Abū ʿAlī Sīnā Balkhī or Ibn Sīnā and commonly known in English by his Latinized name "Avicenna" (c. 980-1037) was a Persian polymath and the foremost physician and philosopher of his time. He was also an astronomer, chemist, geologist, logician, paleontologist, mathematician, physicist, poet, psychologist, scientist, and teacher. His important works include *Al-Shifā'* (an encyclopedic work covering, among other things, logic, physics and metaphysics), *Al-Najāt* (a summary of *Al-Shifā'*), and *Al-Ishārāt* or in full, *Al-Ishārāt wa 'l-Tanbīhāt* (a latter work consisting of four parts, viz. logic, physics, metaphysics, and mysticism). [Trans.]
2. Shaykh al-Ishrāq refers to Shahāb al-Dīn Yaḥyā Suhrawardī (b. 1155), a towering figure of the Illuminationist (*ishrāqī*) School of Islamic Philosophy. After studying in Isfahān, a leading center of Islamic scholarship, Suhrawardī traveled through Iran, Anatolia and Syria. Influenced by mystical teachings, he spent much time in meditation and seclusion, and in Halab (modern Aleppo) he favorably impressed its ruler, Malik al-Zāhir. His teachings, however, aroused the opposition of established and learned religious men (*ʿulamā'*), who persuaded Malik to have him put to death. The appellation *al-Maqtūl* (the killed one) meant that he was not to be considered a *shahīd* (martyr). [Trans.]

an inclination in the human being for him to attain the truths of the world.

You can also see in psychology that this feeling is discussed by the name of "sense of seeking the truth" or "sense of curiosity". When an issue is discussed in a broad sense, it is called "sense of curiosity". This is the same thing which also exists in a child. This feeling can be found in a two- or three-year old child – depending on the children. It is the urge to ask question which a child constantly has when he reaches the age of three. In training and education, the father and mother are also advised [to answer the each question of their child as much as possible and not to discard it]. When uninformed and unaware parents observe that their four years old child always ask a question, they regard it as an act of meddling and say, "Kid! Don't be so meddlesome; talk no more." This is wrong. This is a sense of asking question; this is a feeling of curiosity. This is a feeling of seeking the truth, which has just grown in him, and he asks question and he has the right to do so. Even if he asks about certain things which you are unable to answer or he cannot fully understand the answer, one should not give a reply by intimidation, discouragement and suppression of this feeling [by saying]: "Don't talk; don't be meddlesome!" Again, as much as possible the answer must satisfy and convince him. It is even said that many of the child's messy things [are a product of this feeling] because this in itself is a problem. He makes a mess; he is curious of whatever he gets hold of; he knocks something strongly; he beats something else. Is the human being naturally a saboteur and later on reforms himself as he grows older, or not? It is said that this is a product of the same sense of curiosity in him. He wants to beat something to see what will happen. Now, we do not beat something because we know what will happen afterward; we do experience it many times. As such, for us the problem is already solved and there is no more question left unanswered. For him, however, this problem is not yet solved; he beats in order to see what will happen. The issue of "understanding" (*istifhām*) is a problem in itself. Now, what the philosophers talks about is a higher level; the psychologists apply it even to the children – that the human being, after all, is inclined toward knowledge; that is, he wants to know the truths and realities.

You might have already heard of the famous story of Abū Rayḥān al-Bīrūnī.[1] He was on the verge of his death and he had a jurisprudent (*faqīh*) neighbour. His neighbour paid a visit to Abū Rayḥān and saw him lying on his deathbed while facing the *qiblah*.[2] Abū Rayḥān asked him a question on inheritance (*irth*). The jurisprudent was surprised, saying, "Now, what a timing for asking this question?!" Abū Rayḥān said, "I know that I want to die but let me ask you: Which is better, for me to die without knowing the answer to this question or to die while knowing it?" He answered, "It is better for you to die while knowing it." (This in itself is a reality.) Abū Rayḥān said, "So, give me your answer." The jurisprudent gave his answer. He claimed thus, "I have not yet reached our house when I heard the cry of the ladies in the house of Abū Rayḥān."

Now, this in itself is a feeling embedded in every human being. Those who make use of this sense and keep it in themselves will reach a point when the pleasure of discovering the truth for them is better than any other pleasures. In other words, the pleasure of knowledge for them is greater that any other pleasures.[3]

Regarding the late Ḥujjat al-Islām Sayyid Muḥammad Bāqir Shaftī Iṣfahānī (died 1844), our seniors have also narrated a similar story,

---

1. Abū Rayḥān Muḥammad ibn Aḥmad al-Bīrūnī (973-1048): a Persian Muslim scholar and polymath of the 11 th century. [Trans.]
2. *Qiblah*: the direction where the Muslims face in times of prayers and other acts, which is the *Ka'bah* in Makkah. [Trans.]
3. I do elaborate on these things so as for us to know that these are realities regarding human being and they must be analyzed. I have said before that no subject is in need of explanation and interpretation as much as human being does.

and there is also an apparently exact story about Pasteur.[1] During the night of his wedding, after the solemnization and when the bride was sent to the bridal chamber where women would usually come, the late Sayyid Muḥammad Bāqir went to another room while the women were in the bridal chamber. He told himself, "Now is an opportunity which I am going to utilize to study." He began his reading. The ladies already went out [of the bridal chamber]. The poor bride was left alone. No matter how long she waited for the groom but he did not come. At once the late Sayyid realized that it was already dawn; that is, this man was so engrossed in learning that he totally forgot that it was his wedding night. And similar story was also narrated about Pasteur.

It is narrated about him that on his wedding night, he had an hour before fetching his bride. He went to his laboratory room to engage in his works. He was so engrossed in his work that he remained there until morning, forgetting that the previous night was his wedding night!

Now, where are these? There are realities. This feeling more or less exists in all individuals. Of course, like other feelings, this strong in one individual while weak in another, and it also depends on how much a person nurtures or cultivates it, and for this reason of "knowing," the human being is given preference over non-human beings. Stuart Mill,[2] a famous British philosopher, thus says: "An unfortunate learned is better than a fortunate ignorant."

That is to say that If I were to choose between being knowledgeable while unfortunate and living in poverty, indigence and misery, and being ignorant while fortunate in the sense that everything is provided for me, I will prefer the former. "A lonesome

1. Louis Pasteur (1822-95): a French chemist and microbiologist who was a pioneer in pasteurization and the use of vaccines. [Trans.]

2. John Stuart Mill (1806-73): a British philosopher, civil servant and an influential contributor to social theory, political theory, and political economy. [Trans.]

Socrates[1] is better than a corpulent hog." All these statements show the value of truth for the human being, for what is the meaning of knowledge in essence? Is it other than awareness, access to the world and perception of the same?

This is an inclination which pertains to the subject of truth.

2. Inclination Toward Good and Virtue

There is another inclination in the human being which technically pertains to the subject of "good and virtue". In other words, it pertains to the subject of ethics. This relates to what we call "morality". One is inclined to many things because their beneficial and valuable. One is attached to money because it is of value to him. It is a means which can provides for his material needs. This is very good. Man's inclination to benefit is the same "self-centeredness". That is, he tends to incline to something because he draws it toward himself for his own subsistence or survival. (Of course, as to what this inclination of a living being to protect his life is and what its limitation is a question in itself.) Up to this extent, its analysis is somewhat simpler. There are things, however, to which man is attached not because they are [materially] beneficial but because they are virtuous and "rationally good." Benefit (*manfa'ah*) is emotional goodness while virtue (*faḍīlah*) is rational goodness. Virtue is like man's inclination to truthfulness for the sake of truthfulness in contrast to his abhorrence to lying, and his inclination to God-wariness and purity. In general, such inclinations which are virtue are of two kinds; some are individual while others are collective. Examples of individual [virtues] are inclination to order and discipline, inclination to self-control, whatever we call "dominance over the self", self-discipline, and many other

1. Socrates (circa 469-399 BCE): a Classical Greek philosopher and considered one of the founders of Western philosophy. [Trans.]

individual moral concepts including bravery in the sense of courage of the heart and not the use of force which does not pertain to ethics; it is bravery in contrast to cowardice – and the like. And examples of collective [virtues] are inclination to cooperation; helping others; to be socially in unison with one another; inclination to kindness and benevolence; inclination to self-sacrifice (which cannot be reconciled with the logic of benefit because self-sacrifice means to sacrifice oneself or even one's life); and inclination to selflessness:

> ﴿ وَيُؤْثِرُونَ عَلَىٰ أَنفُسِهِمْ وَلَوْ كَانَ بِهِمْ خَصَاصَةٌ ﴾
>
> But they prefer [the Immigrants] to themselves, though poverty be their own lot. (59:9)

That is, while a person is in utter need of a something, he gives preference to others over himself:

> ﴿ وَيُطْعِمُونَ الطَّعَامَ عَلَىٰ حُبِّهِ مِسْكِينًا وَيَتِيمًا وَأَسِيرًا * إِنَّمَا نُطْعِمُكُمْ لِوَجْهِ اللَّهِ لَا نُرِيدُ مِنكُمْ جَزَاءً وَلَا شُكُورًا ﴾
>
> They give food, for the love of Him, to the needy, the orphan and the prisoner, [saying,] 'We feed you only for the sake of Allah. We do not want any reward from you nor any thanks. (76:9)

In general, therefore, inclination to virtue or moral inclinations, or in other words, inclinations which pertain to the subject of virtue and moral goodness exist in the human being.

3. Inclination Toward Beauty and Aesthetic Value

Third is the subject of beauty. In its absolute sense, there is an inclination to beauty and aesthetic value in the human being – whether in the sense of love of beauty or creative beauty which is called "art". This is another inclination which exists in the human being and no one is devoid or bereft of it. A person tries as much as he can to make the garment he wears to be more beautiful. He [beautifies] his room. Just consider this hall. What is the primary purpose for which this hall was built? It is for the assembly of students, or assembly of the students' parents for the presentation of works, for speech delivery, and in short, for public gathering. Now, that those curtains are such is no longer part of the topic. For instance, does the fact that those curtains are such make the sound more audible? No, but this in itself is essentially [desirable to man and] beauty in essence matters for a human being. In the same manner, one constructs a building in the first place, for his protection from heat and cold, stealing, and the like, but he always combines it with his sense of beauty. That is, he always wants that building, furniture and carpet to be beautiful. This love of beauty is something which exists in man. He loves the beauties in nature. In one place, he sees clear and limpid water. He enjoys seeing a swimming pool or sea. He enjoys seeing very elegant natural scene. He enjoys seeing the sky, the horizon, mountains, and all these things. He sees them as beautiful and is pleased with their beauty.

And the same is true with the issue of art which in itself is a creation of a kind of beauty; it pertains to things which have been called before as "beaux crafts" (*ṣanāyi'-e mustaẓrifah*); for example, a script which is a very ancient art. A very elegant script has an extraordinary value for the human being and he keeps it. Even if a person has seen ten times a Qur'an manuscript which is written in a very beautiful script, he will still desire to look at it for the eleventh time. In fact, even if he has seen it a hundred times, he will still desire to look at it one more time.

Our late father (may Allah be pleased with him) who had also a good handwriting had also a particular inclination to calligraphy. He said, "If a Qur'an manuscript with a very beautiful script were written with my own hands, I could not be able to read it because I would be engrossed with its calligraphy and its beauty such that I could no longer read it. An example of elegant calligraphy is the large Baisonghor Epigraph in front of the Bleached Porch (*īwān-e maqṣūrah*) [in the Shrine of Imām al-Rīḍā (A.S.) in Mashhad]. Baisonghor himself who was the son of Gawharshād thus wrote at the end of this epigraph: "Epigraph of Baisonghor ibn Shāhrukh ibn Amīr Taymūr Gūrkān." Gawharshād was the wife of Shāhrukh and Baisonghor was his son. In the third calligraphy, no one can be like Baisonghor. Prior to him, no one had written such a third script and no one after him could probably be able to do so. Although 'Ali-Riḍā 'Abbāsī – who lived during the reign of Shāh 'Abbās – was an extraordinary calligrapher and whose examples of calligraphy which exist up to now in Iṣfahān or Qum in the tomb of Shāh 'Abbās are so beautiful, [he cannot be at par with Baisonghor.]

One of the dimensions of the Qur'an's being a sign (*āyah*) is aesthetic in nature; that is, rhetoric and eloquence, and one of the greatest factors for the universalization of the Qur'an is aesthetic factor; that is, its extraordinary rhetoric and eloquence.

The point is that inclination toward beauty and its manifestations is also one inclination which exists in the human being.

4. Inclination Toward Creativity and Innovation

Yet another inclination which is the fourth one is creativity and innovation. This inclination exists in the human being in that he wants to create or make something; he wants to create something which does not exist. It is true that in order to address his needs in life, man engages in craftsmanship, creativity and innovation. But just as knowledge is a means in life as well as a purpose in itself for man, [so is creativity for him.] One issue which is discussed nowadays is this: Is knowledge for the sake of knowledge, or is it for the sake of life? The answer is this: It is both; that is, for the human being knowledge is – in the jargon of Islamic seminarians – desirable in essence as well as desirable for some other reasons. In other words, knowledge is desirable by its own nature and desirable as it is a means to solve humanity's problems. It is because knowledge and discovery of the truth is desirable in essence and at the same time, since it is power and ability – "He who is knowledgeable is capable" – as well as a means to solve problems in life, it is desirable by-something-else.

The same is true with creativity. You[1] are better experienced with pupils and you know that when a child makes or builds something, how this gives him mirth and joy and boosts his morale. When you give him a handicraft – "Do this handicraft" – [this makes him happy.] He wants to create something new. In general, innovation of any sort is an act of creation in itself. You call certain individuals as innovators. For instance, you say that in the field of teaching, so-and-so has an innovation; that is, he develops a method. It is possible that other individuals are imitators and emulators; that is, they [just] adopt and imitate the methods of others, but some individuals have the ability to develop a method. In general, in social schemes, state policies, city planning, in matters, for example, which a city mayor should plan and initiate, in planning and writing of books, [some are pioneers while others are imitators]. You can see that many of the books are mere imitation. As popular saying goes, "They inscribe printed books and they print scripts once again." That is, they write the ideas that they have taken from printed books and submit the same once again for printing. It is obvious that there is no innovation in this work. There are individuals, however, whose books are an innovation; they are a creation and initiation. And this inclination exists in every person;

---

1. It refers to the managers and teachers of Nīkān School among the audience.]

that he wants to be a maker or builder.

Something more serious than these is in theories [and theory-formulation]. A person formulates a theory and then proves it. Later on, others will accept his theory. (This in itself is a kind of power and creation.) It is like the one who formulated "transubstantial motion" (*ḥarikat-e jawharī*) as a theory and then proved it, and later on, others follow it.[1] Of course, you are also aware that in certain things, two or three purposes are combined together. For example, a person who composes a poem or a composer in poetry, such as Ḥāfiẓ,[2] does two things at the same time. One is that he "creates" a thing; that is, he satisfies his own sense of creativity. The other is that he creates a "beautiful" – a beautiful poem – that is, he satisfies that aesthetic sense. It is also possible that in doing so, the sense of searching for truth is also satisfied. It is not impossible that one thing could be considered from different dimensions.

5. Love and Worship

The fifth subject is what we call for the time being "worship" or "love and worship". Let us go back to our first proposition that there is no being in the world which is as much as the human being in need of interpretation and explanation, because there are elements which can be seen in him which cannot be seen in other beings. Complexities can be seen [in him] whose explanation and interpretation are not easy but so difficult. It is for this reason that the human being is called the "small world" (*'ālam al-ṣaghīr*); that is, he himself is a universe. The mystics do not accept that the human being

1. This alludes to Ṣadr al-Dīn Shīrāzī (1572-1641), better known as Mullā Ṣadrā Sadr al-Muta'allihīn, the foremost representative of the Illuminationist (*ishrāqī*) School of Islamic philosophy whose magnum opus is *Al-Asfār al-Arba'ah* (*The Four Journeys*). [Trans.]

2. Khwājah Shams al-Dīn Muhhammad Hāfiz Shīrāzī (circa 1325-1391) was the fourteenth century Persian lyric bard and panegyrist, and commonly regarded as the preeminent master of the *ghazal* form. [Trans.]

is a small world. They say that the world is the small human being while the human being is the big world. Mawlawī [Rūmī][1] says,

چیست اندرخانه کاندر شهر نیست   چیست اندرجوی کاندر نهر نیست

What is in the house that is not in the city?
What is in the stream that is not in the river?[2]

The house is a part while the city is the whole. Whatever can be found in the house can definitely be found in the city. It is possible, however, that there are things in the city which cannot be found in the house, as is the case most of the time.

In the same manner, whatever is in the small stream is also in the river. Mawlawī then concludes and says:

این جهان جوی است دل چون نهر آب   این جهان خانه است دل شهری عجاب

This world is the stream, and the heart is like a river;
This world is the chamber, and the heart is the wonderful city.[3]

The case is not the opposite that this man (the heart means man) is the house while the world is the city.

The point I want to drive at is the importance of the human being, and there are many things in him which necessitate interpretation and these instances of simple mindedness on the subject of man are

1. Mawlāwī or Mawlānā Jalāl al-Dīn Rūmī (1207-73): the greatest mystic poet in the Persian language and founder of the Mawlawiyyah order of dervishes ("The Whirling Dervishes"). He is famous for his lyrics and his didactic epic, *Mathnawī-ye Maḥnawī* (Spiritual Couplets). [Trans.]
2. *Mathnawī-ye Ma'nawī*, Book 4, line 810, with slight variation. [Trans.]
3. *Ibid.*, line 811, with slight variation. [Trans.]

utterly wrongly. Everybody has this simple mindedness. Now, a topic which perhaps we need to elucidate is the issue of "love and worship" and in fact it is the issue of "love". This love is an extremely amazing phenomenon in man which is so much in need of interpretation. As far as love is concerned, some consider it nothing but an integral part of the subject of carnal desire, saying that love is the same excitement of the sexual instinct and nothing else. In other words, its alpha and omega is nothing but sexual instinct.

There is another view which holds that love begins with sexual instinct but gets refined later on. It slowly loses its sexual dimension and develops into something spiritual. There is yet another view which basically subscribes to two types of love: (1) corporeal love whose alpha and omega are both corporeal, and (2) incorporeal love whose alpha and omega are both incorporeal.

The issue of love especially if it associated with worship – in fact, every love which reaches the stage of real love (that is, the issue of carnal desire must be separated) will reach the stage of worship in the sense that these two are in fact inextricably interwoven with each other – at any rate, the issue of love and worship in man is an issue which is extremely in need of analysis, interpretation, elaboration, and explanation. It must be investigated what really its origin is. Is this statement which has been attributed to Plato from olden times – and as such, today it is said, "Platonic love" – true? Is there really a non-corporeal and non-material origin of love in man? Is there also spiritual love in him, and if there is, what is it?

Chapter 4: Love and Worship as Proof of Human Inclinations

The discussion was about a series of inclination in the human being which do not exist in animals and we have said that it is these inclinations which have made the human being as an important subject for reasoning, interpretation and philosophy. We have mentioned four of these inclinations in the previous session. Now, we mention, though briefly, another inclination. This inclination, as we have said, is that which can be called "love (*'ishq*) and worship" and we can say that it is of the subject of "love and worship".

I should make an explanation and that is the point that this subject is something very tangible such that there is no ground in the human being for us to call it *'ishq*. *'Ishq* is something above *muḥabbah*. In its common extent, *muḥabbah* (love) exists in every human being. [Different] types of *muḥabbah* exist in the human beings, such as the love which exists between two friends; the love which a student has toward his teacher; usual love and affection which exist among couples; the love which exists between parents and their children. This area also exists in the human being – the area of something which is usually called *'ishq*. In Arabic language, it is said that the word *'ishq* (عشق) originally comes from the root-word *'ashaqah* (عَشَقَة) and *'Ashaqah* is the name of a plant which is called *Pīchak* in Fārsī. It rolls around anything it reaches. For example, once it reaches another plant it will roll around it so much so that it will approximately limit and restrict it and become under its control. Such a state [will appear in a person] and its effect is this – contrary to common love – it digresses a person from his usual state; it deprives him of sleep and appetite for eating; it limits his attention to the beloved alone; that is, it brings a kind of singularity, singleness and oneness in him; that is, it takes all his attention to everything and focuses it to only one thing so much so that this becomes his everything; it is such an intense love.

Such a state cannot be witnessed in animals. In animals, the maximum affections are limited to the same affections which human beings show toward their children, or spouses toward their partners. If ever human beings have enthusiasm, bigotry and the like, these things can more or less also be found in animals. But this state in such form is exclusive to the human beings. As to what is basically the nature of this state has in itself become one of the subjects of philosophy. Abū ʿAlī Sīnā has a particular treatise on *ʿishq*. In the same manner, in the section on theology of his book *Al-Asfār [al-Arbaʿah]*, Mullā Ṣadrā has allotted many pages – approximately 40 pages – on the commentary of the nature of *ʿishq* – what state is this that exists in the human beings. Similarly, today the issue of love is being analyzed in psychoanalysis – what is really the nature of this state in the human beings?

Theories on the Nature of Love

Different theories in this regard have been given. Some have absolved themselves of this word, saying that this is an illness; an unpleasantness; a sickness. It can be said that presently this theory – to regard love as purely a kind of sickness – has no following or supporters. Not only that it is a kind of sickness but rather they say that it is something given (*mawhibah*). Then, the main question here is this: Is love of only one kind or two kinds? Some theories maintain that love is only of one kind and that is the physical love; that is, it has organic or physiological root and it has only one kind. All the forms of love that have existed and do exist in the world with all its traces and properties – love which is called 'romantic' has filled the love stories of literatures around the world, such as the story of Majnūn 'Āmirī and Laylā[1] – are physical love and it is nothing other than this.

Some regard love – the same love expressed by a person to another person which is the subject of discussion – is of two types. For example, Abū 'Alī Sīnā, Khwājah Naṣīr al-Dīn al-Ṭūsī,[2] and Mullā Ṣadrā consider love to be of two types. Some regard love as purely sexual love – which is called metaphorical love and not real love – and believe that other forms of love are spiritual love – that is, psychic love, in the sense that in reality there is a kind of attraction between two individuals. The root of physical love is instinct. It ends when the lover meets the beloved and the fire of carnal urge is extinguished, for this is its very end. If its beginning is internal secretions, it will naturally end with its partition. It will begin there and end here. They claim, however, that sometimes a person reaches a point in love which is beyond these things. Khwājah Naṣīr al-Dīn describes it as "alikeness between souls" (*mushākalatun bayn an-nufūs*), in the sense that there is a sort of

---

1. *Majnūn wa Laylā* is a classical Arabic story of star-crossed lovers based on the real story of a young man called Qays ibn al-Mulawwaḥ al-'Āmirī from the northern Arabian Peninsula in the Umayyad era during the 7th century. [Trans.]
2. Muḥammad ibn Muḥammad ibn Ḥasan al-Ṭūsī, better known as Khwājah Naṣīr al-Dīn al-Ṭūsī (597-672 AH/1200-73): a Persian polymath and prolific writer—an astronomer, biologist, chemist, mathematician, philosopher, physician, physicist, scientist, theologian, and *marja' al-taqlīd* (religious authority). [Trans.]

uniformity between souls. In fact, they assert that there is a seed for spiritual and psychic love in the human soul. In reality, if it has also a soul, it is mere stimulant of the human being, and his real object of love (*ma'shūq*) is a Metaphysical Reality in whom the human soul is united, to whom it reaches and whom it discovers. And in reality, the human being's Real Beloved is within him. (For the meantime, we are mentioning [pertinent] assumptions and theories.)

It is in this context that stories are narrated, saying that love (*'ishq*) appears when the lover (*'āshiq*) regards thinking for the beloved (*maḥbūb*) as dearer and more lovable than the beloved himself or herself. It is because the beloved himself or herself and the initial ground for stimulation is within the human being and within himself he becomes accustomed to another Reality – with the same image of the beloved which exists in his soul, and in reality it is not the image of this object (apparent beloved) but rather the image of another object – and he becomes comfortable with it.

This story is narrated even in books of philosophy: After Majnūn recited all those poems and couplets about his love for Laylā and his separation from her, one day Laylā came to the wilderness, in front of him and calling him. Majnūn raised his head and asked, "Who are you?" She answered, "It is me, Laylā. I come to you" (while thinking that now Majnūn would rise up and tightly embrace his beloved whom he missed a lot for their long separation). He said, "No. Go away."

لِي غِنيٍ عَنْكَ بِعِشْقِكِ.

That is to say, "I am fed up loving you and I abhor you!"

Incidentally, we read a similar story in the biography of Shahriyār,[1] a famous poet of our time. Shahriyār was a graduating medical student, right here in Tehran in a boarding house. (He was

1. Sayyid Muḥammad Ḥusayn Behjat-Tabrīzī (1906-88), mainly known by his pen name, Shahriyār, was a legendary Iranian Azerbaijani poet who wrote in Azerbaijani (Azeri Turkish) and Fārsī languages. [Trans.]

from Tabrīz.[1]) There he fell in love with the daughter of the boarding house's owner and how infatuated he was! For whatever reason, the young lady was not infatuated with him. Like Majnūn, he was willing to relinquish everything – work, occupation and studies – just because of her. Many years afterward, in one of their encounters, that lady along with her husband met him and paid him a visit. As she approached him, he was engrossed with himself. He told him, "No, I have no business with you at all. I am already fed up with my earlier feelings and I am already used to it. Even if you are divorced with your husband, I will have nothing to do with you." There is a poem in this regard which he had composed after this lady's visit to him, in which he expressed his emotional state saying, "How comes I am accustomed to her love while I have no affection to her?"

Now, I will briefly say this so that you would pay attention to an aspect of Islamic mystical literature: This issue of one of those issues which are extremely worthy of attention and analysis. Mullā Ṣadrā recites poems which, I think, are those of Muḥyī al-Dīn ibn 'Arabī;[2] that is, they seem to be those of 'Arabī. He does not say who the composer of these poems is. He only says, "Someone says..." Yet, I guess they are those of Muḥyī al-Dīn ibn 'Arabī; they appear to be his. As he expresses the point that some forms of love are not physical but spiritual, he expresses it in this way (and it is indeed an excellent poem):

---

1. Tabrīz: the provincial capital of Eastern Azerbaijan in the north-western part of Iran. [Trans.]

2. Muhyī'd-Dīn ibn al-'Arabī, or in full, Abū 'Abd Allāh Muḥammad ibn 'Alī ibn Muḥammad ibn al-'Arabī al-Ḥātimī al-Ṭā'ī (1165-1240) was the celebrated Arab Andalusian Sufi mystic and philosopher whose magnus opus is *Al-Futuhāt al-Makkiyah* ("The Meccan Openings"). [Trans.]

أُعَانِقُهَا وَالنَّفْسُ بَعْدُ مَشوقَةٌ   إِلَيْهَا وَهَلْ بَعْدَ ٱلْعِنَاقِ تَداني

It says, "I am amorously kissing and caressing her (beloved) and I sense that my soul still craves for her. Is there anything closer [in expressing intimacy] than *mu'āniqah* (amorously kissing and caressing someone)?!"

It wants to convey that if two bodies try to get closer to one another, they will certainly meet and once this happens, it will come to an end.

وَأَلْثِمُ فَاهَا كَيْ تَزولَ حَرارَتِي   فَيَزْدادُ مَا أُلْقي مِنَ ٱلْهَيَجَانِ

It says, "I kiss her lips so that my heat will mellow down. I sense that it intensifies even more." Now, the philosophical conclusion it wants to arrive at is this:

كَأَنَّ فُؤَادِي لَيْسَ يُشْفىٰ غَليلُهُ   سِوىٰ أَنْ يُرىٰ ٱلرُّوحانِ يَتَّحِدَانِ[1]

That is to say, "It is impossible for this fire within me to be put off unless two souls shall be united together."

As such, this theory is one which divides love into physical love and spiritual love; that is, it recognizes a kind of love which is different from physical love in terms of the origin – in the sense that its origin is not sexual but rather the human being's soul and natural disposition (*fiṭrah*) – and also different from sexual love in terms of the end-purpose because sexual love ends with the satisfaction of the carnal desire, but this love does not end just like that. This is also one theory.

For the meantime, we do not want to engage in these philosophical discussions and to put forth the arguments brought

---

1. *Asfār al-Arba'ah*, vol. 7, 179.

by the philosophers to prove this kind of love, which is also called 'Platonic love'. We just want to mention some lines which are simple discussions, and they are the following:

That which is obvious is that human being appreciates love in the sense that he regards it as something worthy of appreciation, whereas that which pertains to carnal desire is not so. For example, human being has craving for eating or desire for food which is something natural. Does the mere fact that it is a natural desire necessitate that it is worthy of great appreciation? Have you seen so far even a single person in the world who praises his craving for a certain food? So long as it is related to [sexual] desire, love is also like craving for eating and not worthy of great appreciation. At any rate, however, this reality (love) has been sanctified and a great deal of literatures in the world comprises sanctification of love. As far as individual or social psychoanalysis is concerned, this is extremely worthy of attention – what is this [phenomenon]?

The Lover's Annihilation in the Beloved

More surprising is the fact that a person is proud of sacrificing everything for the sake of his beloved and of showing that he is non-entity and nothing before her. That is, it is a source of pride and honour for him to have nothing vis-à-vis his beloved, and whoever is there is none but the beloved. In other words, it is "the lover's annihilation in the beloved". We have mentioned something similar in the field of ethics. In ethics there is something, such as self-sacrifice or altruism, which is seemingly incompatible with logic. Altruism is incongruent with self-centeredness. Self-sacrifice is inharmonious with self-centeredness. Yet, you can see that speaking of good manners, man highly appreciates munificence, beneficence, altruism, and self-sacrifice, regarding them as virtues and holding them in high esteem and regards. Here the issue love (*'ishq*) is also different from the issue of carnal desire (*shahwah*), because if it is carnal desire, it means to desire for something for oneself. Here lies the difference carnal desire and something else. When one is in love with someone else and the issue is that of carnal desire, the objective is taking possession and benefiting from the connection with the beloved. In love, however, the issue of connection and taking possession [of anything] is not a concern at all. The issue being discussed is the lover's annihilation (*fanā'*) in the beloved. That is, once again, it is incompatible with the logic of self-centeredness.

As such, this issue in such form is extremely worthy of discussion and analysis. What is this in the human being? What state is this and where does it originate that only for the beloved's sake that one is willing to absolutely surrender and nothing from his self, identity and I-ness shall remain? In this regard, Mawlawī (Rūmī) has very elegant poems which are extraordinary in the mystical literature:

عشق قهّار است ومن مقهور عشق چون قمر روشن شدم از نور عشق

Love is the All-subduer, and I am subdued by Love:
By Love's light I have been made illuminated as moon.[1]

This is the issue of worship. That is, love draws a person to a point where he wants to create an object of worship out of the beloved and to regard himself as servant to his absolute master (beloved) and to reckon himself non-entity and nothing in front of the beloved. What category is this? What is the reality of this [state]?

We have said that one theory maintains that absolute love has sexual root and end-point; it moves along the same line of sexual instinct and continues until the end which is also sexual in nature.

Another theory is the one we have mentioned. Our philosophers emphasize this theory. They believe in two kinds of love, viz. sexual-physical love and spiritual love. And they say that there is a room

1. *Mathnawī Ma'nawī*, Book 6, line 902, with slight variation. [Trans.]

for spiritual love in every human being.

There is a third theory which attempts to combine the two [mentioned] theories, [the theory of Freud[1] which recognizes spiritual love.] Freud, the well-known psychoanalyst who regards everything – love of knowledge, doing good, virtue, worship, and everything else – as originating from sexual instinct, considers love to be primarily sexual. His theory today, however, is no longer acceptable; another theory has been formulated. The said theory propounds that in "love" some properties can be found which are incompatible with sexual dimensions. In other words, it is not dependent on the sexual urges or excitement which is its epicentre, because sexual matter is like hunger; hunger is a natural condition; when the body is in need of food and there is a series of urges, there is hunger and if there are no such urges, then there is no hunger. In sexual need, the same is true. When there is this physical need, there will be urges to whatever extent, otherwise there is no such [physical need]. "Love", however, does not possess such properties; as such, they have explained in such a way that as far as the initial stage of love is concerned, it is sexual, but as far as the end-point or quality is concerned, it is non-sexual. In other words, it starts as something sexual; its origin is carnal desire but later on, it will change quality and condition, and in the end, it will transform into something spiritual.

In his book *The Pleasure of Philosophy*, Will Durant,[2] the famous

1. Sigmund Freud (1856-1940): the founder of psychoanalysis who founded the International Psychoanalytical Association in 1910 and whose view on psychoanalysis was reached through his study of the effect of hypnosis on hysteria. Among his numerous and well-known works are *The Interpretations of Dreams*, *The Psychopathology of Everyday Life*, *Introductory Lectures in Psychoanalysis*, *Humor and Its Relation to the Unconscious*, *The Ego and the Id*, *The Problem of Anxiety*, and *The Future of an Illusion*. [Trans.]
2. William James Durant (1885-1981): a prolific American writer, historian, and

historian, has a discussion about love. He subscribes to the same theory, refuting and rejecting Freud's theory. He says that the fact is that later on, love changes direct, path and even changes characteristic and quality. That is, it will totally come out of the sexual state. He regards as incorrect the foundation of Freud's theory.

Our view in putting forth the issue of love is more on that inclination that the lover finds himself being annihilated in the beloved, and we call it "worship". This is something which is incompatible with material reckonings.

Wiliam James' Statement

In his book *Religion and the Mind*, William James[1] says that because of a set of inclinations which exists in us and has made us attached to the nature, there is also another set of inclinations which exists in us and these are incompatible with material reckonings and natural considerations, and it is these inclinations that connect us to the metaphysical, and whose explanation and interpretation is that which the Muslim philosophers have made, believing that this state of annihilation which the lover experiences is actually the stage of his perfection. This, [in essence,] is not annihilation and turning into nothingness. If his real beloved is this physical and corporeal entity, then annihilation cannot be justified – how could one incline toward his or its own annihilation? In reality, however, his real beloved is another Reality and this (outward beloved) is His (Real Beloved's) manifestation and representation, and in fact, he

---

philosopher. [Trans.]

1 . William James (1842-1910): a pioneering American psychologist and philosopher trained as a medical doctor, considered the originator of the doctrine of pragmatism and whose best-known work is *The Varieties of Religious Experience* (1902). [Trans.]

shall be united with More Perfect [Being] than himself and with More Perfect Station than himself, and in this way, this soul shall attain his own perfection.

Russell's Statement

The Westerners call these kinds of love "Oriental love" and they even sanctify it. In his *Marriage and Morals*, Bertrand Russell[1] says: "Nowadays, even in the realm of imagination, we cannot comprehend the spirit of the poets who talk about their annihilation in their poems without having the least attention to the beloved."

He wants to say that in the forms of love that we usually know of, we know love as a means and preliminary step toward union. (There are many statements in this regard.) He says that in Oriental love, love is basically not a means but the objective in itself. He then great appreciates it, saying that it is this love which bestows greatness, glory and identity to the human spirit.

Justification for the Abovementioned Five Subjects

Now, let us deal with the main subject at hand. What do we know of and how do we explain these five subjects which we have discussed in these two sessions, viz. truth and knowledge, art and aesthetics, goodness and virtue, innovation and creativity, and love and worship? Generally speaking, they have two basic explanations. One explanation is that all these things emanate

1. Bertrand Russell (1872 - 1970): a British philosopher, mathematician and man of letters. Initially a subscriber of idealism, he broke away in 1898 and eventually became an empiricist. His works include *The Principles of Mathematics* (1903), *Principia Mathematica* (3 vols., 1910-1913) in collaboration with A.N. Whitehead, *Marriage and Morals* (1929), *Education and the Social Order* (1932), *An Inquiry into Meaning and Truth* (1940), *History of Western Philosophy* (1945), and popularizations such as *The ABC of Relativity* (1925), as well as his *Autobiography* (3 vols., 1967-69). [Trans.]

from man's natural disposition (*fiṭrah*). Love for truth (truth-seeking) is an inclination which has been engrained in man's spiritual nature. The human being is a being which is composed of body and spirit, and his spirit is something divine:

﴿ وَنَفَخْتُ فِيهِ مِن رُّوحِي ﴾

And I have breathed into him of My spirit. (15:29)

There is a non-natural element in the human being, as well as natural elements. The natural elements have attached him to nature, while this non-natural element has linked him to non-natural and non-physical things. That the human being is inclined toward the truth and loves it is a desire which is related to his spirit and his spirit's nature. Beauty is an inclination in his soul. So is moral virtue as well as inclination to creativity, innovation and invention. So is the inclination to adore a beloved which in reality is a ray of worship of the Real Beloved. That is, the human being's Real Beloved is the Sacred Essence of God, the Exalted, and whenever he is spiritual in love with any other being, this rekindles the flame of the real love which is love of the Real Being's Essence which is expressed in such a form. This is one kind of explanation for all those [subjects].

Justification Based Upon Negation of Emotional Inclinations

Naturally, another explanation is [to say] that [sense of] goodness is not intrinsic (*fiṭrī*). Once it is not intrinsic, we must look for an explanation of all these things from outside the human being. Let us deal with its clearest manifestations. For example, for what purpose is the human being's inclination to knowledge and high regard for it? They say that the human being has no difference with the animal. What the human being desires by instinct are the same matters for his subsistence. They are things [which are related] to his subsistence and livelihood as well as the same physical-natural matters that must be provided for him. As a result of this subsistence and livelihood as well as these physical needs, however, the human being becomes in need of a set of other needs which take various forms. For example, the human being will be in need of law. Why will he be in need of law? It is because he provides for the means of his subsistence. It is obvious that he cannot live alone, and people are forced to live together. Their needs and interests necessitate that they live together. After living together, they will feel [the need that] they should believe in a sort of limit or restriction among themselves; so they will have no option but to promulgate certain rules. These rules are laws, yet they will still observe them because the interests of them all necessitate that they observe these rules. For example, they will promulgate [the principle of] justice because their interests necessitate so. Once we all see that we are in need of this social living and that this social living is also impossible without justice, we say, "Therefore, let us all submit to justice." I want justice so that you could not oppress me. In turn, you also want justice so that I could not oppress you. But to say that I want justice for the sake of justice itself is basically meaningless. Then, one realizes that the more he is knowledgeable and acquainted with nature the better for his physical life. Knowledge helps a lot in his subsistence, and in fact, the best means and finest tool for physical life is no other than knowledge. As a result, he comes to highly appreciate it and he assumes it to be worthy of appreciation; otherwise, knowledge must have essential sanctity – that I want knowledge for the sake of knowledge itself has no meaning. Knowledge is a tool, but no tool is as useful as knowledge for the human being's material life and comfort. As such, as he realizes that knowledge is the best of tools, he has great appreciation for it. Sometimes, a set of great appreciations is artificially created (in the sense that they are so much highlighted). For whatever reason, the class which has acquired knowledge has more pieces of information and naturally, they are more familiar than other people and also, they are smarter and more astute, and they can deceive other people because they could make use of others' fruit of work. They will come forward and pretend to believe in an essential sanctity for knowledge – "Yes, knowledge is such and the learned in such. Hence, since we are knowledgeable, you proceed to your work and deliver you products for us to consume."

Similar explanations are also given for art and beauty. So are for creativity and innovation. What is creativity or innovation? Since it is also means for physical life and comfort, [the human being also gives it high regard;] otherwise, it is nothing in and by itself. Love and worship are also basically devoid of meaning because it renders man alien to his self and expels him from himself. That the lover turns into somebody else and then he would express willingness to sacrifice for the sake of the beloved and to give everything along this way is totally incompatible with logic.

[This explanation of the same subjects] is tantamount to washing away the foundation of them all. Naturally, the moral values will become baseless. They have no option but to consider moral values to be part of the assumptions, inventions, machinations, and pursuits of the exploitative classes – what?! Munificence – what?! Kindness – what?! Self-sacrifice – what?! Altruism – what?! In other words, naturally, they cannot justify these things, yet in this regard some schools of thought have such audacity to conclude from their own principles that those principles provide those conclusions. Other schools of thought, however, do not have such audacity.

Audacious and Non-Audacious Sensualists

In the discussion of mental dispositions, we have said that when the tide of sensualist philosophy[1] swept Europe, one group became sensualists, and out of this group some have really remained sensualists, loyal to their being sensualists and audacious in the requirement of prerequisites of sensualism, saying that "We do not have conviction and faith in anything other than that which is perceived by our senses, but we do not also negate anything beyond that." They staunchly upheld these two principles, thus:

We can neither affirm nor deny anything which we cannot sense. (It is an apparently reasonable statement because of the use of 'sense', saying "I sense it; since I sense it, it therefore exists, but 'sense' does not tell me that whatever I cannot sense does not exist, but rather [only] says that I cannot sense [it]."

Regarding so many issues, they said that although the mind accepts them, since we have investigated and realized that they are not tangible, we do not affirm them; for example. The principle of causation. They said that "The principle of causation is not tangible. That which is tangible is that sometimes the events in this universe follow one another; they are in succession one after the other; they are together. Yet, that which we know as 'causation' (*'illiyyah*) and we say that 'A' is the cause of 'B' and what we think of 'causation' is that if there is no 'A' then it is impossible for 'B' to exist, and we say that the existence of 'B' depends on the existence of 'A'. One cannot sense them. They are products of the mind, and since the sensory perception cannot affirm them, we cannot accept them."

1. With a long precedence in the history of human thought and traceable to the Skeptics of Ancient Greece, sensualism is the philosophy which regards the way of knowing realities as limited to sensory observation and experiment. [Trans.]

They are audacious sensualists in the sense that they are sensualists who are totally loyal and devoted to the prerequisites of their school of thought's sensualism, and for this reason, they are worthy of respect.

There are some [sensualists], however, who wanted to be sensualists initially and to be rationalists in the end or conclusion. The materialists are all like this. The materialists, on one hand, are like the sensualists in expressing views on knowledge, and on the other hand, they are like the rationalists in expressing views on issues in philosophy. In other words, they rely on things which the sensory perception is silent about.

Nietzsche's Statement

The same is true as far as the inclinations are concerned. The followers of the school of human materialism – the school of thought which regards the human being as pure matter – are classified into two. We consider one group of them to be audacious materialists we call the other group as non-audacious or hypocrite materialists. Audacious materialists were those who totally embraced the prerequisites of being a materialist, such as Nietzsche.[1] Nietzsche is a materialist philosopher. Regarding the human being, he does not believe in soul and similar things. As a result, his views on the human being are totally based upon his own philosophy. He says, "Throw away that which is called 'morality'. If ever all the moralists throughout the world have come to say, 'Do not follow your carnal desire,' I say to you, 'Follow it!' Why not follow it? If ever all the moralists throughout the world have come to say, 'Hasten to help the weak and fight against the powerful that oppresses the weak,' I say the opposite. If ever you happen to

1. Friedrich Wilhelm Nietzsche (1844-1900): a 19th -century German philosopher and classical philologist who wrote critical texts on religion, morality, contemporary culture, philosophy and science. [Trans.]

encounter a weakling, [you also trample upon his rights.]" Our poet [Sa'dī] thus says,

چو می‌بینی که نابینا و چاه است   اگر خاموش بنشینی گناه است

But if you see a blind man near a well

It is a crime for you to remain silent.[1]

This conveys that it is a sin if you do say something (with the intention of help or warning). If you see someone who fell into a ditch, you even pelt him with stones. Nature, based on the course it has so far been following, dictates that it is the right thing [to do]. Some have turned to be weak while others have turned to be strong. According to the dictate of nature, those who are weak are condemned to extinction. According to the dictate of morality, they are also condemned to extinction. The supreme man is Genghis Khan.[2] Compassion – what?! Compassion is [a sign of] weakness. Self-sacrifice – what?! It is foolishness.

It is this that has negated all human values, and indeed if, regarding the human being, we regard the human being as purely a material being, there is no other option but to negate these [values]. That is, the things we call 'humanity,' 'human inclinations' and 'human sanctities' are all fictitious and baseless. To subscribe to human materialism, on one hand, and to talk about humanity and human values, on the other hand, are contradictory and cannot be justified. Human values are compatible with human disposition and human disposition, in turn, is compatible with the fact that in his nature, the human being has a human origin – the origin of such sacred inclinations; that is, there is a sacred reality in man's nature in whose essence is embedded the desire for excellence. The human

1. *Gulistān*, chap 1 (The Manners of Kings), story 38, with a slight variation. [Trans.]
2. Genghis Khan (1162–1227): the founder, *Khan* (ruler) and *Khagan* (emperor) of the Mongol Empire, which became the largest contiguous empire in history after his death. [Trans.]

being's inward contradiction – a real inward contradiction in an individual which is mentioned in *ḥadīth* and thereafter in our literature – [speaks about this truth.]

A Tradition Concerning the Human Being's Creation

It has been narrated in a *ḥadīth* which has been narrated by both Sunnī and Shī'ah and which in Shī'ah [corpus of *ḥadīth*] has been mentioned in the treatise *Al-Kāfī*[1] in which God, the Exalted, created the angel and fashioned him from pure intellect (*'aql*), and He created the animal and fashioned him from pure carnal desire (*shahwah*), and He created the human being and He mixed these two – the angel's nature and that of animal – in the human being and fashioned him from these two:

> إِنَّ اللهَ تَعَالَى خَلَقَ ٱلْمَلَائِكَةَ وَرَكَّبَ فِيهِمُ ٱلْعَقْلَ وَخَلَقَ ٱلْبَهَائِمَ وَ وَرَكَّبَ فِيهِمُ ٱلشَّهْوَةَ وَخَلَقَ ٱلْإِنْسَانَ وَرَكَّبَ فِيهِ ٱلْعَقْلَ وَالشَّهْوَةَ.
>
> "Indeed Allah, the Exalted, created the angels and endowed them with intellect, and He created the animals and endowed them with carnal desire and He created the human being and endowed him with intellect and carnal desire."[2]

Mawlawī (Rūmī) also recites, thus:

در حدیث آمد که خلّاق مجید　　خلق عالم را سه گونه آفرید

1. *Al-Kāfī*: more fully, *Al-Kāfī fī 'l-Hadīth*, one of the most important Shī'ah collections of *hadīth*, compiled by Shaykh Abū Ja'far Muḥammad ibn Ya'qūb al-Kulaynī (d. 329 AH/941 CE) and divided into three sections: *Usūl al-Kāfī*, *Furū' al-Kāfī* and *Rawdah al-Kāfī* consisting of 34 books, 326 sections, and over 16,000 *ahādīth* that can be traced back to the Prophet and his family by an unbroken chain of transmission. [Trans.]
2. *'Ilal al-Sharāyi'*, vol. 1, section (*bāb*) 6, 4, with a slight difference.

> It is related in the ḥadīth that the majestic God
> Created the creatures of the world three kinds.[1]

He then elucidates the three kinds on the basis of this *ḥadīth* which have been narrated by both Sunnī and Shīʿah. This human composition – in the words of the *ḥadīth* – is from the angelic as well as animalistic dimension (an angelic-animalistic creature). Naturally, this has brought about two opposing inclinations in the human being – downward tendency and downward tendency, heavenly inclination as well as earthly inclination. Thereafter, God has endowed him with intellect and willpower, and He has set him free [to choose] between these two paths:

﴿ إِنَّا هَدَيْنَاهُ السَّبِيلَ إِمَّا شَاكِرًا وَإِمَّا كَفُورًا ﴾

> Indeed We have guided him to the way, be he grateful or ungrateful. (76:3)

He has placed him between two paths and has given him absolute willpower and freedom for him to choose any of the two paths. The conflicts in history also originate from this contradiction in human nature. That is, human beings who have advanced upwardly and intellectually constitute the People of Truth (*ahl al-ḥaqq*) and Army of Allah (*jund Allāh*), while those who have fallen into [the abyss of] bestiality, the base and animal-like human beings [constitute the People of Falsehood (*ahl al-bāṭil*) and Army of Satan (*jund al-shayṭān*)]. The human conflicts in history are not merely the struggle of the deprived against the affluent for the sake of class interests; it is the struggle of the truth-seeking class against the profit-seeking class. Of course, naturally, the deprived class – since it is fortune as well as spectacle for it – it is more inclined to the

1. *Mathnawī-ye Maʿnawī*, Book 4, line 1497, with a slight variation. [Trans.]

truth because for it 'truth' has two characters. One is that it (truth) satisfies its truth-seeking spirit and in the language of the Qur'an, its *ḥanīf* spirit or its *ḥanīfiyyah* character – as we have said *ḥanīf* means 'truth-seeker' and *ḥanīfiyyah* means 'truth-seeking'. The other character is that at the same time, [by adhering to the truth] it could be able to obtain its rights.

The Parable of Rūmī

As such, humanity in this school of thought is the product of the spiritual, divine and celestial dimension of the human being, as opposed to his materialistic inclinations, and then between these two opposing forces he must choose one, and what an extraordinary parable in this regard can be found in Mawlawī (Rūmī's) *Mathnawī[-ye Ma'nawī]*! And Mawlawī is indeed excellent in showing such spiritual and divine issues. In this context, he says afterward that the human being has been created in such a manner that half of him is heavenly while another half is earthly and half of him is celestial while another half is worldly, and that this contradiction always exists and the human being always swing between the two. Sometimes, he swings to this side, and at other times, to that side. There are times when he goes downward and there are times when he goes upward. There is always an inner struggle within the human being. Mawlawī then puts forth a parable – the famous story of Majnūn al-'Āmirī and his she-camel that had just given birth to an offspring. He says that Majnūn's she-camel had just given birth to a young camel. When an animal has just given birth to an offspring, it is so much attached to its young one. This man (Majnūn) mounted this she-camel as he wanted to go along with the animal to pay a visit to his beloved (Laylā). (This is a parable.) He mounted to she-camel and began to set off. As he was already out of the city, the lover began to think about his beloved and plunge into his own world while forgetting the animal. Little by little the halter that was in his hand naturally used to slacken and he became just like a luggage at the animal's back. Little by little, the animal would realize that no one was mindful of itself. It would change direction toward its master's house (where its foal was situated). After a short while, Majnūn would open his eyes and realize that instead of reaching his beloved's residence, he was back in his own barn. Once again, he would turn the animal toward his target destination. He would cover certain distance. Once again, he would be engrossed with thinking about his beloved while being oblivious of the animal. The animal would again think about its beloved and darling which was in the barn [back home]. As it sensed that it was again free, it turned back. This incident would be repeated many times:

همچو مجنون در تنازع با شتر　　　گه شتر چربید و گه مجنون حر
یک دم ار مجنون ز خود غافل شدی　　　ناقه گردیدی و واپس آمدی

Assuredly they are like Majnūn in his struggle against the she-camel:
That the she-camel preponderated while Majnūn was free.
If Majnun forgot himself for one moment,
The she-camel would turn and go back.[1]

Then he says that in the end, Majnūn suddenly dismounted from this she-camcl and thus said:

گفت اي ناقه چو هر دو عاشقيم　　　ما دو ضد پس همره نالايقيم

He said, "O camel, since we both are lovers,
Therefore we two contraries are unsuitable fellow-

1. *Mathnawī-ye Ma'nawī*, Book 4, lines 1533, 1535, with a slight variation. [Trans.]

travellers.[1]

That is to say, "I am a lover and you are also a lover. I am infatuated with Laylā; I have to proceed toward that direction. You are attached to your foal. You must move toward the barn (where you offspring is located). We cannot go together [as fellow-travellers]. Finally, it is either I or you – one of this two. He then makes a conclusion, saying:

> عشق مولی کی کم از لیلاستی　　　　بنده بودن بهر او اولاستی
>
> How should love for the Lord be inferior to love for Laylā?
>
> To become a servant for His sake is more worthy.[2]

The point is that [if we do not regard the human being as purely a material being], then all human subjects, all human peculiarities, all human distinctions, and all matters that distinguish the human being from non-humans can be explained; otherwise, they are all beyond explanation. The explanations that they have given are materialistic [in nature], especially the Marxist explanations. In fact, these are not explanations and they have failed to provide explanations. There is one explanation in this regard, and that is the existentialists' explanation. They have attempted to explain the issue in another way. That is, while accepting the materialist nature of the human being, they could be able to, so to speak, enshroud the human values. We shall elaborate on this, God willing, in the next session.

---

1. *Ibid.*, line 1542.
2. *Ibid.*, line 1557, with a slight variation.

Chapter 5: Spiritual Love: Marxism and the Permanence of Human Values

The first question is about our discussion on the meaning of dispositions (*fiṭriyyāt*) in the [Qur'anic] verse which says, 'Allah has brought you forth from the bellies of your mothers while you did not know anything'(16:78) as well as verses which we call 'verses of tryst and disposition'. We have presented the subject-matter in this way: We have said that the view of Muslim philosophers is that the human being has a set of intrinsic pieces of knowledge (*ma'lūmāt*) in the sense that these pieces of knowledge are not acquired (*iktisābī*) not in the sense that they are actually with him or he has brought them along. To him to bring them along and to have them from the beginning is one thing. For him to realize that they cannot be found through acquisition is another thing. This is in the sense that as much as these [pieces of knowledge] are presented to the mind, it could immediately perceive them without needing for any proof. In the question [time], this has been posed regarding the issue of *'ālam al-dharr* (world of pre existence):[1]

1. *'Ālam al-dharr*: the world prior to the creation of human beings on earth in which God obtained their acknowledgment of His Divinity and Lordship: When your Lord took from the Children of Adam, from their loins, their descendants and made them bear witness over themselves, [He said to them,] 'Am I not your

> "Does this question not arise: What is the Divine commitment and covenant and our affirmative reply "Yes indeed!"? And if because of that affirmation [by us] – as [pieces of] knowledge are either conceptions (*taṣawwur*) or affirmations (*taṣdīq*) – no more argument is left for us, how comes God bears witness to it and gives reference to it?"

No, this has no contradiction with that. Had we reached the point – which we will never reach – when we have correctly stated the verse of pre-existence (*āyat al-dharr*), [it would have been better], but here we can refer you to the exegesis (*tafsīr*) *Al-Mīzān*.[1] In the exegesis *Al-Mīzān* – of course, I have not seen its Fārsī translation, how its translation is, but in volume 8 of *Al-Mīzān*'s [original] Arabic text in which this section has been discussed – it has been excellently and well discussed. In today's discussion, we reach the subjects in which we have to elaborate on it.

Another Analysis of the Nature of Spiritual Love

The second question is this: "How can one regard every type of spiritual love, however the beloved is a common person may be, as the same real love to the Essence of God, the Exalted, and emanating from Him?"

In that theory which we have stated, we have said that firstly, they believe that there are two types of love, viz. physical and spiritual love. In other words, some types of love are spiritual, and not that all types of love are spiritual. Make no mistake about it. According to them, some forms of love of individuals [to one another] are

---

Lord?' They said, 'Yes indeed! We bear witness.' [This,] lest you should say on the Day of Resurrection, 'Indeed we were unaware of this'. (7:172) [Trans.]

1. It refers to *Al-Mīzān fī Tafsīr al-Qur'ān* by 'Allāmah Sayyid Muḥammad Ḥusayn Ṭabāṭabā'ī (1904-81), the renowned Islamic scholar, thinker and philosopher. [Trans.]

spiritual. Now, how can one consider it to be the real love for the Essence of God, the Exalted? That [question] is on the basis of the point that in reality, they want to say that in spiritual love, the Real Beloved is the person. Instead, this person serves as a motivation and manifestation although the lover himself may imagine that she is indeed his real beloved. In reality, however, she is not his real beloved. The mystics (*'urafā'*) basically do not believe in metaphorical love (*'ishq al-majāzī*) as they consider all forms of love to be real, and they say that there is only one Beauty (*jamāl*) who is the Real Beauty and all other beauties are just a ray or reflection of that Beauty. Every beauty with whatever degree it is such is [beauty] depending on the beauty it reflects, and the human being's disposition which searches for perfection (*kamāl*) and beauty does not want limited perfection or beauty. Absolute Perfection and Beauty is what it desires. In other words, that is what the human being's disposition wants but he would mistakenly run after the manifestations of these limited beauties – which shall become real beloved commensurate to their being manifestations – and for this reason, after meeting his beloved, he will get frustrated and look for another beloved. In his unconscious mind, he feels that she is not the one he wants.

There is another question being raised concerning the human being and that is, why the human being is so desirous of things he does not have? Once these things are obtained by him, his burning desire or craving for them begins to wane, and in a sense, he would have a lukewarm feeling for them. This is an issue in itself: why does a person wish for and so desirous of something he does not have. After attaining that which he wishes for and so desirous of, gradually he would have a lukewarm feeling for it. As it is said, the human being looks for diversity and diversion. Why does he look for diversity? Norm dictates that one must slowly get that which he wants and nature necessitates since he wants it. Why will he abandon it afterward and look for diversity? Again, he wants to get something else. He will abandon an object of his desire and look for new object of desire, [and this state of affairs continues] until such a point that this maxim becomes applicable to him: "The human being always looks for anything he does not have." And it is indeed true that the human being looks for something he does not possess, in the sense that he desires for something he does not have and he is fed up with something he possesses. Why is it like that? Some have imagined that this is an essential element of the human nature and disposition. Why is it an essential element of human nature and disposition? Obviously, wandering state cannot be an essential element of human nature and disposition. Neither can we say that one essential element of human nature is that he should always be perplexed and permanently look for change!

The correct analysis of the subject-matter is the view which maintains that the human being will find tranquillity if he attains the thing which is his real and true object of desire (*maṭlūb*). In reality and in the depth of his nature, the human being is not in a state of wandering. This state of wandering that one may experience is due to the fact that he vaguely desires for the truth and strives to attain it; he attains something, thinking that it is the very truth which he desires. After sometime, however, he scrutinizes it from a close distance and his nature or disposition rejects it. Then he will look for something else, and this state of affairs continues again and again. This is the point [in saying] that if he attains his real object of desire, he will attain real happiness which is naturally no other than his real tranquillity in the sense of that which is above all thins. This is what the Qur'an says:

﴿ الَّذِينَ آمَنُوا وَتَطْمَئِنُّ قُلُوبُهُمْ بِذِكْرِ اللَّهِ ﴾

Those who have faith, and whose hearts find rest in the

remembrance of Allah. (13:28)

And then it says:

﴿ أَلَا بِذِكْرِ اللَّهِ تَطْمَئِنُّ الْقُلُوبُ ﴾

Look! The hearts find rest in Allah's remembrance! (13:28)

Alā (look!) is a particle of stimulation (*ḥarf al-tanbiyah*) with the function of emphasis and stimulation – "Pay attention!" or "Look!" *Bi-dhikri'llāh* ("in the remembrance of Allah") is *jarr* and *majrūr*[1] which pertains to *taṭma'inna'l-qulūb* ("the hearts find rest") which takes precedence. When the *jarr* and *majrūr* take precedence over the verb (*fi'l*), it is a sign of restriction. That is, any verbal adjunct which takes precedence over the verb is a sign of restriction; in other words, it conveys the meaning of "only". *Alā bi-dhikri'llāhi taṭma'inna'l-qulūb* means "Look! The hearts find rest in Allah's remembrance *only*!" That is to say that obtaining any other object of desire does not give real tranquillity to a person. It will give a momentary peace of mind so long as he thinks that he has really obtained his real object of desire, but after a short while when his disposition begins to be acquainted with it (his object of desire) and correctly recognizes and identifies it, he will experience a lack of compatibility [between himself and his object of desire] and he will begin to abhor it. The only Reality, which if he 'attains', it is impossible for him to abhor, is God, the Exalted, and this is the time when one's heart has 'attained' the 'Reality' (*ḥaqīqah*), 'Him' and Divine unity (*tawḥīd*).

As such, some say that paradise must be the worst of places in the realm of existence. It is because paradise has a monotonous

1. *Jarr*: to pronounce the final consonant or a word with *i* and to put it into the genitive case (*majrūr*). [Trans.]

condition. Moreover, everyone has everything there, and when one possesses everything, it is as if he possesses nothing. When a person has no possession, he strives to get one and as he succeeds, this brings joy to him. On the other hand, if he has everything, he is like a grandee's child sources of his joy and happiness are already provided for him from the very day he opened his eyes to the world. Nothing will be new for him, and as such, joy has no meaning for him. For a poor child who walks along the street barefooted, a pair of shoes will bring him unimaginable joy and happiness. As such, in his book *Emile*,[1] Rousseau[2] says that those who drown their children in enormous fortunes bring them up in a way of having no feeling for joy or pleasure. They will not really feel happiness for the sources of happiness, but they will express extreme sensitivity to pains. In other words, he cannot endure even a minor pain. On the contrary, children who have been brought up from the beginning in difficulties and sufferings do not show sensitivity to pain because they are used to it. That is, enduring difficulties is easy for them, nay they do not difficulty at all, and on the contrary, even the smallest source of joy will bring them extreme joy and happiness.

They say that it follows, therefore, that paradise must be most tiresome and kill-joy of all places, because all sources of joy and happiness are readily available there. In fact, it can be considered a

1. *Emile*, or *On Education* or *Émile*, or *Treatise on Education* (1762): a treatise on the nature of education and man written by Jean-Jacques Rousseau, who considered it to be his *magnum opus*. [Trans.]

2. Jean-Jacques Rousseau (1712–78): a major philosopher, writer, and composer of 18th-century Romanticism, whose political philosophy heavily influenced the French Revolution, as well as the American Revolution and the overall development of modern political, sociological and educational thought. [Trans.]

prison and the worst of prisons.

In one passage of the Qur'an, it is as if it gives answer to this argument, saying, thus:

﴿ خَالِدِينَ فِيهَا لَا يَبْغُونَ عَنْهَا حِوَلًا ﴾

> to remain [forever]in them, from where they will not seek to shift. (18:108)[1]

In other words, the inhabitants of paradise shall not desire change; that is, paradise for them is not tiresome.[2] Why? It is because if paradise is like a garden in this world – though an eternal garden – in the sense everything else is earthly and the human being has the same quality of humanness, it is definitely like that. Simply put, if paradise will be made for the human beings who are in this world and the supposed immortality shall be given to them therein, this argument (that paradise is boring for being monotonous) shall become valid. The fact, however, is that for its dweller, paradise is the pinnacle of Divine blessings. That is, for him even corporeal paradise and physical pleasures are also treated as Divine munificence in the sense that unless a person possesses Divine knowledge and gnosis (*ma'rifah*), he cannot be able to discern the meaning of paradise. For a paradise dweller, the quintessence of pleasures is that now he is a Guest of his own Creator, partaking in his Creator's banquet. That is, he is along with the Truth and when one is along with that Truth, the problem of weariness, diversity, change, and shifting will have no more meaning. In other words, anything other than God or what is called Divine munificence,

---

1. The context of the passage is as follows:

﴿ إِنَّ الَّذِينَ آمَنُوا وَعَمِلُوا الصَّالِحَاتِ كَانَتْ لَهُمْ جَنَّاتُ الْفِرْدَوْسِ نُزُلًا * خَالِدِينَ فِيهَا لَا يَبْغُونَ عَنْهَا حِوَلًا ﴾

As for those who have faith and do righteous deeds they shall have the gardens of Firdaws1 for abode, to remain [forever]in them, from where they will not seek to shift. (18:107-108)

2. There are other relevant Qur'anic verses in this regard.

Divine grace, Divine blessings, or Divine banquet cannot be the everlasting object of desire for the human being, and it is only God who is the everlasting object of desire for the human being. In paradise, there is possibility for the human being to experience boredom, exasperation, monotony, and "to go somewhere else". "Somewhere else" has no meaning there. "Somewhere else" can be imagined in things which are limited, and you can certainly say that "somewhere else" is inconceivable for him (dweller of paradise). We fell from one place to another. We have been talking about the issue of spiritual love. The subject extended up to this point.

Love According to the Mystics

My purpose is to point that the mystics maintain that all forms of love are real:

عشق حقیقی است مجازی مگیر　　　این دم شیر است به بازی مگیر
Love is real, don't take [it] metaphorically.
This is lion's tail, don't play with [it].

They reject the philosophers who consider love to be of two types. They claim that even in metaphorical objects of love, the lover – while being unaware himself – loves the object of love in view of the fact that she is a ray of Him (Real Beloved). According to them, it is really impossible for a human being to love someone (or something) other than God. Muḥyī al-Dīn [al-'Arabī] thus says:

ماَ أُحِبُّ أَحَد غير خالقه.

"I do not love anyone other than his Creator."

(It is because of such statements that a number of jurists (*fuqahā*) have strongly criticized him.) He says that he has not been in love so far with anyone other than his Creator, although the Most Exalted has been hidden under the names Zaynab, Su'ād, Hind, etc.[1] He is hidden under the names of the metaphorical objects of love. He is the Real object of love. Mawlawī (Rūmī) has poems in this regard. He thus sings:

جرعه‌ای بر ریختی زان خفیه جام بر زمین خاک من کأس الکرام
From that hidden goblet You have poured out of the cup of the noble
A draught over the dusty earth.[2]

He mentions it as a parable. He wants to say that a mouthful of the Divine love was poured onto the ground, and if ever a person likes a fellow earthly being, his beloved is just like the mouthful [of the Divine love] which was poured onto the ground.

هست بر زلف و رخ از جرعه نشان خاک را شاهان همی لیسند از آن
From the draught thereof there is a trace on the locks and cheeks:
Hence kings[3] lick the earth.[4&5]

This mystic says that if everybody embraces and licks the ground it just means that there is something in that mouthful [of Divine love that was poured on the ground].

He then says:

---

1. Sayyid 'Alīkhān's commentary on *Ṣaḥīfah al-Sajjādiyyah.*
2. *Mathnawī-ye Ma'nawī*, Book 5, line 372.
3. By 'kings' it means that which is the highest level and it refers to those whose coquetry is more extreme.
4. It wants to convey that the body of this human being is nothing but dust.
5. *Mathnawī-ye Ma'nawī*, Book 5, line 373.

جرعه خاک آمیز چون مجنون کند   مر شما را صاف او تا چون کند

Since the draught, when mingled with dust, makes you mad,
Think how its pure essence would affect you![1]

He says that this metaphorical object of love (*ma'shūq-e majāzī*) is like a particle of the mouthful [of Divine love] that was poured on the ground. It has made you behave like that. If this gets flattened – that is, if you attain the Truth Himself – then what else are you desirous for?!

There is no contradiction, therefore, that apparently – that is, in one's thinking – the beloved is another person. In reality, however, the real beloved is not the person but rather the Manifest (*ẓāhir*) who manifests Himself in that form.

Are Human Values Changing?

The third question which, perhaps, is necessary for us to discuss more is this:

> "In justifying the lack of contradiction between defending human values and materiality (about our previous discussion that there is a sort of contradiction between materialist philosophy and acceptance of human values), a Marxist can say, "We do not regard the human being as a fixed creature (and naturally, human values are also not fixed) and in line with social system, we regard him as evolutionary. As such, in every period, the human beings have moral values which are peculiar to that period and to which one may rely. Feudalistic morality is different from communistic morality, but in a particular historical stage, the proletariat class can talk

1. *Mathnawī-ye Ma'nawī*, Book 5, line 375.

> about a set of communistic moral values. There is no contradiction, therefore, and acknowledgment of changing moral values does not necessitate acceptance of human dispositions and metaphysical things."

It is a good question and argument which we must address. The first point is that the human being is an alterable being; it follows that human values are also a set of changing values. In other words, since the human being is not fixed, it naturally follows that the values are not also fixed. This is one subject.

Another subject is that as [the human being and human values] are not fixed and are alterable, they are also evolutionary. Then we have to ask, "What is the criterion for evolution?" In this regard, we must have a separate discussion. Then they say, "As such, in every period, the human beings have moral values which are peculiar to that period and to which one may rely. Feudalistic morality is different from communistic morality."

Here propositions have been made the basis, and one [of them], perhaps, has been presented a bit incorrectly. One is the issue that human values are not fixed and that they are changing. This is the same ethical relativity. That is, among the human values, those things which are related to morality are alterable; [this is] the issue of alterability and relativity of morality. This is argument correct? Are human values, including moral values, really alterable? Are these few things which we have mentioned [viz. the five subjects on the emotional dispositions] really alterable and changing? For example, we have said that truth-seeking is a value for the human being. Is this an alterable value? In other words, during the periods, for example, of primitive communal life, farming, slavery, feudalism, capitalism, and communism, has this value changed for the human being? Is this fixed in the form of value for the human being?

Secondly, if values were changing, does it mean that every value is correct during its period and condemned in another period? Let us consider, for instance, feudal morality. Can we approve and uphold this morality which we call 'feudal morality' due to the fact that it was related to the period of feudalism? That is, should we have to see what had been considered morality during that period, [and those things we must affirm], although the morality of knowing them, for example, is as follows: Although it is a myth, Ḍahhāk[1] has to come one day to kill a young man so that he could his brain as food to the serpents on his shoulders, or should we not? There is a set of fixed principles at work. Pharaoh's acts during his time were also condemned; it is not [correct to say] that "Since they belonged to Pharaoh's time, his acts were correct during his time. We are in a different time and we should not also impose the values of our time to that of Pharaoh and Moses (A.S.). Pharaok belonged to a different time and whatever was regarded by them during that time as morality is correct morality." Can we say so?!

Thirdly, these statements are based upon class morality. As a rule, it is exactly like that. That is, Marxism cannot uphold human morality – morality which is morality for all human beings. In accordance with these statements, for example, during our time which has an example of all these systems – example of feudalism, example of capitalism and example of communism – we have to say that morality for a community is really one thing (communist morality) and another thing for a capitalist (capitalist morality). This is what a communist would say to a capitalist – and vice versa – "You cannot impose your morality to me because you are not in my situation and I, in turn, am not in your situation. If I were in your situation, I would have accepted your morality, and if you

1. Ḍaḥḥāk: a tyrant king in Iranian mythological history. [Trans.]

were in my situation, you would have accepted my morality. As such, neither I could say something against you, nor you could say something against me. No communist can condemn a capitalist on moral ground. Neither can a capitalist condemn a communist on moral ground. It is because there is no common intrinsic human morality [on the basis of which] a communist could be able to disapprove a capitalist, and vice versa. And there is nothing common. Each one can say, in reply to the other, "My morality belongs to me while your morality belongs to you. You cannot have my morality and I cannot have your morality."

Morality, therefore, depends not only on the [different] periods, but also on the class characteristics. For example, in all these parts of the world in which the feudal system governs, the correct morality for them is none other than the feudal morality.

Our contention is that on account of being human, the human being has a set of moral precepts and these moral precepts has remained from his primitive period the way it is correctly presented up to this industrial period of his.

Dr. Hashtrūdī and its Refutation

Incidentally, two or three nights ago, I read in the newspaper an article which was very interesting and I intended to read it to you on one occasion. Today, as our discussion has also reached this relevant point, I will read it to you now. In *Kayhān*[1] newspaper (8th of Tīr),[2] there was [a script of] an interview with Professor Hashtrūdī with the title, "Our Reporter's Interview with Mr. Hashtrūdī" and with the subtitle, "Earthly Man Comes Out as Celestial Being." Sometimes, he would tell about some strange

1. Founded in 1943, *Kayhān* is one of the longest-running national dailies in Iran. [Trans.]
2. [In 1356 S.A.H (29 June 1977)].

things. He has a set of words in these regards which he always repeats. [For instance,] the pyramids of Egypt have not been made by human beings on earth but rather by other human beings that came from a planet more progressive in civilization, and accordingly, it is impossible for these [pyramids] to have been made by human beings at that time, and these like that. Recently, he has established a 'moral philosophy' for himself. That is, he has invented a sort of humanism from himself. In the said interview, Mr. Hashtrūdī has made some preliminary remarks in which he has condemned today's knowledge and civilization, saying that since the outcome of knowledge and civilization is currently to the detriment of humanity, they are currently condemnable. We shall quote part of his statements. He says, "No rule is absolute. All rules are relative. Perhaps you are told that mathematical rules are absolute. Mathematical rules are not also absolute."

The *Kayhān*'s reporter says:

> "With this logic that no ruling is absolute, Professor Hashtrūdī, a veteran mathematician of Iran, wages war against all unkindness, calling the people from various regions and nations to hoist the banner of all kindness and for them to consider one another as brothers and sisters."

Here I have thus written: His statement that no ruling is absolute is a ruling in itself. [By the way,] is it absolute or not? One time we say, "No rule is absolute," except this rule that no rule is absolute. This is no longer absolute. Why the exception in this case? If no rule is supposed to be absolute, then there is no reason for it to accommodate any exception. The logicians say that some propositions (*qaḍāyā*) are impossible (*muḥāl*). These propositions are generally correct; there is certainly an exception. For instance, one would say, "All my statements are lies." This cannot be true in a way that all its manifestations are correct, because if all his statements are indeed lies, then his statement that "All my statements are lies" must be included. If this last statement of his were a lie, it follows then that all his statements may not be lies; otherwise, this [last statement] cannot be a lie.

Now, among the statements which cannot be true is this: "No rule is absolute." If this should be true, then it will include itself. If it includes itself, it follows that it is not absolute. Once this is not absolute, it then follows that we have absolute rules. In other words, since this is not absolute, then we are supposed to have a set of absolute rules. This is one.

Another point is this statement [by the reporter]: "[He] calls upon the people to hoist the banner of all kindness and for them to consider one another as brothers and sisters." This gentleman must be asked, "Is this moral instruction that all people must consider one another as brothers and sisters an absolute or a relative rule? Does it belong to a particular period, or [is it true] at all times? Was this instruction for all times – past, present and future – good or is it good only for the present time? In the same way, is it true at all places and under all circumstances for all people, or only for some people?" Then the reporter says:

> "The inalterable rules of the Middles Ages have shattered during our century, not only losing their credibility but are also replaced by new rules which are in no way absolute. The great wisdom of Socrates and the transcendental ethics of Kant, with all rhctoric and pomposity, have turned into hypocrisy, lie, self-affirmation, self-centredness, and egoism. Einstein[1] has

1. Albert Einstein (1879-1955): German, Swiss and American mathematician and atomic physicist who stimulated a revolution in physics by discovering the

> destroyed the scientific credibility of the absoluteness of time and space. On the other hand, through the sexual theory of Freud, the foundation of morality which was considered to be an absolute divine endowment has collapsed. Now, as all rules are relative, we should not engage in fratricide just because so-and-so does not recognize a rule which is acceptable to us. A rule which is acceptable to us is absolute as far as we are concerned but this same rule may not be absolute for others. As mathematical rules are not absolute and everything is relative, how can some people, under the pretext of absolute rule, engage in fratricide and make use of technology along this line?"

These wars are essentially remnants of the absolutist rules of the Middle Ages; that is, during the Middle Ages the people [considered] their rules [to be absolute]. His point is that, for example, the followers of a certain religion regarded themselves as [following] the truth – absolute truth – while their opponents were [following] falsehood – absolute falsehood. The same was true with their opponents, and this state of affairs used to lead to killing. We must understand to that extent that nothing is absolute. If I say that what I say is the truth, even if it is true, it is not absolute truth. If we say that so-and-so is wrong, even he is really wrong, he is not wrong in absolute sense. I am relatively true as well as relatively wrong. He is also relatively true as well as relatively wrong. As such, let us come together and be brothers to one another. This is the essence of his [reporter's] statements.

He then mixes moral precepts with mathematical and other issues,

---

theory of general relativity and for which he received the Nobel Prize in physics in 1921 and is often regarded as the father of modern physics. [Trans.]

saying that all this Socratic ethics – as they recently claim – is actually a kind of self-love, lie and hypocrisy.

This gentleman must be told, "With this utterance of yours now, you condemned hypocrisy; you condemned lying; you also condemned self-affirmation, self-love and egoism. Of course, this statement [of yours] that such is the essence of Socrates' wisdom is baseless." That is, they have said that this (Socratic ethics) is a kind of self-love garbed as 'ethics'. Well and good, we have accepted that Socrates' wisdom is a kind of self-love, self-centredness, sense of self-affirmation, pretension, hypocrisy, and the like which appears to be 'ethics', and we condemn Socratic ethics, but as a result, we accepted that we absolutely negated them and considered them anti-ethics in the absolute sense. Is hypocrisy anti-ethics in the absolute sense or in the relative sense? Is telling a lie anti-ethics in the absolute sense or in the relative sense? Is self-love or self-centredness anti-ethics in the absolute sense or in the relative sense? If these are anti-ethics in the relative sense, it follows that Socratic ethics is also relatively true and is not totally negated. You want to say that Socrates' wisdom is totally abrogated on account that such and such are its inward nature. In this case, therefore, you have accepted in the absolute sense, your stance that they [are anti-ethics].

A person cannot believe in morality and at the same time, regards morality as alterable and relative. (This is our point, and we will also discuss [later].) In other words, in terms of principles morality is at least equal [with inalterability and absoluteness]. We have moral principles (*uṣūl*) and secondary elements (*furū'*) of morality. Secondary elements of morality are difference from its principles. The principles of morality are either moral, inalterable and absolute, [or not moral]. And if we take out inalterability and absoluteness from morality, it will no longer be 'morality'. Yes, it will become just like a set of courtesies – a set of contractual rules such as by-laws, and not something sacred or something which is really virtuous and good...[1]

1. [Unfortunately, the remaining parts of Professor Muṭahharī's lecture were not recorded.]

Chapter 6: The Evolution of Human Originality

... [According to the deniers of human originality,] all these concepts which we call human originality, human nobility and human dignity are purely imaginary. Some of these deniers, however, say that these are fictions the acceptance of which by the people is necessitated by human society's welfare and interests although they are not real. For instance, honesty has no primacy at all over lying and deception. There is no difference for a person who wants to be honest or to be dishonest. If all people decide to be dishonest, it will be to their own detriment. In order for all people to serve their interests better and obtain the least harm, they have no option but to accept these superstitions. Then some philosophers came and inculcated these ideas to the people: "Nobility dictates that one should be honest and not dishonest" until such a point that these are inculcated in their minds. These are superstitions which are useful to people's wellbeing, otherwise they are purely imaginary by themselves. There is another group of those who regard these [concepts] as imaginary. This group also regard these as imaginary and does not encourage them at the same time. They encourage acting against these [concepts]. For instance, Nietzsche says that some [individuals] have coined these fictions for their own interests. If a person could be able to go against them, he must do so.

A Comparison Between Nietzsche's and Marxists' Views

The second view, therefore, is these [concepts] are imaginary such that we should regard them as superstitions which are useful for humanity, or superstitions which may not even be useful. In this context, Nietzsche has a view which is the exact opposite of that of the Marxists. The Marxists say that moral concepts – especially religious moral concepts – have been invented by the wealthy and noble class in order to appease the deprived class and put a stop to the revolution or uprising of the deprived class. Accordingly, religion has been coined by the exploiting class. Nietzsche says the exact opposite of this subject. Since his philosophy revolves around the axis of evolution of human generation (considering perfection as achievable only through power) and the emergence of powerful human being (superman), he says that religion, morality and these things are actually invented by weak class which is condemned by nature to extinction, in order to put a stop to the strong class. In the nature's law of evolution, the weak are basically condemned and they must be doomed to extinction – sometimes there is nothing above weakness – and the strong must remain so that a stronger generation would come into being and nature will reach its perfection in the strong and in the weak. The weak are beings which are meant to be extinguished and they must be extinguished, and to empower the weak is a grave mistake. Concepts like religion, faith, justice, equity, self-sacrifice, altruism, selflessness, and the like are invented by the weak. As they realized that they cannot fight against the strong through physical power, they came forward to coin these ideas and concepts and through which they were able to put a stop to the advancement of the strong. In his logic, religion is invented by the weak in order to put a stop to the strong, as the right is always in the hands of the strong – "Might is right" as they say. That is, the right is in the hands of those who have emerged victories in this natural struggle for survival. As such, he totally negates all religious, ideological and moral concepts and ideas, saying that these are hindrances to evolution. This is the second view.

There are other views, however, which accept the originality of humanness (*insāniyyah*) (in the sense that they are not superstitious). These views really affirm reality for humanness although without considering it to be intrinsic. These views are of two groups. One group refers to those who want to acknowledge them (religious and moral concepts) and at the same time, deny their innateness. They put forward the same issue which was raised in one of the previous questions, saying that in this universe, there is no inalterable truth; there is nothing permanent. What thing is permanent in this universe in that humanness must be permanent?! [Accordingly,] humanness – in the same sense of human originality – is also an alterable reality, following particular exigencies of time. Every time and in every exigency of time, human originality and moral originality is something in accordance with that time and circumstances of the time. At that time, such indeed is morality which is sacred and another thing is humanness. As circumstances of the time change, however, they also change and will be replaced by another set of things. Such is humanness at that time. This originality, therefore, is alterable, changeable and also – as we have said earlier – not absolute. It is relative; in addition, it changes according to [the exigency of] time. Even in the same time, under various conditions and circumstances, it also varies. For instance, class condition naturally makes morality variant and numerous. For every person in each circumstance – social circumstance – morality is one thing which is difference from the thing considered to be morality by other individuals under another set of circumstances. We have discussed this subject in the previous session [and] there is not much needed to repeat [here]; I will just add one thing.

The Meaning of Evolution of Human Originality

This assumption, as we have said, is based upon the point that there is nothing permanent in this universe and all things are changeable. This, however, is not only on the basis of change, but on the basis of change and evolution. Here we would like to elaborate a bit on this subject. If we said that human originality evolves, what 'evolution' could mean such that it would be different from absolute change? We cannot regard every change as evolution, because degradation or decay is also a [form of] change. It is possible for a person to be more perfect in terms of his humanness and it is equally possible that his change is the opposite, just as what we call 'moral decadence'. Does 'moral decadence' have any meaning at all although in the same time, or none? There is no option but [to say that] it has meaning; it cannot have no meaning at all. We have to say that every condition that comes after another condition is evolution! It is obvious that it is not so. Evolution (*takāmul*) means taking a step toward the path of perfection (*kamāl*). That is, the evolving entity changes its station and passes through each of the phases. Apart from the lack of permanence and not being stationary in one place, there is another thing and that is, this change leads toward perfection in the sense that we consider the origin (*mabda'*) and then we say that it evolves from it. That is, it advances forward and reaches a stage a bit higher than the previous one.

If the path, therefore, is not the path of perfection, that change, change of stage and moving [from one point to another] is not perfection. If the path wants to be that of perfection, we take into consideration one thing. Then we have to say that [that entity] must have the element which it possessed at the beginning – which we have regarded as perfection – in the next stage in a more advanced form.

Let us take into account, for example, perfection in science as well as in technology. A society which is in a particular level of science, learning, information, and discovery of the secrets of nature as well as in a particular stage of technology moves to another stage. Now, can we call every change as 'perfection'? If in the next period of time, these people become more ignorant and unaware and their technical-industrial capability becomes weaker, can we still say that they have evolved in view of the fact that they have differed from their past? For example, the number of the literates was more in the past [and] now it has decreased. The level of literacy and knowledge was higher before [and] now it has gone down. Can we say that it has evolved simply because it is not the same as before? No. We say that it has evolved when in the succeeding period that society has reached a higher stage quantitatively, qualitatively or both; that is, if in the previous period, for instance, the number of literates was 50% [and] now it has become 60% quantitatively and if it has the highest level of knowledge and learning and the minimum level of literacy was to have a bachelor's degree and now the minimum level is a master's degree. The same is true in the field of industry. That is, [the society] is in possession of that which it had before with some addition; in other words, it possesses them in a higher level.

As such, speaking of evolution (*takāmul*) we have to consider a 'beginning of evolution or perfection' and then consider the path from that beginning – how a thing along that path moves from one phase to a higher phase. We call this 'evolution'.

Types of Evolution of Human Society

1. Evolution in Man's Relationship with Nature

Let us deal with the evolution of human society. The evolution of human society is of many types.[1] There is a time when we say that

1. In the discussions on *The Philosophy of History*, the author has dealt with it under the section on 'evolution'.

human society has developed in the sense that in the field of technology – that is, in the human being's relationship with nature – [it has progressed.] The human being has a relationship with nature. He is at war and competes with nature and he wants to dominate it. He wants to become the overlord and employ nature under his command. Evolution in this case has a very good meaning and there is no doubt that in its relationship with nature, human society has developed. That is, if we take into account the totally of periods of time, that which is called 'technology,' 'industry,' 'exploitation of nature,' or 'domination of nature' [has progressed and] increased day by day.

2. Evolution in Collective's Structural Relationship

Another issue is evolution in the human beings' relationship with one another but the point is the collective's structural relationship. What does it mean? It means that in terms of organization, society is like a living organism. The simpler and less complex it is, the more unified and homogenous it will become. The more it is developed, the more it will become more complex in terms of members, components and organs; the division of labour more extended; and the whole structure far more complex.

From this perspective, there is also no doubt that human society has developed. For example, let us consider today's Iranian society and Iran's society fifty years ago. Take into account the occupations and professions. Take into consideration the fields of studies. Keep in mind the government posts. Previously, this society was like an infant animal with very limited limbs. You can see that day by day other limbs would be developed. For instance, in terms of occupation in the sense of work which is a means of trading in – those who provide means at the disposal of individuals – previously, if one would take into consideration types of occupation right here in Tehran, perhaps they can be summed up in ten occupations. That is, the condition of society would not necessitate more than this. In villages that you would visit, you would see a single shop in which perfumes, grocery, butchery, and stationery would be available for sale; whatever you wanted would be available there. As the society expands, however, these occupations multiple and now you can see that as a result of industrial advancement, certain occupations which were non-existing in the past as their areas of endeavour did not exist yet have been invented. One example is selling of cassette tapes in which one's occupation is to record cassette tapes and sell them. Recently, among the recorded cassette tapes, one section of them consists of religious tapes. You can see that a shop comes into being whose concern is to sell religious tapes only.

The same is true in the case of government functions. Let us take into consideration, for example, the ministries. (Now, it is possible that [some ministries] are a bit artificial and exaggerated but some are really necessitated by society.) If during the time of Nāṣir al-Dīn Shāh,[1] there were just one or two ministries which would perform the administrative functions, now if one would really and actually perform the functions of ministries, one function – for instance, water and electricity – is equivalent to the all [ministerial] functions during the time of Nāṣir al-Dīn Shāh.

From this perspective also, [human society has progressed.] In terms of the complexity of communities (and this is not only true in Iran but in the entire world) – that is, the multiplication of occupations and profession and then the division of labour, increase in the number of specialization and expertise whose outcome is going beyond the state of homogeny by the members of society, which in turn, has many impacts sociologically, because the human

1. Naṣīr al-Dīn Shāh Qājār (1831-1896): the Shāh of Persia from September 17, 1848 to May 1, 1896 when he was assassinated. [Trans.]

being is similar to his work and his work is similar to him, and he creates his own work. During the time which occupations were very few, human beings were more homogeneous compared to those of the present in which occupations are so varied, and they are heaven and earth apart from each other. Naturally, between a person who has spent his whole life in one occupation and another person who has spent his whole life in another occupation, there is an extreme difference and they are actually two spirits. And this is a serious problem which has intentionally or unintentionally come into being.

In this [aspect], therefore, evolution is also meaningful. That is, we say that during the first period the human beings were like a single living organism in the sense that they were like one group whose mission is to perform a single work. In this regard, the human society has progressed from one period to another. In other words, it has in the next period whatever it had with an addition, and whatever it has in the new period, it will also have in the upcoming period with an addition. In sum, in these periods, it has those [things] in a higher level.

As such, evolution (*takāmul*) is not absolute change. Evolution requires a criterion.[1] That is, whatever [a thing] has possessed in the previous phase – which we also consider to be a kind of perfection – it will also possess in greater quantity and more perfect form. In other words, in evolution there must be one specific pivot and one specific direction with such conditions.

3. Evolution in Humanness

Now, if we regard the principles of human values are intrinsic and

1. According to philosophers, every motion or movement (*ḥirikah*) requires a distance (distance in its general sense). If a movement's distance differs, it is no longer one movement. In the evolutionary movement, the distance must be only one.

inalterable, it is only then that 'evolution' becomes meaningful. For example, we have said that the issue of truth-seeking is one of the human values. If in this issue of truth-seeking, truth-inclination and truth-loving, the pioneering human being was also truth-seeker and truth-lover, and in the succeeding era, he has progressed in the area of truth-loving in the sense that he became more truth-lover, more truth-seeker and more inclined to the truth than he was in the past, it follows that he has progressed. The same is true in the case of inclination to beauty. If beauty – and in other words, inclination to beauty – is a criterion in itself and has a specified meaning, evolution in this domain might be meaningful. The pioneering human being loved beauty. The present human being also loves beauty. That which the pioneering human being used to love the present human being also loves in a higher level. So is the case of art which creates beauty. That is, in the same sphere that the pioneering human being used to create beauty, the present human being has also progressed. Since the same thing exists, progress has meaning. The same is true with goodness, moral virtue, love, and worship.

If from the beginning, however, we regard 'evolution' as mere change such that we do not even believe in the unity of direction for it, in the sense that we do not believe in an criterion for it, and we say, for example, that the past human being in the past periods of time used to regard truth-seeking as a value, then the criterion for humanness was truth-seeking, but if today this criterion changes, then truth-seeking is no longer [the criterion] and it must be something else. In this case, how come do you call it 'evolution' (*takāmul*)? That the criteria are inalterable is different from the fact that the human being is inalterable. They confuse these two. They imagine that if we regard as inalterable the criteria of humanness – which are identical with the pivot and path of humanness – we must have also regarded the human being as inalterable. It is like saying that if the earth's orbit around the sun is a fixed and specified orbit, it means that in its movement the earth revolves around the sun along an elliptic orbit and its distance from the sun cannot be less and more than such-and-such distance. Such is the distance during spring season. Such is the distance during autumn season. Such is the distance during winter season, and such is the distance during summer season. Another would say, "It follows that you regard the earth as fixed." No. The earth is in motion, but it is moving in this fixed orbit. To be fixed means that the earth turns around this orbit in a certain station. The earth, however, can move in two ways (revolution around the sun and rotation). One is that it moves in a specified orbit – now, that orbit may be straight, curved, elliptic, circular, or whatever it may be – and the other is for it to have a random movement. Sometimes it moves in this or that direction. At other times, it swings in this way or that way. At times, it revolves back to its earlier station, and the movement continues on and on. Of course, in spatial movements or motions, one cannot be assumed to be 'evolution' because of a certain reason.

As such, the fact that the orbit of the movement is fixed and that its direction is determined does not necessarily mean that the moving object is motionless and fixed. It is like saying that if a specific route is determined for the Apollo [11][1] from here (earth) up to the moon and this route has been written earlier on a sheet of paper and it is even specified, for example, that in 48 hours and so-and-so minutes and so-and-so seconds it would be in a particular point of the route and it is known on which part of the moon it

1. Apollo 11: the spaceflight that landed the first humans on the Moon, Americans Neil Armstrong and Buzz Aldrin, on July 20, 1969, at 20:18 UTC, with the third member of the mission, Michael Collins, having piloted the command spacecraft alone in lunar orbit until Armstrong and Aldrin returned to it just under a day later for the trip back to Earth. [Trans.]

would land, then we could say that Apollo [11] is fixed. It is not so. Its route is determined. For its route to be determined does not necessarily mean that the object itself is static. Its being static means that it will remain in a particular distance, not a bit closer to the earth or a bit away from it.

Natural Disposition and the Evolution of Human Society in Humanness

Those who have regarded the evolving nature of the human being as identical with the randomness of the criteria for humanness have succumbed to this mistake. That is, we have said that if we believe in human disposition in the sense that we regard the criteria for humanness as fixed such that their root is the human disposition, humanness (*insāniyyah*) becomes meaningful and sensible. Not only humanness but also the evolution of humanness will become meaningful and sensible, and as such, today, there is this doubt among the scholars, and in the philosophy of history this subject is extensively discussed – has the human being progressed in what is called 'humanness' and 'spirituality' (*ma'nawiyyah*), or not? In his book *The Lessons of History*,[1] Will Durant has thus allotted a section for this discussion: "Is Progress Real?" Of course, humanity's progress in technology is real, but [the question is:] is humanity's progress in humanness real?

As such, this question is raised now: that there is no doubt that in terms of science and technology and his relationship with nature, the human being has progressed and there is equally no doubt that

1. *The Lessons of History* is a 1968 (New York: Simon & Schuster) book by historians Will and Ariel Durant, which presents an overview of the themes and lessons observed from 5,000 years of world history, examined from 12 perspectives, viz. geography, biology, race, character, morals, religion, economics, socialism, government, war, growth and decay, and progress. [Trans.]

in terms of the society's structural systems, he has progressed, but that which is doubtful [is his progress in humanness]. It is even said that in this regard, the word 'progress' must be taken out because such a thing does not simply exist. What is [the opinion of] the author of history book? He himself opposes this idea, saying that it is not so; the human being has also progressed in human aspects although its tone is different from that of other evolutions. It is not synchronized with them and it is very slow. He, however, mentions some views in this regard and then says that it is no true that the human being has no progress at all in these aspects.

Marxism and the Evolution of Human Society in Humanness

The Marxists have no option but to deny any criterion for humanness and to regard evolution as merely a label, something ceremonial and a tool of production. There is no doubt that the tool of production has evolved. They say that the tool of production which has evolved in every stage necessitates morality. Since the necessitated morality of the stage of evolution is a tool of production, then we argue that the said morality has evolved, whereas these (tool of production and morality) are not compatible at all with one another. First of all, we do not accept the premise that in every period, the tool of production – in whatever level of progress it reaches – necessitates only one morality. In the principles of morality, we do not accept this premise. The tool of production, in whatever stage it is, has the same principles of morality. It is like someone saying that that "Betrayal against someone's property or chastity is only considered to be betrayal, stealing or rape, as the case may be, which is something bad, if it is committed using candle (for lighting). But, today, with this electricity and electrical energy, do you again say that it is bad if a person steals something or rapes someone?! Conditions have changed." These have no correlation with each other.

In addition to this, such an argument is basically a negation of human originality or essence; that is, human originality is basically senseless. We call evolution of the tool of production as human evolution. As such, humanness, for its being human-related, does not evolve. The tool of production has evolved and – as they say – in every stage where it evolves, it necessitates particular relationships (and all these relationships, like law, government, art, beauty, and ethics are superstructure, and they all products, dependent on and parasites of the tool of production). And since this tool of production necessitates them, we say that it has evolved. Other than labelling, it cannot be any other thing; otherwise there is nothing which is real such that we would say that there is something that has evolved. Rather, something has been abrogated and something else has replaced it. Whenever something is abrogated and something else has replaced it, can it be called 'evolution'? It is possible for it to be plain progression, or retrogression, or possibly nothing but retrogression. With which criteria can we say 'evolution'? With no criterion at all. It is only that since the tool of production has evolved, we say that a certain thing has also evolved!

As such, this issue of changeable morality in the sense that even the moral principles are changeable can never be the solution to the question of the human originality.

Existentialism and Human Originality

Meanwhile, there is another theory which is existentialism. They (existentialists) have also really attempted to build the edifice or foundation of human originality without touching on the question of materiality of the universe and corporeality of the human being.

They have raised an issue which had already been raised by others prior to them.[1] The first issue which they have put forth and whose way here is different from that of Oriental philosophy is that in Oriental philosophy – such as the statements of Abū 'Alī Sīnā – they say that we have two types of 'good',[2] viz. tangible good and rational good. These are things which the human being desires from the tangible and material aspects; in other words, the desires of these physical dimensions of the human being and the desires of his spiritual aspects. If ever they use the word 'benefit' or 'gain' sometimes they do so in relation to tangible good, and it is even possible for them to use it for rational good. They say, for example, that knowledge is good, though rational good. But water and bread are good, though tangible good. And the human being is compelled to pursue that which he considered to be 'good' from the depth of his being. In essence, he is in pursuit of his own 'good'. If we ask, "What is the criterion for good?" they say that the criterion for good is perfection; that is, the stage in the human being's existence reaching which promotes good and perfection is realized.

In European philosophy, since they do not want at all to believe in anything tangible to be real and true, they say that reality is that which is material and tangible; otherwise, it is not reality. As such, naturally, they could not say that the human being has two types of good. Those who say that "There are two types of good" believe in two types of reality. They acknowledge two levels of reality for the human being as well as for the world of existence.[3] Within his

1. Most of these philosophies are traceable to the philosophy of Hegel. The primary roots of both Marxism and existentialism are traceable to the philosophy of Hegel, and it is rightfully said that Hegel has changed the face of Europe's philosophy.
2. 'Good' (*khayr*) is a desire which emanates from the depth of human essence.
3. There are actually more than two levels. What are meant are the two levels related to the human being.

tangible reality, the human being is in pursuit of tangible good and within his rational reality, he is in pursuit of rational good. And from this perspective that he is in pursuit of good anyway, in both aspects, there is one [good]. If he is in pursuit of knowledge, he is in pursuit of a reality which is "rational good". If he is in pursuit of money, it is also a reality; he is in pursuit of a reality which is a tangible one.

Since the basis of their work is what is called 'reality', i.e. tangible and physical, they came [forward] and said that the human being is either in pursuit of good – which is nothing but material benefit or gain – or in pursuit of something which is actually nothing; it is mere 'value' – the same phrase 'gain and value' which was introduced in European philosophy and what a grave deviation in human philosophy! It is in this context that they say that the human being either in pursuit of gain – that is, something in which there is good and naturally, the intellect urges him to do so as it is logical as well – or he is in pursuit of things in which there is nothing good, and the intellect also discourages him to do so but he still pursues them. He does something irrational and illogical. He pursues a set of irrational and illogical works which logic or the intellect does not urge him to pursue, yet he still does. Such a contradiction or such a state of affairs which is called 'irrationality' exists in the human being. He pursues things which do not bring any good in him, and thus, they are not compatible with the intellect. Yet, are all actions of the human being compatible with the intellect?! He does something irrational and illogical. They have regarded these acts as man's illogical actions. Naturally, they made no progress in justifying these things which they called 'value' and not 'good'; that is, those things that the human being pursue without being good and chosen. How could these values be justified? 'Good' is that which is tangible and material; these are not tangible or material. Is beauty tangible and material for a person?! Does it have what is called 'volume' in the sense that it can be contained? Is virtue basically real?! Is the truth real?!

These became a set of illogical and irrational issues for humanity, but on the other hand, in the end they realized the difficulty in informing the society that all these things are fictitious; that is, they have to say the inevitable implication of Nietzsche's view and others that these things are fictitious; that the reality is that which is gain; anything which has no gain is not real; the intellect does not also encourage it to be pursued. Those who were courageous enough have revealed it. Those who were not brave enough indirectly revealed it in a different way. One said that values have evolved. Another said something else... The existentialists came forward and found a solution and that is, they said that the difference of values with the realities and truths is that the values are a set of producible things and not a set of discoverable things.[1] Discoverable things are those things which are real. Through reason, knowledge and argument, the human being discovers that which is real. Values, however, are things which the human being coins and invents. They

1. There is a book entitled *Jidāl bā Mudda'ī* (*Debate with the Pretender*). It is an interesting book. It is said that one of these Marxist leaders was interviewed by someone and this person claims that he has published the text of the interview with some modifications. He (author) writes an introduction and expresses all curses to the interviewer and then he says, "Now, I will publish exactly that interview." This book is divided into two. Its first part is about the value of life, living, progress, and more or less, about this issue of values, and the second part is about modern poetry. The critic poses odd questions. Initially, he is a proponent of the philosophy of nihilism, or at least, he defends the philosophy of nihilism there; that everything is nought and nil, and that life has only one direction and that is suicide. He is a proponent of the philosophy of suicide. Now, as to why this gentleman does not commit suicide himself is something that we must ask from him. This person wants to refute this view. Gradually his discussion leads to this issue of values. In this connection, he follows the logic of existentialism (because regarding these issues, Marxism is untenable – so untenable) and says that values are a set of producible things and not discoverable.

do not exist before in that they could be discovered; the human being creates them.

This is all the arguments of existentialists regarding the issue of values, and thus, this expression has been made a lot in today's literature: "Man creates values." This is while this statement is absurd. "Man creates values" – what does it mean?! This statement means that in nature itself, *īthār* and *ithrah*[1] (in Arabic jargon), for example, are the same; justice and injustice are equal; that there is essentially no difference between justice and injustice. Yet, the human being gives value to justice. Then he distinguishes justice from injustice, as having value. The human being gives value to it, just as he gives value to *īthār* and distinguishes it from *ithrah.* If you say now that justice is better than injustice; honesty is better than dishonesty; trustworthiness is better than treachery; these are [actually] essentially the same. It is this human being that gives value to them.

These gentlemen should be asked, "What does 'Man creates value' mean?" There is a time when "Man creates value" in the sense that he gives reality to something which is not real; that is, it was not real before and then he gave reality to it and it became real.

It is clear that these are not things which the human being has to make. The creative power of the human being is the same technical and industrial power which is applied on something physical which he shapes or forms. And you accept that in this context, shape, form and materiality are non-existent. As such, "Man creates them" in the sense that he gives them actual reality has no meaning at all. And granted that he wants to give reality, has 'spirituality' basically real or not? You say that spirituality is not real at all. In this case, how

1. *Ithrah* means to give preference to one's own self while *īthār* means to give preference to another person over one's own self.

can the human being give reality to something which is unrealistic?! The human being's creatorship in this regard is that which we call 'convention' (*i'tibār*) and it means any contractual matter. For instance, you are a group whose members cooperate with one another in this school. You can see that if you want your cooperation to bear fruit, you must be organized, and if you want to be organized, among yourselves there must be a management board, an executive board and the like, and one person must be elected as president of this school. You choose a certain person as your president, saying that "Mr. A is our president." Here you granted presidency to Mr. A; that is, presidency which was non-existent before was given him by you. Here you created and coined [something], but this creation is something conventional and contractual. In other words, it has no reality; that is, now in your realm of imagination, mentality, convention, and contract, Mr. A was different from Mr. A an hour ago when he was not yet president. In the actual and real world, however, he is the same person as he used to be before. Grant of presidency means is a contract, a validation and something which is acceptable to and assumed by the mind due to certain necessity. That is, it is something being permitted (*mujāz*). Validation is the ultimate human power of creatorship in such matters.

The widest possible meaning of "Man creates value," therefore, is that the things which we call 'values' are not real. Humanity grants 'value' (*arj*) to them. In reality, there is no 'value' for humanity, yet humanity gives 'value' to them.

Once again, it is a negation of originality or essence (*iṣālah*) and it can be a conventional and imaginary matter. Recently, the important issue is that in contractual matters, the human being can have contract in the 'means' and not in the 'ends'. We say, for example, that the value of paper bill is a nominal value; that is, it is contrary to the gold which, as it is useful to the human beings – as it has multiple uses, being rare to find as well as having multiple uses – whether for ornamentation purpose or other purposes, it is in itself relatively valuable for the human being. [Paper bill has no value in itself.] We give value to paper bill in lieu of gold in order to achieve certain objectives. We give value to it in order to ease transaction. As such, paper bill has no value in itself. In other words, this piece of paper, for example, which is labelled 1,000 *tūmāns*[1] in our hands, has no difference at all with another piece of paper with the same size in terms of real value. In terms of nominal and conventional value, however, the former is different from the latter so much so that we have set it as a means to achieve other objectives.

As such, if we regard human originality or essences are creatable matters in view of the fact that to create means to give reality, then it has no meaning here, and to create here has no meaning here except giving nominal value. This means that all these things are means for other ends, for they cannot be nominal by themselves and the objective at the same time. "To be nominal and the objective at the same time" is like the following case. A person has no objective; he gives nominal value of a certain thing to be his objective and that thing becomes his objectives. It is exactly the same case with the Arab idolaters who came to make their own idols. Afterward, they would worship the same objects that they had made.

﴿ أَتَعْبُدُونَ مَا تَنْحِتُونَ ﴾

> Do you worship what you have yourselves carved? (37:95)

The objective is that which is above your level and you exert all your efforts to achieve it. The thing which you make and grant value is that which is in your hand and it is lower than you in level.

---

1. *Tūmān*: every *tūmān* is equivalent to ten Iranian *rials*. [Trans.]

Human Essences as Intrinsic

As such, this is not also the solution to the problem, and let us return back to the same conclusion we have drawn earlier that this human originality or essences are only sensible, meaningful and real if they are a set of intrinsic matters for the human being, integral elements in the human disposition and they themselves are a set of realities which draws the human being toward his own reality. Just as the human being in tangible good moves along with his tangible reality toward tangible realities, they are also realities toward which the human being moves with his rational reality. Also, the human perfection can only be conceived with this assumption, and if we rob the human being of it, perfection in humanity will have no meaning although perfection in the means may be meaningful.

The values, therefore, are the same real good things. It is equally baseless to say that we have to divide into two the things that the human being pursues, viz. gains and values, and then we have to say that the values which are futile and absurd are illogical and the intellect never dictates that they must be pursued, yet one still pursues them. The human being does crazy and irrational things. Now, although it is not irrational to say that it is against the dictate of reason, finally it is not rational either and it is equal to a crazy action. In other words, it is a sort of half-wittedness, but half-wittedness is good as well as necessary. Again, to say that "It is good as well as necessary" is basically meaningless. Finally, we have no option but to regard them as a set of half-wittedness for the human being. Let us proceed in our discussion.

Now, the intrinsic nature of religion is put forth. What do those who say that religion is intrinsic mean? What is their basis that religion is intrinsic? In other words, what are the indications that religion is intrinsic? Do those indications exist in religion or not? These are parts of the questions posed earlier: "What are the indications of being intrinsic? Is religion intrinsic or not? What are the theories about the origin of religion?" One theory is that it is intrinsic. Which theories oppose this theory of the intrinsic nature of religion? The article I have mentioned in the previous session is approximately about this subject, "Theories on the Origin of the Emergence of Religion." Mr. ... was supposed to deliver a lecture regarding this article.

Approximately 20 years ago, a publication called *Nashriyyeh-ye Sālāneh-ye Maktab-e Tashayyu'* (*Annual Publication of the Shī'ah School of Thought*) was used to be published in Qum. Perhaps seven or eight issues were published annually. Three or four issues were published quarterly. In the said annual publications – I remember very well that it was in the first issue – Engineer Bayānī translated an article entitled *Dīn yā Bu'd-e Chahārum* (*Religion or the Fourth Dimension*). An introduction and an epilogue were also written by Engineer Bāzargān[1] for that article. The said article – if you can find it – is very good for this discussion (theories on the origin of the emergence of religion). The theories have been mentioned there. Of course, the writer himself of the article is an advocate of the intrinsic nature of religious feeling.

1. Engineer Mahdī Bāzargān (1908-1994) was among the main founders of the Freedom Movement of Iran. Upon the culmination of the Islamic Revolution in Iran, he was appointed as the head of the provisional government; however, he decided to step down one day after Iranian students stormed the US embassy (Den of Espionage) in Tehran. Later, however, he became the Member of Parliament for Tehran during the first session of the Islamic Consultative Assembly. [Trans.]

Chapter 7: The Foundation and Origin of Religion

One basic benefit for us of knowing their[1] theories about the foundation and origin of religion is that we would understand the essential nature of fanaticism for non-religiosity. We have been always told about religious fanaticism that religious people are fanatic and since they are fanatic, they express views out of utmost fanaticism. Let us see what balderdashes those who are fanatic in non-religiosity – that is, their foremost assumption is the negation of religion – have found to justify this negation, for it is impossible for a neutral person to have this extent of balderdashes. Let us also see how in the end they will be trapped in explaining [the nature of] religion. In other words, you will definitely realize the utter paltriness of their theories.

A branch of science named 'religious sociology' has come into being in Europe. At the outset, this branch of science chooses something as the 'axiom' (*aṣl-e mawḍū'*) just as every branch of science has an axiom which cannot be proved at the beginning as it is considered to be 'given' (*mafrūḍ*). Then, on the basis of this axiom, one's views are explained. In religious sociology, from the beginning, the assumption is that religion is a phenomenon that comes into being as a result of interaction in society. In other words,

---

1. [It is worthy of note that prior to Professor Muṭahharī's lecture, there had been a lecture about an article on the topic "Theories on the Origin of Religion" written by a certain Anwar Khāmeh.]

it has no divine or metaphysical origin, and this [religion has having divine origin] is not part of the assumption at all. If we are told, for example, about the reason for the emergence of the notion of 'unlucky 13,' – to investigate how this notion of 'unlucky 13' became prevalent to the people – since a person realizes that logically there is no difference between the number 13, 14 or 12, such that there is a possibility of a rational or empirical reason for it, he says that it must have a non-logical root. What is that non-logical root?

Regarding religion or religious belief, at the outset their basis is that religion cannot have a logical root. Now, as it has a non-logical root, the question is: what is this non-logical root? So, their axiom is that [religion is no logical and divine root].

Initially, the writer of the article gives a brief historical background and then says that the first person to systematically analyze this issue is a very famous materialist philosopher named Feuerbach[1] who is also one of the two intellectual foundations of Karl Marx.[2] Feuerbach is [also] a German and known as a mentor of Marx, but not in the sense of formally becoming Marx's teacher in a classroom setting. It rather means that Marx has benefitted a lot from his ideas and quoting from him. Marx's ideas have two foundations. In terms of logic and frame of mind, he is a follower of Hegel;[3] that is, the dialectic logic [and in terms of social philosophy, he is a follower of Feuerbach.] Hegel, however, is not materialist; he

1. Ludwig Andreas von Feuerbach (1804-1872): a German philosopher and anthropologist whose thought was influential in the development of Marxist dialectic. [Trans.]

2. Karl Heinrich Marx (1818-83): a German philosopher, political economist, historian, political theorist, sociologist, and communist revolutionary, whose ideas played a significant role in the development of modern communism and socialism. [Trans.]

3. Georg Wilhelm Friedrich Hegel (1770-1831): a German philosopher, one of the creators of German idealism, and along with Immanuel Kant, one of the most influential philosophers of the Age of Enlightenment. [Trans.]

has a unique kind of thinking such that some say that he is an idealist while not believing in God at the same time. Others say, however, that he believes in God. No, he believes in God but his conception of God is somewhat different from those of others. Feuerbach's popularity in materialist thinking lies in the same analysis he has made about religion, and his analysis is that he has said that religion is born out of the human being's feeling of self-alienation. 'Self-alienation' has also been introduced for the first time in European philosophy by Hegel. It is something in the philosophy of man which is called 'self-alienation'. Perhaps, the correct term for it is 'alienation with the self' in the sense that there are many contributory factors for the human being to be alienated with himself. Now, this in itself is a problem: how can a person be alien to his own self? Is such a state of affairs possible at all? It is because alienation – and also its exact opposite which is kinship – involves two parties. In this case, how can a person be alien to his own self? This means that a person mistakenly identifies himself to be another person. In other words, a person has a reality; he has a real self. Then he thinks to be his own self something which is a 'non-self'. Instead of doing for himself, for example, he works for that 'non-self'. We have presented this issue – though not lengthily but just concisely – in the book *Sayri dar Nahj al-Balāghah* (*Glimpses of Nahj al-Balāghah*).[1]

Losing the Self Means Forgetting the Self

I remember that approximately twenty years ago – one or two years after I had come to Tehran (and I came to Tehran in 1331 S.A.H) – we had a private session for exegesis *(tafsīr)* [of the Qur'an] at the residence of one of our merchant friends in which I used to attend to share [my] exegesis. [Real] exegesis cannot be made; it was a discussion on selected verses and a meeting for admonition and

1. See Murtaḍā Muṭahharī, *Glimpses of Nahj al-Balāghah*, trans. Sayyid 'Alī Qulī Qarā'ī (Tehran: Ahl al-Bayt (A.S.) World Assembly, 2011), 262-275. [Trans.]

reminding. For me this issue was raised there for the first time. A point from the Qur'an struck me attention at that time and I remember that I presented this point in the said gathering. Afterward, I have also put forth many times that it can be inferred from the Qur'an that occasionally a person has a feeling that he keeps distance from his own self (and I used the word 'distance' there). One becomes away from his own self, for this expression has been used oftentimes in the Qur'an: to lose the self (self-losing). Losing has the same meaning used in gambling or in commercial transaction – so-and-so lost, is at a loss, or loses his assets. This is while to believe in this state of affairs is very problematic for a person, because when one loses something which is in his own possession it means that it is given to someone else. But how is it possible to say that a person lose himself? The Qur'an says:

﴿ قُلْ إِنَّ الْخَاسِرِينَ الَّذِينَ خَسِرُوا أَنْفُسَهُمْ ﴾

> Say, 'Indeed the losers – the real losers – are those who ruin themselves'. (39:15)

In other words, the one who loses his property is not the real loser. It is something secondary in importance. The real loser is the one who loses his own self; he gives away his self elsewhere. 'Self-oblivion' means to forget one's own self. From a philosophical perspective, this is also problematic notion because a person's knowledge of himself is an intuitive knowledge (*'ilm al-ḥuḍūrī*) and intuitive knowledge is unforgettable. Acquired knowledge (*'ilm al-ḥuṣūlī*) is forgettable; that is, the essence of man's being is basically knowledge and his self is the same knowledge of himself about himself.

Rūmī's Statement

To lose the self means to forget the self. This, for me, at that time, was something to think about. Of course, later on, I realized that the philosophers, the Muslim mystics (*'urafā'*) in particular, have understood it many years before us, also relying much on it – what and who this real 'I' is. In fact, the foundation of mysticism (*'irfān*) is to find the real 'self' and the real 'I'; that is, to see through the veils of the imaginary 'self' and the imaginary 'I' and to attain to the real 'I'. In other words, 'to lose the self,' 'to mistaken the self,' 'to lose the self,' and 'to give away the self' are concepts which can be very well inferred from the Qur'an and later on they have also been well explained and interpreted. One of those excellent interpretations and allegories which is indeed a masterpiece is an allegory which Mawlawī (Rūmī) has expressed. As you know, he deals with a subject in the form of an allegory. The human being mistakes his lower self as his higher self, or you may say, he mistakes his carnal and physical dimension as his spiritual-celestial dimension which is his real self. That is, he thinks of his self as such.

The allegory is as follows. Imagine that someone owns a piece of land. He begins to build on that piece of land. He brings building materials. He bricks; he brings land plasters, cements and soil; he brings lumber and steel, and a very magnificent house is built there. The following day, he wants to go to his own house. As he wants to move into the new house, he goes there. Suddenly he realizes that his mistake of erecting the house on his neighbour's plot. The piece of land he owns is elsewhere; this plot is owned by somebody else; whatever he built is erected on another's plot. According to the law, he has no right to take something from his neighbour. The neighbour says, "I didn't tell you to build [here]; you yourself came here and built. Come and take away everything [you put up]." And if he wants to dismantle the house, he has to spend some more money. So, he is forced to abandon it and go. In expressing these amazing spiritual subtleties, Mawlawī (Rūmī) thus sings:

در زمین دیگران خانه مکن   کار خود کن کار بیگانه مکن
کیست بیگانه، تن خاکی تو   کز برای اوست غمناکی تو

Do not make your home in others' land,
Do your own work, don't do the work of a stranger.
Who is the stranger except your own earthen body?
For the sake of which is your sorrow.[1]

That is to say, "Your whole life, you work for your body and your carnal self and you imagine that you work for yourself."

تا تو تن را چرب و شیرین می‌دهی   گوهر جان را نیابی فربهی
گر میان مشک تن را جا شود   وقت مردن گند آن پیدا شود

So long as you are giving your body greasy and sweet,
You will not see fatness in your essence.
If the body be set in the midst of musk,
On the day of death its stench will become manifest.[2]

That is to say, "If you set your body in the midst of musk your whole life, [at the time of death, its foul odour will be revealed]."

مشک را بر تن مزن بر جان بمال   مشک چه بود؟ نام پاک ذو الجلال

Do not put musk on your body; rub it on your soul.
What is musk? The holy name of the Glorious.[3]

Similarly, the Qur'an states, thus:

﴿ وَلَا تَكُونُوا كَالَّذِينَ نَسُوا اللَّهَ فَأَنْسَاهُمْ أَنْفُسَهُمْ ﴾

1. *Mathnawī-ye Ma'nawī*, Book 2, lines 263-264, with slight variation. [Trans.]

2. *Mathnawī-ye Ma'nawī*, Book 2, lines 265-266. [Trans.]

3. *Mathnawī-ye Ma'nawī*, Book 2, line 267, with slight variation. [Trans.]

> And do not be like those who forget Allah, so He makes them forget their own souls. (59:19)

It affirms the correlation between 'finding the self' and 'finding God'. The Qur'an asserts that only those who have found themselves have really found God and those who have found God have found themselves:

مَنْ عَرَفَ نَفْسَهُ عَرَفَ رَبَّهُ.

"Whoever knows his self knows his Lord."

In the same manner,

مَنْ عَرَفَ رَبَّهُ عَرَفَ نَفْسَهُ.

"Whoever knows his Lord knows his self."

According to the logic of the Qur'an, they are inseparable. If a person imagines that he has found his real self without finding God, he is mistaken. This is one of the principles of the gnostic knowledge of the Qur'an.

This subject which is called today as 'self-alienation' or to be more precise, 'alienation with the self' has a long precedence in Islamic teachings. That is, it begins with the Qur'an and it has more than a thousand years of precedence and a specific trend. In Europe, this subject starts with Hegel and after him, other schools of thought put it forth [without necessarily identifying this 'self'!] It is because the first question about it is this: what is this 'self' that talks about alienation? You have just said that the human being is alienated from the 'self'. Before anything else, identify to us this 'self' and then 'alienation with the self' or 'self-alienation' must specified. Without discussing about the 'self', without identifying the 'self' –

and even without negating the 'self' – [they talk about 'self-alienation'.] The foundation of these materialist philosophies is that the 'self' is essentially a nominal entity. All materialist philosophies maintain that the human being has no 'self' of his own; the 'self' which you imagine is an abstract concept. A series of conceptions continuously come and go one after the other. You imagine that among them there is a 'self'; it is not so; there is no such 'self'.

On one hand, the foundation of their philosophy is that there is no such 'self' at all, and on the other hand, they come forward and coin the philosophy of 'self-alienation' for the people, and this is very amazing!

Origin of Religion According to Feuerbach

Mr. Feuerbach who is a materialist philosopher has made odd remarks. He has attempted to psychologically and sociologically analyze religion and religious belief on the same basis we have mentioned. First of all, the assumption is that religion has no logical foundation. He says that the human being has two-pronged existence. (This notion itself is taken from religion.) The human being has a higher and lower existence. It is the same thing which we call the celestial dimension and earthly dimension. The earthly dimension of the human being is his animalistic dimension; like any animal, his concern is nothing but to eating, sleeping, anger, and carnal desire, while his celestial dimension is his very humanity, which Feuerbach consider to be another part of man's being and he has no option but to treat it as something innate – and it is the same dimension which possesses a set of virtues, viz. nobility, honour, compassion, goodness, kindness and the like. Then he says that the human being (and he has no option but to affirm that all human beings are like that) yields to lowliness; that is, he submits to the lowly dimension of his being. After submitting to the lowly dimension of his being, he realizes that the celestial aspects are not compatible with his being, for he himself now has degenerated into a lowly animal. Consequently, while having these nobilities and essences, he concludes that these elements are beyond him and creates 'God' on the basis of his self.

A European philosopher has said that it is thus mentioned in the Torah, "God created mankind in his own image"(1:27) in the sense that He set Adam as manifestation of His attributes of perfection. That European philosopher said so, but the fact is the opposite. The human being created God in his own nature. In other words, since the human being has an innate excellent nature in which are embedded all this nobility, perfection, compassion, and the like, which he separated from his self and he became alienated with his self. Then he thought that these are beyond his being, failing to realize that all these are within his self.

From then on – according to him – the human being became alienated with his self. In other words, he separated certain elements which were in his being from his self, assuming that these are beyond his being. He (the European philosopher) says, however, that this metaphysical dimension gradually gets closer. Initially, it was far away from the human being; in the gods of primitive religions it was very far. Then in the God of Judaism [it got closer]. The God of Judaism is similar to the human being; like a man, he has feelings or emotions, gets angry and is pleased. In Christianity, He gets even closer. He comes in the form of human being who is the Christ and the Christ is God Himself. In fact, He has undergone an arch; initially, the human being had separated these attributes from his being, putting them far away, and there had been no relationship between the Far Being and the human being. Then little by little, the said Being has returned and came toward the human being. As He turned into the Christ, He has become so closed and become a God-Man (because in Christianity the Christ is God; that is, He is man and God, and He is a human being and Divine at the same time). There is only step lacking. The more man knows himself, the more he keeps himself far away from this 'self-alienation'. Suddenly, he reaches a point where "It is indeed I myself and these attributes are all mine and not by anybody else." So, nothing has been left except one more step. (This is while Islam has come after Christianity and has been more perfect than Christianity, yet it has strongly negated all this God-Man dimension, Divinity of a man who is the Christ, his Godhood, and his Sonship of God.)

According to Mr. Feuerbach, religion will soon cease to exist. That is, the more the human being knows himself, his need for thinking about God becomes lesser and once he completely knows himself, there will be no more room for religion in his life, and instead of worshipping God, he will worship himself; instead of praising and glorifying God, he will praise and glorify himself.

Refuting Feuerbach's Theory

One of the aspects that could refute this theory is that which should be said to Mr. Feuerbach: "You do not believe in God at all and you recognize the human being as primarily purely materialist. So, how can you reconcile this duality in his being?" It is religion which could be able declare that it regards the human being as an earthly being as well as a celestial being:

﴿ فَإِذَا سَوَّيْتُهُ وَنَفَخْتُ فِيهِ مِن رُّوحِي ﴾

'So when I have proportioned him and breathed into him of My spirit... (38:72)

On one hand, "I have proportioned him" (that is, "I have perfected him and I have completed him in terms of faculties and organs"). There is something else, however, which follows it: "and I have breathed into him of My spirit" or in *Sūrat al-Mu'minūn* it is thus stated:

﴿ وَلَقَد خَلَقنَا الإنسانَ مِن سُلالَةٍ مِن طينٍ ﴾

> Certainly, We created man from an extract of clay. (23:12)

Until such a point that it states thus:

﴿ ثُمَّ أنشَأناهُ خَلقًا آخَرَ ﴾

> Then He produced him as [yet] another creature. (23:13)

To become another creature [is important as it is related to the dual dimension of man's being.] They can say, "Yet what can you say?"

Secondly, on the basis of this philosophy, we have to accept that no one in the world is left with his innate nobility. It maintains that in his innermost being, the human being has duality. Then, as he degenerates in social life, he falls into that lowly dimension, his base self and bestiality. He comes forward to separate the higher dimensions and nobility of his being from his self. From here, the belief in religion starts. This means that first of all, we have to assume that all human beings have fallen into the abyss of bestiality, and secondly, all these fallen ones must be assumed to be 'religious'. This is while firstly, the human being has been always of two types: those who have kept their human nobility – and there have always been such people at all times – and those who have fallen into the abyss of bestiality. Secondly, we have to see which groups are those who incline to religion – and incidentally, this is part of our proof – in other words, those who are the 'customers' of religion. Are they the noble men – those who have maintained within themselves human essences – are inclined toward religion, or are they those who have fallen into the abyss of bestiality? In this regard, even non-religious individuals have no denial, and as such, they say that if ever you can see religious people, this religiosity stems from their innate nobility. It has nothing to do with the religion to which they are inclined; it is related to their nobility. In other words, the real customers of religion can always be found from among the noble individuals. You say that as the human being loses his nobility and falls into the abyss of bestiality, this state of affairs is to origin of his belief in God. This is while the truth of the matter is the contrary. Those who sense this nobility within themselves and maintain their human originality are the ones who have belief or faith in God and religious precepts. At any rate, the theory is this gentleman is a refuted theory.

Religion as a Product of Ignorance According to Auguste Comte and Spencer

As a whole, this notion they have expressed that religion is a product of ignorance has been expressed in two ways. The remarks made by Auguste Comte[1] is different from the one quoted from Spencer[2] and others. That is, these are two [different] forms. Auguste Comte's view on the issue is an explanation of the causes of events. That is, he wants to say that humanity has naturally acknowledged the principle of causation, however, since the ancient people were not aware of the main causes of events, they would attribute these events to a set of unseen beings, gods and the like.

1. Auguste Comte (1798-1857): a French philosopher and social theorist. [Trans.]
2. Herbert Spencer (1820-1903): an English philosopher, prominent classical liberal political theorist, and sociological theorist of the Victorian era who developed an all-embracing conception of evolution as the progressive development of the physical world, biological organisms, the human mind, and human culture and societies. [Trans.]

They would see, for example, the coming of rain; since they were not aware of the cause of the coming of rain, they would say that it was the 'god of rain'. A storm would come; they were not aware of the cause of storm; so they would say it was the 'god of storm'. So were the other phenomena.

According to him, therefore, this is mere thinking for the human being; in the same manner, regarding monotheism (*tawḥīd*) we say that this is only related to the degree of cognition.

Spencer and others have presented the notion in another way and that is, the human being believed for the first time in his dual being in the sense of duality of the body and soul since he could see living and dead people in a dream, the dead ones in particular. Those who died would come to appear in his dream. Then he would conclude that those who would appear in his dream were real beings out there that came to him and since he knew that their bodies were already buried, he believed that they have souls. Since then, he believed that all of us human beings have bodies and souls. Then he generalized all things in the sense that he believed in all things to have spirits. He believed in the sea to have a spirit; he believed in the storm to have a spirit; he believed in the sun to have a spirit, so on and so forth. In times of difficulties and encountering these forces of nature – just as he would offer a present and make a vow when facing a powerful individual – he would occasionally make an appeasement and acts like that. He would begin doing such acts and gestures – that is, worship – in facing forces of nature. (Spencer explains the issue of 'worship' by identifying its first appearance.) And then from there worship of the forces of nature came into being.

Thus, Auguste Comte only gives a theoretical and intellectual explanation of the subject. Spencer has identified the root of worship: how it began for the first time; how the worship of the forces of nature began; and these acts such as appeasement and giving of gifts and bequests which a person would do to another person more powerful than him. Just as they would give gifts for fellow human beings, they would offer sacrifices for these spirits. Just as they would practice appeasement when dealing with fellow human beings, they would worship, glorify and adore these spirits.

According to this theory, with the disappearance of ignorance in the sense of knowing the causes (as Auguste Comte theorized), belief in all things to have spirits; sea to have a spirit; the earth to have a spirit; rain to have a spirit; and even the human being himself to have a soul was naturally doubted or negated. In this case, worship has no sense. That is, with the expansion of knowledge, religion is automatically negated.

The writer of an article rebuts that this notion is not correct for certain reasons. One of the reasons is that experience shows the opposite. He says that we can see that both religious and non-religious can be found among the ignorant people; both religious and non-religious can also be found among the learned people. The question of religiosity or irreligiosity has nothing to do with ignorance or knowledge. If religion were indeed a product of ignorance, the more illiterate a person is, the more religious he must become; the more literate or learned a person is, the more irreligious he must become. As such, the highest ranking scholars must definitely be irreligious, whereas the scholars are not so. Then writer asserts that so-and-so as well as so-and-so and even Darwin[1] were not irreligious.

> "...A point in this article of Anwar Khāmeh is that there are two quotations which, in my opinion at least, seem to be very erroneous. One is this quoted poem of

1. Charles Robert Darwin (1809-82): English naturalist and one of the strongest and best-known defenders of organic evolution, whose most important work is *The Origin of Species by Means of Natural Selection* (1859). [Trans.]

Mawlawī (Rūmī):

ابلهی شو تا بمانی دین درست

Be fool so as to keep the religion upright.

And another is a poem by Abū'l-'Alā al-Ma'arrī. [1] Notwithstanding the opinions about him, at least this poem of his is probably not recited for this purpose [that religion is a product of ignorance]. He thus says,

إثنانِ أهلُ الأَرْضِ ذُو عَقْلٍ بِلاَ دِينٍ ۞ وَآخَرُ دَيِّنٌ لاَ عَقْلَ لَهُ

The earth's inhabitants are of two sorts: those with brains, but no religion,
And those with religion but no brings.

I think both of these [poems] are a reproach for the elitist religious who, for example, would excommunicate (*takfīr*) others, and as a reply to them, and not in that sense that these sociologists [wanted to believe] that they (poets) really believed that religion is a product of ignorance.

Of course, Abū'l-'Alā al-Ma'arrī is a philosopher and man of learning but he is also a poet of an ascetic order; that is, he is a person who says different things on different occasions, and as such, it is clear that Abū'l-'Alā is not so enlightened. Evidently, I do not have an extensive study on the personality of Abū'l-'Alā; This is only the extent of what I know about him. In the words of Abū'l-'Alā, monotheism, religiosity and Islam are also much emphasized, and words which are against them can also be found.

Regarding the [alleged] poem of Mawlawī (Rūmī), I have not

1. Abū'l-'Alā al-Ma'arrī (973-1058): a blind Arab philosopher, poet and writer, known as a controversial rationalist and sceptic of his time for attacking the dogmas of religion. [Trans.]

found its reference. Concerning him, no one could give such possibility. My guess is that most probably, as he is a mystic, at logger heads with philosophers and wants [to state] his view on total submission (*taslīm*), he wants to say that so long as a person does not submit to the truth, [he will not attain it]; he must put aside everything from himself and go there. Any mystic always thinks that way. He would say that one should take away whatever you possess and these are [manifestations of egoism (*anāniyyah*)], and come forward himself. He (Mawlāwī) even interprets in that way the tradition – عَلَيْكُم بِدِينِ الْعَجَائِزِ (With you is the religion of *ajā'iz*). Of course, its being really a *ḥadīth* is not clear. At any rate it is narrated as such. That is, *'ajā'iz* is taken by him from *'ajz* (عجز) which means a state of despondency and hopelessness. In many poems of Mawlawī, the intellect is condemned, but the condemned intellect is that 'rational' intellect vis-à-vis the mystical love. That is, in case of contradiction between reason and love, he condemns reason and clings to love. Of course, such is mysticism (*'irfān*). He says,

آزمودم عقل دوراندیش را   بعد از این دیوانه سازم خویش را

I have tried far-thinking intellect;
Henceforth I will make myself mad.[1]

He says so not in the sense they want him to say.

Religion as Originated from Weakness and Fear According to Russell

It is said that another theory considers religion to be a product of the human being's weakness and fear. It is the same question of fear. Perhaps the person who lays most emphasis on it is Russell. It is

1. *Mathnawī-ye Ma'nawī*, Book 2, line 2332.

good to read some quotations from him.

The book *Barguzīdeh-ye Afkār-e Russell* (*A Selection from Russell's Ideas*) is a book on education, and it explains his social order in this way:

> "Belief in God and life after death gives us this possibility to continue our life with lesser righteous animosity toward the sceptics. That is, belief in religion makes us less daring. A very large group of people lose their faith to these religious laws in the ages in which despair and hopelessness swiftly dominate human being. They have to deal with individuals who have no religious upbringing at all with much more disappointments. Christianity gives reasons why we should not be afraid of death or the hereafter but in order to attain it, it fails in adequate teaching of animosity. This is while enthusiasm for religious faith is substantially a product of human fear. The proponents of religion show inclination to the idea that "Some types of fear should not be taken into consideration." In my opinion, he is seriously mistaken in this regard. That we will let someone resort to pleasing beliefs in a bid to escape from fear can never be called 'living in the best way possible'. So long as religion seeks refuge in fear, human value and station will continue to be undermined."[1]

The writer also quotes from Russell's *Human Society*,[2] thus:

> "I think the human being that could not tolerate the existence of life's mortality without the acceptance of

1. *Barguzīdeh-ye Afkār-e Russell* (*Selection from Russell's Ideas*).
2. Most probably it refers to Russell's *Human Society in Ethics and Society* (London: George Allen & Unwin, 1954). [Trans.]

comforting myths is a weak and threatened being. Definitely such a person is declaring such a truth in part of his being that what he accepts is nothing but a myth or fiction, and their acceptance is merely for the sake of tranquillity in his being, but he has no courage to face such ideas. It can even be said that since he is aware of the illogical nature of his ideas, it follows that he is biased toward them and avoids discussing and arguing about them.

"Description of the subject is that the human being can see phenomena and are afraid of them, and because of his fear of them, he needs to change his worry and agitation to a sort of tranquillity. He could not discover this tranquillity through science or real knowledge of the phenomena that would subsequently lead to a suitable solution for him. Inevitably, instead of real cure, he resorts to a tranquilizer and he comes to create a cold heart for himself. By believing in fate (*qaḍā*) and predestination (*qadr*), for example, he solves undesirable things in life for himself. By believing in paradise and that paradise in the price of our sufferings here (in this world), he makes easy for himself the undesirable things; so on and so forth..."[1]

Criticism and Analysis

I shall return to the point I have mentioned in the beginning. Perhaps, I have not been able to explain it correctly. Our scholars on the principles of jurisprudence (*uṣūl al-fiqh*) have a [certain] term. They say that a certain proof rules over yet another proof or

1. *Barguzīdeh-ye Afkār-e Russell* (*Selection from Russell's Ideas*).

a certain proof takes precedence over yet another proof. Their point is that sometimes two proofs cannot conflict with each other because one proof depends on a condition which ceases to exist with the appearance of the other proof. Once the condition for its existence ceases to exist, the proof will not also exist. It does not mean that the two proofs are contradictory; there is no chance for them to conflict with each other. Now, if I will discuss it, we will digress far away [from the subject]. Those who are acquainted [with the principles of jurisprudence] know it.

As I have said, their assumption is that logic cannot be the origin of religious thought. As such, let us now deal with illogical matters, viz. fear, ignorance, etc.

They must be told that sometimes the origin of a person's inclination to an idea, no matter how false it may be, is still logic and not anything beyond logic. For thousands of years, the people were thinking that the sun revolves around the earth and that the earth is static. Have we ever investigated the reason why the people used to believe that the earth is the centre and that the sun and the stars revolve around it? For example, was it fear of the dead, and things like that? No. We say that logical thinking process [has made the people arrived at this conclusion.] No factor beyond thinking and logic is at work, although the assumption was incorrect. The people used to observe; it seemed as though the sun and the stars revolves around the earth. They arrived at this conclusion based on what they used to observe. This is not a proof other than seeing and thinking by the human being. There is no external proof. It is like [belief in the unlucky number] 13; we could not say that there another factor involved [other than the human mind].

They must be asked, "Is the human being the same human being of the past thousands of years? Fortunately, the relics which we have now from people of the past thousands of years – apart from the issue of the prophets – in science and technology, craftsmanship and even in thought and ideas, some of them are extremely impressive and many of them have no more traces at the present. The oldest books which have been obtained from China and others speak of philosophical thoughts which are so fine and excellent that they have brought astonishment to the people of today. You can see that some personalities of today like Hashtrūdī could not believe that the pyramids of Egypt were built by human beings at that time. That is, these [pyramids] are a showcase of advanced technology and craftsmanship so much so that they say that these were built by other beings from other planets who came [on earth for that purpose]. Is the human being that same human being of the past who did not think much and drag himself toward religion and [belief in] God? The fact that you say that he used to think about happenings and conclude that they have causes is very good. Let us push him a step forward. What is the cause? This is a simple step that the human mind would be able to reach and he would not just remain on the first step; he would not just remain on calling [the Supreme Being] *Ilah* or *God.* He says that this rain is something that comes and goes; he then investigates it and asks about it. This is an integral part of the primitive ideas of man. There is no need for a person to go to school or attend a formal lesson; in fact, every person could quickly understand that whatever he sees is in the form of something overwhelmed (*maqhūr*) and subdued (*marbūb*).

The Qur'an and the Question of Knowing God

Look, what miracle the Qur'an has shown in narrating a story of Ibrāhīm (Abraham) (A.S.) who is one of the most ancient prophets (prior to Judaism, Christianity and the like). It also narrates about the young Ibrāhīm (A.S.); [it narrates] about Ibrāhīm (A.S.) as a person [who is isolated from society due to a particular reason].

This is a very extraordinary point that the Qur'an particularly narrates this story that due to a particular reason Ibrāhīm (A.S.) used to be isolated from society and to live in a cave.[1] During the first time that he saw the outside world, when he saw a bright star, this caught his attention and he said, "*Hādhā rabbī*" (either in the form of question or affirmation); that is, "This is my Lord, Nourisher and Schemer." One night he observed that after sometime its place somehow changed and faded away. He observed that the characteristic possessed by himself who was looking for his own *Rabb* (Lord and Nourisher) – that is, to be overwhelmed, subdued and subjected – could also be seen in that which he called, "This is my *Rabb*." He said,

﴿ لا أُحِبُّ الآفِلِينَ ﴾

> I do not like those who set. (6:76)

He saw the moon which is bigger. He said, "This is my *Rabb*." When he saw that the moon has also the same characteristic of being subdued, he was surprised. He sensed that he has the *Rabb* but not this one. "Amazing! I was mistaken again."

﴿ لَئِن لَّمْ يَهْدِنِي رَبِّي لَأَكُونَنَّ مِنَ الْقَوْمِ الضَّالِّينَ ﴾

> Had my Lord not guided me, I would surely have been among the astray lot. (6:77)

1. I have said time and again that Ibrāhīm (A.S.) is the *ḥayy ibn yaqẓān* of the Qur'an. *Ḥayy ibn yaqẓān* refers to a hypothetical person who the philosophers suppose to let let grow up in a cave or where he could not see anybody and get to know anybody's idea. One day, they will bring him in the outside world to see how he would think. But the Qur'an has a *ḥayy ibn yaqẓān* who is a real person at the same time.

He saw the sun and said,

﴿ هٰذا رَبِّي هٰذا أَكبَرُ لَمّا أَفَلَت... ﴾

'This is my Lord! This is bigger!' But when it set.... (6:78)

He suddenly relinquished all of them; that is, he considered them all. It was a very simple assessment: "All these that I saw have one thing in common. All these things are in motion, subdued and subject to be moved." That is, he saw the whole universe as a single subdued unit. The Qur'an states the primitive man's thinking also reached this point that the whole universe is a single subjected unit. So, the *Rabb* is the One who does not possess this characteristic of theirs:

﴿ إِنِّي وَجَّهتُ وَجهِيَ لِلَّذِي فَطَرَ السَّمَاوَاتِ وَالأَرضَ ﴾

Indeed I have turned my face toward Him who originated the heavens and the earth. (6:79)

They must be asked, "Is anthropology more accurate that way, or the way you say so?"

Also, the Verse of Pre-existence (*āyat al-dharr*) – if you study the exegesis *Al-Mīzān* and we will discuss it if we cover it – [refers to this subject].

﴿ وَإِذ أَخَذَ رَبُّكَ مِن بَنِي آدَمَ مِن ظُهُورِهِم ذُرِّيَّتَهُم وَأَشهَدَهُم عَلَى أَنفُسِهِم أَلَستُ بِرَبِّكُم قَالُوا بَلَى ﴾

When your Lord took from the Children of Adam, from their loins, their descendants and made them bear witness over themselves, [He said to them,] 'Am I not your Lord?' They said, 'Yes indeed!' (7:172)

The Qur'an says that [this matter is related to] training and education [and nothing else]. The primitive man, the middle man and the man at the end of time are one and the same in this respect, and this is an integral part of his natural disposition (*fiṭrah*): "Am I not your Lord?" That is, the human being feels that he and anyone else who possesses the characteristic that he has is subdued (*marbūb*), and the *Rabb* is other than the subdued because a *rabb* who is subdued is one of those who are subdued.

When a subject has such a logical basis – that is, logic is sufficient enough to let man reach that point – what sickness a person is suffering from in that he looks for such justifications and analyses?! It is like a situation when the door of this hall is open. One day, we see that there is somebody inside the hall. Then we ask, "Did this person come inside through the hole of the air conditioner? Did he make a hole in the wall? Did he make a hole in the ceiling?" They will say, "The door is open; he comes inside through the door." Another day, the door is closed. When we see that there is somebody inside the hall, we will look around the hall to know through which way he comes inside. But when the door is open, it is a kind of sickness if one would think of another way how that person gets inside.

Now, is the Qur'anic logic stronger or their logic? The Qur'an particularly mentions the story of Ibrāhīm (A.S.) – Ibrāhīm (A.S.) who had not seen the outside world for approximately sixteen years and not gone anywhere else other than the cave. It states that the primitive man (in reality, it wants to refer to the most primitive of people to mean his unsullied natural disposition) who is the same most ancient man also arrives at the same conclusion on the basis of his natural disposition; that is, this is the simplest of problems. This is one side of the issue.

The other side is this: could the primitive men have not been able to see the same amazing order in the universe? Was the primitive man not planting trees? When he would see that a seed, a simple object, is buried in the ground and then it would turn into a tree with all its leaves, buds, flowers, and fruits, was he not amazed? Could he not see his bodily constitution? Was he not astonished by all these orders in that we say that these same things [prompted the human being to incline to God and religion?]. Now you say it is wrong. I ask, "Are all these things not enough to urge him to arrive at this thought? Considering the existence of all such basis for human thought[1] and the openness of such logical and mental windows, how can we overlook all these things?" Then we ask, "Was fear the reason why the human being thought about God? Was it caused by ignorance and unawareness of the causes [of events]? Was it the cause why he could see [the dead] in a dream and realized the duality of spirits? When such a door is open, what insanity is this and what is the reason that one would look for these [causes]?! He should not look [for such other causes]; that is, has had such a logical mental basis. Firstly, such amount is already enough for the primitive man [to be able to think about God]. Secondly, history shows that during the times which are called 'pre-historic period' – with such magnitude of historical relics – many learned men (whom we call 'prophets' and by others as 'philosophers') had already existed to be sufficient enough to inform the people.

> "We can say that the human being's ignorance of a set of bases led him to commit mistake in his thought..."

It is ignorance and innate belief in causality, because if there were no belief in causality, mere ignorance is not enough. I have made the expressions 'first step' and 'second step'. I have said that the first step is that man says that such an event will not happen

---

1. When we say 'basis for human thought,' we mean that man reaches such a point in his thinking although he might be mistaken; just like his notion of the earth's motion or the sun's motion.

without a cause. The human mind – even a three or four years old child – when something happens to him, will look for its cause or reason. For instance, when a three or four years old child hears a sound – whether it has meaning or something else and whatever you want to say – he will look around to see the origin of the sound. That is, his mind cannot accept that the sound just spontaneously appears without any origin. As such, the primitive man was always looking for cause.

Let us deal with the second step. I want to say that the second step is a very simple step. It is not a step which necessitates that it should be the twentieth century now so as for the human mind to reach the level how a cause by itself comes into being (the question of the cause of a cause). Then this question comes to the fore: is there any Entity which is the Cause of all things, or none? This question had been posed by the human being from the very beginning. When this question is posed, the answer which is mentioned by the Qur'an is embedded in man's natural disposition. It says that as a person sees *marbūbiyyah*, i.e. change – when he sees that things change, and come and go willingly and unwillingly – he looks for the factor [or factors] of change. As he sees that all those things he is looking for have the same characteristic; that is, he feels that all these are destined to be alterable as well on which a certain power or powers rule over, control or influence them, this question is immediately entertained in his mind: is there a power which is always dominant, inalterable and cannot be dominated, or none? This query is very natural.

I have said that here by saying 'logical thinking' I do not mean a logical thinking which is totally correct or not correct. That is one issue and that logic guides a person is another issue. Sometimes, logic leads a person to a certain point, though it may be incorrect.

After all, it is a way of thinking that guides a person; that is, the human being has a guide within himself. In other words, his sensory perceptions, and not any factor beyond his sensory perceptions, have guided him up to that point. As I have said, on the issue of the static nature of the earth and the sun's motion, it was incorrect, but these sensory perceptions, and not any factor external to him, had entangled man with this error for thousands of years. Now, as this error has already been detected, let us see if its cause is a dream or something else. No, the human being has a feeling; he thinks. He thinks on the basis of his feelings. He would apparently see that the earth does not move while the sun would change location and go higher and higher. Then he thought that his feeling was not wrong and there was no reason beyond the mind and sensory perceptions.

Our point, therefore, is that for these issue why one always looks for a cause beyond logic and the sensory perceptions? We have to look for the cause beyond the mind and sensory perceptions when we have no explanation according to our mind and sensory perceptions. We have to say that it is because it has no explanation whatsoever; hence, something beyond the sensory perceptions must have been the cause.

That which they call 'ignorance' is something different from what you call so. The issue is not that the human being thinks and reasons out but commits error in his reasoning. It is the same ignorance that a philosopher has in his own philosophy and a scientist in his own field of science. The ignorance that they refer to is that ignorance which is purely fear. For example, a person dreams and in his dream he feels his dual dimension and then concludes that all things have a soul or spirit.

> "He immediately associated the coming of rain to something which he calls 'God'."

It is the same principle of causality.

> "This is exactly my point. Because of lack of knowledge of the real physical cause, they would immediately associate [something] to a metaphysical factor."

No, they accept the issue of the principle of causality to some extent. That is, in their statements also – especially that of Auguste Comte – it is such that from the beginning, man attempted to analyze but he just stopped there and looked for illusions. One would say that the human mind has not gone a step further. It just accepted the principle of causality, and then did not go further. It is as if the human being could not be able to think beyond that and he just stopped there. Since [his] thinking has not been able to solve this case, he has made assumptions and sheer illusions which can never be compatible with any thinking or logic. That is, it is not that the logic is wrong; but rather, it is only the place of illusion and assumption that is responsible for his illusion. We say that it is not so. It is this logical thinking of man that has made him reach that point from the beginning to the end. Even if we assume that it is incorrect, it is a sort of [logical] mistake. [That is, it is man's thinking and logic which has made him arrive at this mistake.][1]

1. The last few minutes of Professor Muṭahharī's remarks have unfortunately not been recorded.]

Chapter 8: Love and Worship

Let us answer the questions. One question is as follows:

> "Although in Arabic language the word *'ishq* (love) is used with the same meaning in our language (Fārsī), unfortunately, in the entire Qur'an and Islamic traditions (*riwāyāt*) this word and its derivatives cannot be seen. Cannot this be a proof of the non-spiritual means of this concept?"

Another Review of the Issue of Love

It can be known from the totality of questions that this topic of *'ishq* which we have discussed elicits so many questions and perhaps it would have been better if you did not touch on it in the first place. They have written that this word in Arabic language is used in that sense, and unfortunately, in the entire Qur'an and Islamic narrations this word and its derivatives cannot be seen. First of all, it is not true that this word and its derivatives cannot be seen [in the entire Qur'an and Islamic narrations]. In the traditions (*aḥādīth*) [this word has been used] although only in a few instances, but there are. Regarding *'ibādah* (worship), there is this tradition:

طُوبىٰ لِمَنْ عَشِقَ ٱلْعِبَادَةَ وَأَحَبَّهَا بِقَلْبِهِ وَبَاشَرَهَا بِجَسَدِهِ...

"Blessed is he who loves worship, loves it with his heart

and performs it with his body."[1]

Also, it is stated in a famous tradition that apparently, when the Commander of the Faithful (A.S.) [along with his troops] was on his way to Ṣiffīn; that is, in the Battle of Ṣiffīn[2] which was along the way from Kūfah to Shām[3] – toward the military camp of Mu'āwiyah – they reached the land of Naynawā (Karbalā). He took a handful of soil there, kissed it and then said:

أيهٍ لَكِ أَيَّتُهَا ٱلتُّرْبَةُ، لَيُحشَرَنَّ مِنْكِ أَقْوَامٌ يَدْخُلُونَ ٱلْجَنَّةَ بِغَيْرِ حِسَابٍ.

"Blessed are you [and] for among you will be a group who will be resurrected and be admitted to paradise without any reckoning."

---

1. *Al-Kāfī*, vol. 2, 83.
2. Battle of Ṣiffīn: the battle fought in the year 37 AH between Imām 'Alī *(A.S.)* and the Governor of Syria (Shām), Mu'āwiyah, for the so-called avenging for the killing of Caliph 'Uthmān. But in reality it was nothing more than Mu'āwiyah who had been the Autonomous Governor of Syria from Caliph 'Umar's days not wanting to lose that position by swearing allegiance to Imām 'Alī *(A.S.)* but wanting to keep his authority intact by exploiting the killing of Caliph 'Uthmān, for later events proved that after securing the government he did not take any practical step to avenge 'Uthmān's blood, and never spoke, not even through omission, about the killers of 'Uthmān. At the head of an army, Mu'āwiyah decided to wage war against Imām 'Alī and when they reached an area close to the Euphrates River, called Ṣiffīn, he confronted Imām 'Alī's troops. The two parties fought each other in 90 battles. When Mu'āwiyah found out he could not defeat Imām 'Alī, he resorted to a trick contrived by 'Amr ibn al-'Āṣ and told his men to hang copies of the Qur'an on their swords and at the same time called for the end of the confrontation through arbitration. The trick was successful and Imām 'Alī finally yielded to arbitration. The Battle of Ṣiffīn lasted for 110 days in early seventh century CE. For a brief account of the battle, see *Nahj al-Balāghah*, Sermon 123, "To exhort his followers to fight," footnote 1. [Trans.]
3. Shām: the capital of the Umayyad dynasty. Up until five centuries ago, it included Syria of today, Lebanon and parts of Jordan and Palestine. [Trans.]

The Imām (A.S.) then said:

> مُنَاخُ رُكَّابٍ وَمَصَارِعُ عَشَّاقٍ.
>
> "[Here shall be] the landing-place of riders and place of execution of lovers."[1]

Here the word *'ashshāq* (lovers) is used for the companions of Imam al-Ḥusayn (A.S.). This tradition exists in the books of *maqtal*[2] such as the book *Nafas al-Mahmūm* by the late Ḥājj Shaykh 'Abbās Qummī.

As such, the notion that this word (*'ishq*) and its derivatives cannot be seen at all in the Qur'an and Islamic narrations is not true at all; it is there although in only a few instances.

Secondly, one day they say that this word can nowhere be found. In this regard, we say that a word cannot be the subject of discussion. If something is undesirable for Islam it is its meaning which is undesirable, and not the word itself such that we would say that Islam abhors such a word. When *muḥabbah* (love) reaches such a state, [it is called *'ishq*.] It is a state which robs a person of a moment to think and decide; it overpowers the intellect and willpower; as such, it is a condition which is similar to insanity; that is, reason is no longer in control:

> قیاس کردم تدبیر عقل در ره عشق
> چو شبنمی است که بحر می کشد رقمی
>
> In love's path, I considered that the deliberation of wisdom

1. Shaykh 'Abbās Qummī, *Nafas al-Mahmum*, 206.

2. *Maqtal* which literally means the place or event of killing usually refers to *Maqtal al-Ḥusayn* which is the title of various books about the death of Imam al-Ḥusayn and his companions in the Battle of Karbalā in 61 AH, and written by different authors beginning from the eighty century, the earliest and most famous extant of which is written by Lūṭ ibn Yaḥyā ibn Sa'īd ibn Mikhnaf al-Kūfī or Abū Mikhnaf (died 774 CE) for short. [Trans.]

Is like a little night-dew that, on the sea, draweth a mark (wrinkle).[1]

In the conflict between reason and love, victory is always considered to be in the hands of love and control in that of reason:

نیکخواهانم نصیحت می‌کنند خشت بر دریا زدن بی‌حاصلست
شوق را بر صبر قوت غالبست عقل را با عشق دعوی باطلست

My well-wishers admonish me,
Making bricks in the sea is futile.
Yearning prevails over the power of patience.
Reason is rendered void by the love's calling.[2]

Such a state is called *'ishq*. The main flaw of this state is that it is beyond man's control. This is unexplainable. Certain things, if they happen, are beneficial provided that one deals with them in a good way, but they themselves, just like any tragedy, are unexplainable. A tragedy may have very beneficial effects to a person but they cannot just be explained. It cannot just be said to a person, "Let yourself experience a tragedy and suffer from a calamity for they are very channel for one's refinement. This thing which is called *'ishq* is also something which, if it happens, may possibly destroy a person, or refine him. Be that as it may, it is something unexplainable. If ever the mystics (*'urafā'*) have encouraged it, they have a claim; their claim is that a perfect man (*insān al-kāmil*) is like a person knows very well how to swim. If someone else does not know how to swim, he (that expert) would throw him onto the sea. If he sees that he would be drowned, he could easily save him anyway. They believe that if a perfect man is along with a faulty

1. *Dīwān-e Ḥāfiẓ*, couplet 471. [Trans.]
2. *Dīwān-e Ash'ār-e Sa'dī*, couplet 72. [Trans.]

person, he can supervise and take care of him, not allowing him to fall into the pit of perdition.[1] It is like the swimming exercise that children undergo in the swimming pool. A child cannot be encouraged to be in the swimming pool alone, but there is no problem in the presence of a lifeguard. He is watching every swimmer. Anytime he sees that there is someone drowning, he will save him.

Also, they believe that it (*'ishq*) is something which, if it happens, gives focus and composure to a person; that is, it will detach him from thousands of entanglements. One basic flaw we have is that in our soul hundreds of roots are linked to hundreds of things, and not to a single thing. Spiritually and conceptually, we are attached to hundreds of things. It is like [the situation of] a person or an animal with different chains linked to hundreds of places. If one of them is severed, there are still ninety nine. If two of them are severed, there are still ninety eight. In order for a person to be one with God in action and all chains [attached to him] be originating from God, these chains must be severed so as for him to be connected to Him and thereby be [a manifestation of this verse]:

﴿ فَمَنْ يَكْفُرْ بِالطَّاغُوتِ وَ يُؤْمِنْ بِاللهِ ﴾

> So one who disavows the Rebels [ṭāghūt] and has faith in Allah... (2:256)

They believe that even this thing called 'calamity' (*balā*) ends up in *'ishq*, for a person would be detached from those hundreds of things (chains) and be connected to the One, thereby giving him a state of concentration and focus. Then, they claim that the mere fact that this concentration – although the focus is a false manifestation and object – is acquired by him, there is a possibility that under the supervision of a perfect [man], this concentration would be taken

1 For the meantime, it is not our concern if this belief is correct or not.

away from there and be channelled to the Real Object of concentration. On this basis is what they have said.

The other question is this:

> "Is [the Fārsī word] *parashtesh* used in the sense of *'ubūdiyyah* (worship)? If it is so, then given your explanation to *parashtesh* as the ultimate level of *'ishq*, what we can call the worship of the servants [of God] who only perform it as a duty?"

Real Worship

There is a clear answer to this [question] and that is, it is part of the definite principles of Islam that in worship sincerity (*ikhlāṣ*) is a requirement:

﴿ وَما أُمِرُوا إِلاّ لِيَعْبُدُوا اللهَ مُخْلِصِينَ لَهُ الدِّينَ ﴾

> Yet they were not commanded except to worship Allah, dedicating their faith to Him. (98:5)

And one of the types of sincerity, nay its highest level, is that the object of worship (*ma'būd*) of a person should not be his carnal desire. Now, whenever there is the carnal desire, naturally a kind of polytheism (*shirk*) is also there. There is no dispute about it, but there is a time when a person's polytheism is not in the conventional sense of polytheism. In reality, it is *tawḥīd*; that is, *tawḥīd* in worshipping other than God and most people are 'unitarians' (*muwaḥhid*) in worshipping other than God.

It is said that during the years when he would deliver speeches in famous pulpits in Tehran, one day the late Shaykh Ja'far Shushtarī[1]

1. Shaykh Ja'far Shushtarī (died 1303 AH): a prominent Islamic scholar and jurisprudent (*faqīh*) known for his power of speech, piety, strong memory,

mounted the pulpit and said, "O people! All prophets came to invite you to *tawḥīd* (monotheism); I have come to invite you to *shirk* (polytheism)." This provocative statement caught the attention of many people. He then said, "All prophets have come and said, 'Worship God alone and work for the sake of Him alone.' I say, 'Work a bit for the sake of God; that is, all your works must be sincerely not for the sake of other than God.'"

A work which is sincerely for the sake of other than God means a work which a person does solely for the sake of the world which has nothing to do with God at all. In some works, however, a person takes God as a means for his carnal desires. Although in doing so God is a means and not the end, such works are still a form of knocking at the door of God's House: "I know that it is God in whose hands are the ability to perform all works in this world; it is God who can be able to solve our worldly problems. Had it not been for the worldly problems, I would have not knocked on the door of God's House; now I will do so but for the sake of worldly problems." There is no doubt that this in itself is a type of polytheism. That is, it is a kind of worship in which God is not the objective but just a means for the fulfilment of selfish desires. God, the Exalted, however, accepts from a person such types of polytheism which are hidden polytheism. That is, the same thing which a person wants to be given to him.

The same is true in the hereafter. If a person performs an act of worship for otherworldly desires, God, the Exalted, will grand him those otherworldly desires. This, however, is not worship in the real sense of *'ibādah* or worship of God as He should be worshipped. God is worshipped when He is worshipped for the sake of none but Him alone. That is, this is the only real worship and real sincerity.

---

and many works including *Uṣūl al-Din* (or *Al-Ḥadā'iq fi'l-Uṣūl*), *Khaṣā'iṣ al-Ḥusayniyyah*, *Majālis al-Bukā'*, and *Manhaj al-Rishād.* [Trans.]

The rest is nothing but different shades and levels of polytheism but they are hidden polytheism. Such hidden polytheism incurs no punishment in the hereafter. There is no doubt, however, that these are [types of] polytheism. That is, *tawḥīd* does not consist of only one level and shade. There is even a tradition – very strange it is – which states, thus:

> إِنَّ دَبِيبَ ٱلشِّرْكِ فِي ٱلْقَلْبِ أَخْفىٰ مِنْ دَبِيبَ ٱلنَّمْلَةِ ٱلسَّوْدَاءِ عَلىٰ ٱلصَّخْرَةِ ٱلصَّمَاءِ فِي ٱللَّيْلَةِ ٱلظَّلْمَاءِ.
>
> "Indeed the creeping of polytheism in the heart is more hidden than the creeping of a black ant on a black rock during dark night."[1]

(This shows that *tawḥīd* is amazingly particular.) That is, the secretive appearance of polytheism in the human being's heart remains so hidden from him that it is like the movement of a black ant on a black rock at a dark night. As the ant is black, the night is dark and the rock is black, can the eyes still see it?! As such, we have real worship and metaphorical worship. Real worship is what this [tradition] refers to:

> مَا عَبَدْتُكَ خَوْفًا مِنْ نَارِكَ وَلاَ طَمَعًا فِي جَنَّتِكَ بَلْ وَجَدْتُكَ أَهْلاً لِلْعِبَادَةِ فَعَبَدْتُكَ.
>
> "I do not worship You out of fear of Your hellfire and not out of desire for Your paradise, but rather worship You are You are the One worthy of worship."[2]

---

1. [In *Biḥār al-Anwār*, vol. 72, section (*bāb*) 98, 96, it is as follows:
إِنَّ ٱلشِّرْكِ أَخْفىٰ مِنْ دَبِيبَ ٱلنَّمْلِ فِي ٱللَّيْلَةِ ٱلظَّلْمَاءِ عَلىٰ ٱلمِسْحِ الأَسْوَادِ.
"Indeed polytheism is more hidden than the creeping of the ant during dark night on a black rock."]
2. *Biḥār al-Anwār*, vol. 41, section (*bāb*) 101, 14, with a slight variation.

The Parable of Sa'dī

How excellent Sa'dī narrated this story. Of course, it is a parable and allegory, and its forepart is not intended. You know that one allegorical love is that one between Sulṭān Maḥmūd and Ayyāz. He narrates that Ayyāz is being discredited before Sultān Maḥmūd, thus: "By the way, what merits does he have? What distinction does he have? He is not that handsome and good-looking. Why are you so fond of him and why do you love him so much?" One day Sulṭān Maḥmūd wanted to practically show them why it is such and that the reasons are not what you supposed; it is something else. It is not because I am fond of his outward appearance. My true and devoted servant is he who loves me for my own sake. In *Bustān*, it is thus narrated:

یکي خرده بر شاه غزنین گرفت
که حسني ندارد ایاز اي شگفت
گلي را که نه رنگ باشد نه بوي
غریب است سوداي بلبل بر اوي!
به محمود گفت این حکایت کسي
بپیچید از اندیشه بر خود بسي
که عشق من اي خواجه بر خوي اوست
نه بر قد و بالاي نیکوي اوست
شنیدم که در تنگنایي شتر
بیفتاد و بشکست صندوق در

A certain one took up reproach against Maḥmūd of Ghaznīn,
Saying, 'Ayyāz has no (great) beauty. Oh wonder!
'The rose, which has neither colour nor perfume,
'The nightingale's passion for it is wonderful.'
One uttered this matter to Maḥmūd;
He writhed much on himself, in reflection,
Saying, 'Oh sir! My love is for his disposition,

'Not, for his stature, and good height.'
I heard that, in a defile, a camel
Fell; and, a chest of pearls broke.[1]

It is narrated that in journey he had undergone, Sulṭān Maḥmūd ordered to intentionally loosely tie the camel loads and as they passed by a valley, he ordered that a chest of jewels – which he usually had along – be intentionally detached from the camel so as for it to fell and be opened, thereby letting gold, pearls and expensive jewels fall into the valley.

به یغما ملک آستین برفشاندوزان جا بتعجیل مرکب براند
The king expanded his sleeve for plunder;
And, thence urged his horse with speed.[2]

That is, he said everyone shall take possession of whatever he would get. He said this and whipped his horse and went ahead.

سواران پی در و مرجان شدند ز سلطان به یغما پریشان شدند
The horsemen (of the retinue) went after the pearls and coral;
They became, in search of plunder, separated from the king.[3]

Such permission for plunder was announced and everybody rushed to the valley so as to get a precious jewel.

نماند از وشاقان گردن فراز کسی در قفای ملک جز ایاز
Of the attendants, neck-exalting, there remained

1. *Bustān*, chapter 3 on love, 112. [Trans.]
2. *Ibid.* [Trans.]
3. *Ibid.* [Trans.]

None, behind the king, save Ayyāz.[1]

The king once looked behind and saw that none remained with him and it was Ayyāz; the rest went after the booty.

نگه کرد کای دلبر پیچ پیچ   ز یغما چه آورده‌ای؟ گفت هیچ
من اندر قفای تو می‌تاختم   ز خدمت به نعمت نپرداختم

He glanced, saying, 'Oh one heart-enchanting, fold in fold!
'What hast thou brought from the plunder?' He replied, 'Nothing.
I galloped in rear of thee;
I quitted not service for wealth.[2]

That is to say, "I prefer rendering service (to you) over wealth." As this point is reached, Saʿdī concludes thus (as the parable ends):

خلاف طریقت بود کاولیا   تمنا کنند از خدا جز خدا
راز دوست چشمت بر احسان اوست   و دربند خویشی نه دربند دوست

It is contrary to religion, that the friends of God
Should ask for anything, save God, from God.
If, as to a friend, thy eye is intent upon his beneficence,
Thou art in the desire of thyself, not in the desire of thy friend.[3]

This is real worship. We should not regard as an act of worship which is not. Out of His kindness, God would overlook these acts of

1. *Ibid.* [Trans.]
2. *Ibid.* [Trans.]
3. *Ibid.* [Trans.]

polytheism from us.

Let us assume that this word (*'ishq*) has not been used; so what? This word has not also been used in relation to God except in that statement,

طُوبىٰ لِمَنْ عَشِقَ ٱلْعِبَادَةَ وَأَحَبَّهَا بِقَلْبِهِ وَبِاشَرَها بِجَسَدِهِ...

> "Blessed is he who loves worship, loves it with his heart and performs it with his body."

Or, it has rarely been used. Yet, it has been used in that sense as well. Do you not read in *Du'ā' Kumayl*,[1] thus:

وَاجْعَل... قَلْبِي بِحُبِّكَ مُتَيَّماً

> "And make my heart enthralled by Your love"?

Mutayyam (enthrallment) is the same state which we call *'ishq* (love). In some other expressions similar to this can be found in *Du'ā' Kumayl.*

There is another question in this regard, and again it is related to the issue of love, carnal desire and the like. We have pointed out that those who have said so, first of all, claim – it is not my concern if what they say is correct or not – that *'ishq* are of two types. Accordingly, one type of it is basically carnal desire (*shahwah*); they call it 'physical' which, they advised, must be relinquished. There is

1. *Du'ā' Kumayl* (Supplication of Kumayl): The supplication of Prophet Khizr (A.S.) taught by Imām 'Alī (A.S.) to one of his loyal companions and staunch supporters of Islam, Kumayl ibn Ziyād. Usually offered on every night preceding Friday *(Laylat'ul-Jum'ah)* individually or in congregation after *Ishā'* prayers, this supplication envisages divine teachings and solid foundations of religion in order to enable everyone to follow the right path for becoming a worthy Muslim. [Trans.]

another type which, they say, is not carnal desire, but something spiritual. Moreover, although it is spiritual, it is essentially not in itself a sort of perfection (*kamāl*) for the human being. Accordingly, when a person has such a spiritual state and experiences an insane-like state, its salient feature is that it will take a person away from all things other than the Beloved (*ma'shūq*), separating him from them, and make him ready to be detached from the creation and to focus on the Beloved alone.

The Story of Zulaykhā

The story of Zulaykhā as narrated in traditions is like that. Zulaykhā fell in love with Yūsuf (Joseph) (A.S.). In place of *'ishq* the expression of the Qur'an is as follows:

﴿ قَدْ شَغَفَهَا حُبًّا ﴾

He has captivated her love. (12:30)

It is said that, apparently, *shaghafahā* means that her whole heart was captivated by him; her heart was essentially under his control. Such a state was felt by this lady. Later on, this lady who used to follow the religion of her husband – a form of polytheism or something else – would become monotheist (*muwaḥḥid*) and a perfect monotheist as such. In the stories of the prophets (*qiṣāṣ*), it is mentioned that in the end, Yūsuf (A.S.) gave attention to Zulaykhā but she was not longer interested in him. He would say, "I am Yūsuf; I am the same person to whom you did something." Whatever he would say, she was no longer interested in him. He would ask, "Why?" She would answer, "Now, I have found someone else; that is why I am no longer interested in you." The same state of the heart which was undoubtedly something bad in her own level [turned into this state]. That is, if the same metaphorical love to Yūsuf had not suddenly took her away from everything else and not catapulted her to such a spiritual state, in the next stage she would not have attained the stage of Divine love so much so that she would no longer pay attention to Yūsuf. They make such remarks.

Chapter 9: The Innate Nature of Religion

It can be said that you want to say that they have three different remarks on the explanation and expression of religion.[1] It can be said, however, that three remarks are not three different remarks; they are all manifestations of a single theory, a single assumption and a single remark.

In a theory which others regard ignorance or fear as the cause for the emergence of religion, in reality, they have not paid attention to the social factor and their attention is focused on the individual factor. In other words, they have given a psychological explanation and not a sociological one. They have maintained that the human being – due to the same reasons we have mentioned earlier, i.e. either due to his ignorance or because of his fear of the same – has inclined to religion. Accordingly, religion might have also existed during the period which they call 'primitive communal period'. That is, during the period when, according to them, the issue of classes and ownership was not yet extant, religion might have also existed, for its original is something personal, individual and psychological.

1. [Prior to the speech of Professor Muṭahharī, there had been a continuation of the lecture about the article mentioned earlier.]

Marxism and the Origin of Religion

This is not the case in the Marxists' theory. Accordingly, we must necessarily accept that during the primitive communal period, religion could not have existed. Religion has emerged after [the emergence of] ownership and after the division of society into two groups, viz. the exploiters and the exploited, the rich and the poor. (This is one difference.) Religion, therefore, has been concocted by the ruling class. According to their theory, we must acknowledge that the initial concocters of religion belonged to the ruling class. The earlier theories, however, have nothing to do with classes; they do not distinguish between the ruler and the ruled, for accordingly, there is no difference between them. As such, if ever history shows that it is not so, in the sense that if history shows that all religions, or most of the religions, have emerged from classes other than the ruling class, naturally their theory would be refuted. They argue that religion has been concocted by the ruling class in order protect their interests. They observe that this class has a set of privileges while the other class has a set of deprivations. In order to protect these privileges, they needed a spiritual and internal factor, and that internal factor for the ruled class must naturally be in the form of faith and belief. Expectedly, the ruling class is faithless for it is the one that has made the sacred being. It is only the ruled class which has faith, and therefore, this class must have faith and belief. Now, what is religion for the ruled class? First of all, it is a sort of tranquilizer for them. They are told, "Whatever they give in this world will be compensated in the other world; don't be sad; for this reason, there is no need for you to stage a revolution." In this case, all teachings of religion must be meant for submission and surrender. If ever there is [this belief in] fate and predestination, so that you could say, "Hey, it is useless; do you want to go against fate and predestination?!" If it is meant to appease the feeling of being cheated, they say, "There is recompense in the hereafter." Accordingly, therefore, all teachings of religions are meant for submission, surrender and appeasement. Meanwhile, there are teachings in religions – in Islam, for example – which are meant for the opposite; that is, teachings which are meant for revolution and uprising. Not only that religion has not emerged from the ruling class but more important than that, sometimes it would emerge from the ruling class and at other times, from another class, with the aim of advancing the interests of the ruled class and calling for uprising or revolution.

This fact is incompatible with those remarks. According to them, it cannot be the other way round. Within the core of these teachings, nothing [should be contrary to the interests of the ruling class]. In these very social orders which we are in, is it possible that one day, one would hear from the mass media – newspapers, radio and television – a campaign instigating the people against the ruling clique? No. Whatever the ruling clique (which controls the media) says is intended to justify itself and it is not possible to say otherwise. As such, it is the ruling class which concocts religion, and in its teachings there must be elements of hopelessness such as fatalism and predestination as well as palliative elements [such as] promises in the hereafter. And naturally, we must assume that the religious class is ignorant, because if they are not ignorant, they will not submit to such teachings.

From this perspective, therefore, we cannot criticize them for having different theories in this regard; that is, the fact that they say that religion is invented by the ruling class and the fact that it has taken advantage of the ignorance of the masses are not conflicting. The first theory attempts to prove that due of their own ignorance, the masses themselves concocted religion for their own selves. They maintain that the ruling class took advantage of the ignorance of the masses and concocted religion [for them].[1]

Refuting the Marxist Theory

One of the weak points of this theory has something to do with the history of religions. That is, the history of religions shows that since the ancient times when the human beings lived on earth – since that period which they call 'primitive communal period', traces of [the practice of] worship have been extant. Max Müller[2] even believes that contrary to the common notion that religion had begun first as worship of nature, objects, idolatry and worship of different deities and has reached the level of the worship of One Supreme Being, paleontology has proved – and continues to prove – that since the most ancient times, worship of One God has been extant.

According to this theory, therefore, first of all, during the 'primitive communal period', there is no possibility of the existence of religion [which we have pointed out to be incompatible with the history of religions]. Secondly, during these periods which are called the Period of Classes – for instance, during the period of feudalism – we must necessarily acknowledge that the initial advocates and proponents of all religions have been from the ruling class. This [notion] could not reconciled also with the definitive and indisputable history of religions; it is incompatible with the Judaism

1. One theory which we possibly do not have is that one may possibly say that the deprived class itself has invented religion for its own consolation. The Marxists have brought to the fore the 'consolation' factor but they assert that the ruling class concocted it (religion) for in a bid to console them (deprived class).
2. Friedrich Max Müller (1823-1900), more regularly known as Max Müller: a German philologist and Orientalist, and one of the founders of the western academic field of Indian studies and the discipline of comparative religion. [Trans.]

and the Israelite people; it is also irreconcilable with the history of Christianity. It cannot be compatible with the history of the Israelite people because firstly, genetically and racially Mūsā (Moses) (A.S.) was apparently connected with the deprived and exploited class, but in terms of the class condition, he was associated with the exploitative class because he grew up in the Palace of Pharaoh with much pomp and glory. That is, he grew up like a prince because they (Pharaoh and his wife) had no child then and he was treated as such. In the House of Pharaoh, Moses (A.S.) would rise up against Pharaoh and he would do so for the sake of the exploited class. This condition defies any amount of Marxist explanation. Or, in order to explain this, we may point to a tribal, racial or genetic cause, which in any case, is still incompatible with Marxism, because the Marxists believe that history is essentially a struggle between classes and not a racial conflict. In other words, either [we have to consider it to be racial] bigotry in that after growing up and realizing that he was not related to Pharaoh by blood but rather to other people, Moses (A.S.) stage an uprising for the sake of racial bigotry – something which is incompatible with Marxism – or, if we do not say so, whatever we would say will not be congruent with the lifestyle of the Pharaoh.

Secondly, Moses (A.S.) would actually stage an uprising in the House of Pharaoh for the sake of the Israelites. As such, it is the group of the exploited that would stage an uprising. The uprising was not that of the Pharaoh's lot. It was an uprising against the Pharaoh's lot; that is, it was an uprising of the Israelites. Hence, this, once again, is totally repugnant to their remarks that religion has been concocted by the ruling class. [According to this theory,] we have to say that the Jewish religion was concocted by the Pharaoh's ruling clique so as to create a sense of submission and surrender on the Israelite people. This is while the Jewish religion came to the fore to urge and instigate the Israelite to stage an uprising:

﴿ وَتِلْكَ نِعْمَةٌ تَمُنُّهَا عَلَيَّ أَنْ عَبَّدْتَ بَنِي إِسْرَائِيلَ ﴾

> As for that favour, you remind me of it reproachfully because you have enslaved the Children of Israel. (26:22)

﴿ يَا قَوْمِ ادْخُلُوا الأَرْضَ الْمُقَدَّسَةَ الَّتِي كَتَبَ اللهُ لَكُمْ ﴾

> O my people, enter the Holy Land which Allah has ordained for you. (5:21)

All of these are a sort of incitement: "Do not be afraid." "Be steadfast and patient." "Rely on God." "God does so and so."

Islam itself is such a religion:

﴿ وَنُرِيدُ أَنْ نَمُنَّ عَلَى الَّذِينَ اسْتُضْعِفُوا فِي الأَرْضِ وَنَجْعَلَهُمْ أَئِمَّةً وَنَجْعَلَهُمُ الْوَارِثِينَ ﴾

> And We desired to show favor to those who were abased in the land, and to make them imāms, and to make them the heirs. (28:5)

﴿ وَعَدَ اللهُ الَّذِينَ آمَنُوا مِنْكُمْ وَعَمِلُوا الصَّالِحَاتِ لَيَسْتَخْلِفَنَّهُمْ فِي الأَرْضِ... وَلَيُمَكِّنَنَّ لَهُمْ دِينَهُمُ الَّذِي ارْتَضَى لَهُمْ وَلَيُبَدِّلَنَّهُمْ مِنْ بَعْدِ خَوْفِهِمْ أَمْنًا ﴾

> Allah has promised those of you who have faith and do righteous deeds that He will surely make them successors in the earth... and He will surely establish for them their religion which He has approved for them, and that He will surely change their state to security after their fear. (24:55)

It is the promise for the people from whom others took away the vicegerency on earth and "We shall give you the vicegerency on earth; We shall set the earth as your inheritance":

> ﴿ إِنَّ الْأَرْضَ لِلَّهِ يُورِثُهَا مَنْ يَشَاءُ ﴾
>
> The earth indeed belongs to Allah, and He gives its inheritance to whomever He wishes. (7:128)

> ﴿ وَلَقَدْ كَتَبْنَا فِي الزَّبُورِ مِنْ بَعْدِ الذِّكْرِ أَنَّ الْأَرْضَ يَرِثُهَا عِبَادِيَ الصَّالِحُونَ ﴾
>
> Certainly We wrote in the Psalms, after the Remembrance (Torah): 'Indeed My righteous servants shall inherit the earth'. (21:105)

Ṭāhā Ḥusayn[1] has written an elegant book entitled *Al-Wa'd al-Ḥaqq* (*The True Promise*) which Mr. Aḥmad Ārām has translated (into Fārsī) under the title *Wa'deh-ye Rāst.* This book *Al-Wa'd al-Ḥaqq* is inspired by this very verse:

> ﴿وَعَدَ اللَّهُ الَّذِينَ آمَنُوا مِنْكُمْ وَعَمِلُوا الصَّالِحَاتِ لَيَسْتَخْلِفَنَّهُمْ فِي الْأَرْضِ﴾
>
> Allah has promised those of you who have faith and do righteous deeds that He will surely make them successors in the earth. (24:55)

Twenty individuals who all belonged to the class of the slaves, downtrodden, deprived, and lowly have been chosen and this Qur'anic promise enlivened and animated them – such as 'Ammār ibn Yāsir, Abū Dharr al-Ghiffārī, and 'Abd Allāh ibn Mas'ūd – [and he has talked about them]. It is one of the very good and interesting books which must be recommended to the children and youth. The history of Islam is essentially such a history; 'Abd Allāh ibn Mas'ūd would come forward to fight with Abū Jahl, his master. That is, it is the conflict between the slaves and the masters. This state of affairs is basically incompatible with this hypothesis. The teachings which

1. Dubbed 'The Dean of Arabic Literature,' Ṭahā Ḥusayn (1889-1973) was one of the most influential 20th century Egyptian writers and intellectuals. [Trans.]

stipulate that

﴿ لا يُحِبُّ اللَّهُ الْجَهْرَ بِالسُّوءِ مِنَ الْقَوْلِ إِلا مَنْ ظُلِمَ ﴾

> Allah does not like the disclosure of [anyone's] evil [conduct] in speech except by someone who has been wronged. (4:148)

or this passage which states, thus:

﴿ وَالشُّعَرَاءُ يَتَّبِعُهُمُ الْغَاوُونَ ★ أَلَمْ تَرَ أَنَّهُمْ فِي كُلِّ وَادٍ يَهِيمُونَ ★ وَأَنَّهُمْ يَقُولُونَ مَا لا يَفْعَلُونَ ★ إِلا الَّذِينَ آمَنُوا وَعَمِلُوا الصَّالِحَاتِ... وَانْتَصَرُوا مِنْ بَعْدِ مَا ظُلِمُوا ﴾

> As for the poets, [only] the perverse follow them. Have you not regarded that they rove in every valley, and that they say what they do not do? Barring those who have faith and do righteous deeds... and aid each other after they have been wronged. (26:224-227)

which permits [the oppressed] in this regard [to express his being oppressed] through poetry, satire and propaganda campaigns, or prohibit backbiting except in such cases – which are not just one or two teachings – cannot be compatible with such logic. That is, such notions are dictated remarks, which must be accepted without being compatible with the reality!

Is Religion a Product of Ignorance?

More important than this is the logic of those who used to regard religion as merely a product of ignorance of individuals and to view the issue from a psychological perspective, and the writer of the article also criticized it. He said that if it is really so, then as the people become more learned and literate, religion must also reciprocally wither away. Just compare this: In the past when religion was a product of the people's ignorance, with the coming of knowledge – just as darkness ceases to exist with the coming of light – religion must have been supposed to cease to exist accordingly. According to this theory, religion is supposed to be totally extinguished commensurate to the advancement of knowledge. That is, there must be no religious among the learned. This is while it is said that no less than Russell says, "We can observe that there are both religion and irreligious among the class of ignoramuses."[1] There are also religious and irreligious among the class of the learned. In fact, perhaps, the most learned of people in every period – even during our time – as we can see, also adheres to religion. According to their logic, it is basically impossible for Einstein to be adhering to any religion or religious belief, or for Max Planck,[2] William James, Bergson,[3] Charles Darwin, and the like who are regarded as preeminent scientists. In the book *Darwinism*, [Behzād] writes that notwithstanding the Church's violent excommunications against Darwin, he remained devoted and believer in One God. He did not identify Darwin, the initiator of the same Darwinism which has been much utilized by the Marxists, as irreligious. I read elsewhere that at the moment of death, he put a copy of the Bible on his chest and kept it so until his last breath. This fact cannot be compatible with such notions.

Another point is that according to the Marxists, as class distinctions cease to end, religion will also spontaneously wither away. That is, there will be no more need for you to wage war against religion. According to their logic, as you extinguish

---

1. From among our very own ignoramuses and rowdies who know nothing but to create hullabaloos, are there more religious, or irreligious? There are both religious and irreligious from among them.

2. Max Karl Ernst Ludwig Planck (1858-1947): a German physicist, father of quantum physics, and winner of the 1918 Nobel Prize for physics. [Trans.]

3. Henri-Louis Bergson (1859-1941): a major French philosopher and evolutionist. [Trans.]

ignorance, religion will also naturally cease to exist. According to their logic, as you remove class distinctions and create a socialist society, automatically religion will also cease to exist. Its falsity [became clear] in the socialist countries themselves. The socialist countries themselves are the best evidence to refute these [notions]. For what reason that they have still many propaganda campaigns against religion in Soviet countries? Class distinctions [supposedly] no longer exist, but they still say time and again to wage war against religion as it is winning the hearts of the youth. This is while as the cause ceases to exist, it is expected that the effect will also cease to exist. You claim that the cause for the emergence of religion is the class distinctions. Here in your society which has no classes, why are there those who incline to religion? It follows that there must be another cause. Or, in other countries – in Muslim countries, for example – our assumption must be as follows. The fact that one of the Muslim countries became socialist, the doors of the mosques are automatically supposed to be closed. Yet, we can see that Muslim countries themselves have no concern, nor do we have for them. Countries are becoming socialists and there is no threat for them at all. If ever there are few irreligious individuals in socialist countries, a great number exists in class-based countries. In class-based countries now, which groups oppose religion more, those of the ruling class or those of the ruled class? [It is obvious that it is those of the ruling class; this is while according to Marxism, religion is invented by the ruling class.] These are social realities which we are facing. How can these be reconciled with the logic of these [Marxist] individuals? How can they explain these [social realities]?!

Will Durant's Statement

Although Will Durant is an irreligious person himself, in his book *The Lessons of History*, he has certain terms which are obviously expressed out of malaise and anger. He cites the reasons given for the emergence of religion and says that these are not accurate. In conclusion, he says, "Religion has a hundred lives; no matter how many times you kill it, it will be revived once again." And this is a fact. There is no need for you to say that it has a hundred lives. Just say that it has a spirit and that is enough. In other words, it is intrinsic (*fiṭrī*). Why do you say that it has a hundred lives?! Man's natural disposition cannot be killed. He says that all of these waged war against religion and religious belief everywhere and according to their claim, they were able to uproot it [but it emerged again]. Any custom, if there is a campaign throughout a generation for its extinction, cannot be able to survive in the succeeding generation. He says that no matter how extent it is suppressed, it emerges again and again.

"He must be told that [it is such] until your last breath."

It is really such; until your last breath. Even this writer of the article who himself is a materialist person says something very good in this regard. He thus says about the theory of classes he mentions:

> "According to this theory, productive and progressive classes such as the working class have no attachment to religion (that is, they have essentially no attachment to it; they are not concern of it) because their way of thinking is a product of their progressive and scientific condition in life! The exact opposite is the exploitative and non-progressive classes which are in need of religion for the protection of their interests."

Now, this person gives his reply, thus:

"This theory is not so compatible with the realities,[1] and proofs and data show the opposite. The farmers are perhaps the most

---

1. Anwar Khāmeh (writer of the article) was one of the leading communists in Iran and he used to promote these notions for many years.

productive class and yet the most religious of all. The intellectuals, on the contrary, are generally non-productive, yet they are the least of all classes to incline to religion. (It has nothing to do, therefore, with the issue of the class of intellectuals and the like.) The unemployed and the jobless show less interest to religion compared to the employed and workers. Among the workers in the industrial countries, there is more inclination to religion in the present century than in the past century, more in the recent decades than in the earlier decades. More importantly, in Soviet and people's democratic countries in which, as they claim, class distinctions have been eliminated and all individuals are productive, religion has not been obliterated; in fact, it has exerted even further greater influence."[1]

How these [facts] can be explained? This is nothing but a failed theory, but still they repeat the same remarks again and again. Beforehand, they had concocted and fashioned elegant terminologies which they repeat time and again. In other words, they make more than ever these remarks while being coated with these very elegant terminologies. No one seems to analyse whether these remarks are valid or not.

The unique theory of Max Müller that there had been monotheism prior to polytheism is an existing theory, but it does not have many proponents. Most theories maintain that polytheism had existed prior to monotheism. Of course, according to the logic of religion and Islam [in particular], monotheism did exist prior to polytheism; that is, polytheism is a deviant [way of expressing] monotheism. Their theory is that polytheism had existed before monotheism. Everywhere, however, history shows that there are human relics, and as they claim, primitive communal living is indicated by these

1. A quotation from the article on the topic "Theories on the Origin of Religion" written by Anwar Khāmeh.

relics. In other words, wherever there are human relics found, there are also relics pertaining to worship. I am not saying this as a citation of others' theory – of course, it is a religious theory, but I do not say this as others' theory – that [wherever there are human relics found,] there is also relic of 'monotheism'. Wherever there is a relic of human way of living – be it communal, non-communal or individual – there is also a relic of worship. There is no relic yet of human way of living being found which does not have any indication of worship in it.

"Some have claimed that during the period prior to fire, no trace of worship has ever been found."

I do not know this in particular but I know for a fact that this claim is contrary to the common view. Moreover, you say that it is still incompatible with the issue the primitive communal living. You say that from the time fire was discovered, [worship also came into being,] The reason why we rejected the Marxists' theory was that according to this theory, during the primitive communal period[1] and prior to the period of agriculture – in which the concept of ownership came into being, as they claim – it was impossible for the concept of worship to have existed. This is while prior to that period, as they themselves implicitly acknowledge, the concept of worship did exist. Now, the issue you have raised that during the periods prior to [the discovery of] fire, no trace of worship has been seen does not disprove anything. In addition, that something has been seen does not necessarily mean that it does not exist at all.

---

1. Of course, the primitive communal period is a period after certain periods. It must be said "during the period of tribal communal living". It is the same period prior to that of agriculture which is the prior of hunting and the like.

Chapter 10: An Examination and Refutation of Durkheim's Theory

The sixth theory mentioned on this subject about the origin of religion and religious belief is dubbed 'return to self-alienation'. Under this label, the theory of the famous French sociologist named Durkheim[1] is mentioned. Durkheim's remarks regarding the origin of religion are presently among the most famous remarks in the world, and I think the writer of this article has somehow mixed his own views. That we should identify Durkheim's theory as a sort of 'return to self-alienation' is perhaps the writer of this article's own expression. That is, I have not come across this term elsewhere. As far as we know of the views of Durkheim, he is a collectivist person. In other words, he gives primacy to the society, and in reality, he ignores individual's entity in the sense that he believes that the society is a real composition of individuals, and not a nominal composition.

Nominal and Real Compositions

We have nominal and real compositions. Nominal composition refers to a collection of things which have a kind of cohesion among

1. David Émile Durkheim (1858-1917): a French sociologist who formally established the academic discipline and, with Karl Marx and Max Weber, is commonly cited as the principal architect of modern social science. [Trans.]

them without losing their individual identities, and their individual identities are not transmuted into the 'collective' identity. For example, we call a set of trees in a particular location as 'garden'. We do not regard a tree as a garden; it is the set of trees which we call 'garden'. Each unit of this set called 'garden', however, has an independent identity. Even if one of these trees is not part of the garden, it still remains a tree; even if it is isolated [from the rest], it is still a tree. Even if there is a change [in the appearance of this garden], it will be very superficial and not profound. For instance, if the identity of a cherry tree in this garden is not specified and it remains so in that if all these trees were not there and there were only this cherry tree, it will remain like that as it is now. So are the other trees. These are what we call 'nominal compositions'.

In real compositions, however, the identities of the composition's component parts are integrated in the 'collective' identity. That is, they no longer possess their previous state. In reality, they will lose their [previous] essence and assume a new one which is that of the collective; for example, chemical and natural compositions. Whatever composition we have in nature is of this kind. For instance, if we regard water as a compound body, we treat it as comprising of two different elements. Those two elements in it have changed into a state and their nature. That is, there is no more oxygen in water as [pure] oxygen and as having a unique entity. There is also no more hydrogen as [pure] hydrogen. They have been mixed together. They have been integrated into the nature of the third entity, and in reality, a new entity has come into being and that is the water. Yes, water can also be decomposed again into its component elements (oxygen and hydrogen), but for the meantime, it is not so. So are the other compositions in nature.

What Kind of Composition is the Human Society?

Now, there is this discussion regarding human society: is human society a real composition or nominal composition? There is no doubt if the criterion is the physical bodies of the members of society, society is a nominal composition; it has no difference with a garden. This individual has all the biological features from the moment his mother gave birth to him. Other individual is also like that. So is yet another individual. If a human being who is born by his mother is confined to a cave where he would grow up, biologically speaking, he would grow up exactly in the same way that a human being grows up in a society. I do not say that there is no difference [at all in other aspects], but there will be no essential difference. His body will not turn into some other body. Nevertheless, unlike animal, human being [has a spiritual dimension.] The animal's identity is identical with its body and spiritual identity is approximately like its own bodily identity. That is, it is least affected by its fellow animals. Mentally speaking also, an animal – given the instinct with which it is created – remains the same whether it is along with fellow animals or not. The human being, on the other hand, has a cultural dimension. Or, in our own jargon, he has a spiritual dimension. He has a dimension which is related to his personality and not to his person. What [dimension] is this? The earlier philosophers have also acknowledged that contrary to the animals which are born with all the functioning and active instincts – concerning the natural disposition (*fiṭrah*) which we have discussed – the human being is born with potential characteristics. In the words of those who do not believe in man's natural disposition, the human spirit at the time of birth is like a *tabula rasa* in which nothing is drawn. It becomes whatever is drawn in it. He is unlike the animal which has been already a finished canvas from the time of birth. Moreover, as we acknowledge man's natural disposition, it means that there is a set of potential talents and abilities in the human being, just as there is a potential fruit or tree in a particular seed. In the jargon of those who do not acknowledge man's natural disposition, at the time of birth, the human being is like a *tabula rasa*; that is, he is a blank page. He becomes whatever is written or drawn in his 'blank page'. There is no difference if you write a verse of the Qur'an in it or, say, something abusive. In the jargon of those who acknowledge man's natural disposition, the human being is like a seed. Now, the seed, as it is a seed, is not an actual tree. It is not a leaf, a branch or a fruit, but it has the inner potential to become these things. If we burn it and turn it into ashes, we will deprive it of the chances to realize its potentials.

It is up to this extent, therefore, that the human being, in any case, is a potential being. It is the society which activates him. That is, it is the society which gives his spiritual entity. A person learns his language from the society [in which he grows up]. He learns his customs, manners, ideas, and beliefs from the society. It is the society which fills his spiritual capacity and moulds his personality. In one way or another, he also exerts influences on his fellows. He is not merely a passive being; he is a passive and active being at the same time. That is, on one hand, he takes [from others]; on the other hand, he gives [to others]. In relation to one person, he may be a learner; in relation to another person, he may be a teacher. And even in relation to his teacher, he is a learner and a teacher at the same time; in one way or another, he imparts his ideas, his spiritual traits, and whatever he learns and initiated; he also receives in kind from him. That is, they mutual influence each other. Psychologically, spiritually and culturally, the members of society are like the elements that constitute water; that is, they mutually affect each other. When oxygen and hydrogen are mixed together, they become compound, affecting each other, and after a series of interactions, a new entity (water) comes into being. Human beings also culturally affect each other, and out of the individuals that assemble together and mutually interaction with each other, there shall come out a real composition called 'community' or 'nation'.

Culturally speaking, therefore, human beings have two kinds of 'self', viz. the individual 'self' and the collective 'self'. In water also, to some extent oxygen and hydrogen are distinct from each other, but in another level, both of them are 'water' and they are united in being 'water'. And if ever each of them could feel its own 'self', it could feel two types of its own 'self'. Oxygen could feel one 'self' that "I am oxygen" and another 'self' that "I am water." Hydrogen could also feel one 'self' that "I am hydrogen" and another 'self' that "I am water." "I am water" is the same 'self' which is common to both oxygen and hydrogen.

In every individual, therefore, there are actually two types of 'self'; one is the individual 'self' while the other is the collective 'self'.

The Origin of Religion According to Durkheim

This is one principle which more or less exists in the words of Durkheim. Although they do not express it in their books the way I have expressed it and we have presented the subject in our own oriental jargon – that is, in the framework of our own terminology – this is their contention and it is obvious here from their words that he has relied on this principle. Durkheim, however, is a person who [has expressed such a theory] within a set of other issues; within the subjects about his predecessors, about primitive tribes that lived in very ancient times, or about primitive tribes that have also existed during our time – it is said that until 18th century and perhaps they still exist until today – and in a sense, about the religions of the primitive people. As you can see, they write all these books and believe that even in that most primitive human condition, a sort of worship had also existed – worship of natural phenomena yet with a form of sanctification of them. They say, for example, that there are traces and relics in some caves. There have been found stones, beads and the like which show that the primitive people held those beads as sacred. They would kiss them and express utmost reverence and awe. There is a dispute whether these were two types of religion or they refer to one and the same. Some are of the opinion that they are one and the same while others assert that they refer to two things.

Another thing which they have said about indigenous societies is the issue of totem and totemism. They believe that the past indigenous societies and some indigenous societies that lived near our time actually used to worship an animal figure with the belief that they were racially one with that animal figure, or basically they descended from that animal figure. The non-scientific version of this belief that human being originates from animal, whose scientific version can be found in Darwinism, can be found in those indigenous societies. For example, one tribe would trace its roots to cow, believing that the very origin of cow-worship and treating cow as sacred in India is that the totem of indigenous Indian societies had been cow. It has evolved, however, and later on, this notion was forgotten but the cow's assumed sanctity remains. Or, some [indigenous society] would regard chicken, for example, as their totem.

Concerning the explanation on how this notion – that they descended from such-and-such animal and then worshipped it later; it is sacred and has an extraordinary power; it is the protector and overseer of the tribe or community; and things like that – was inculcated in the minds of people, they say that Durkheim believes that these are the same manifestation of the collective spirit of human beings, in the sense that since person really feels two types of 'self' within himself, one 'self' – due to the fact that I am Zayd, the son of 'Amr – is a 'self' in contrast to another person's 'self'. This is mine and not yours. And there is another 'self' which is the collective 'self'. (For us Iranians, for instance, "I am an Iranian" is a common 'I'.) Yes, since it is such, this tribe that was worshipping that animal figure was actually worshipping the whole community. They came to believe that all members of this tribe were all descendants of this animal and then if ever they were worshipping it, it was not only because they were traceable to it but also because it was a manifestation of this community, and in reality, we wanted to worship their own community.

Now, the higher and more modern form – in my opinion – of Durkheim's words which they have followed is the very thing which the writer of the article mentioned. There is no need to look at totemism and the like; he has mentioned the first part which I said. He says, "This is a sort of 'return to self-alienation'." In the human being, there are actually two types of 'self', individual 'self' and collective 'self'. Many of the things that a person does are for the sake of his social 'self' and collective 'I'. There is a time, for example, that a person performs self-sacrifice. You interpret self-sacrifice as preferring others over one's self, and then you try to explain and analyze why a person who is naturally expected to work for himself – as he usually feels – gives preference to others than to himself. It is something which cannot be reconciled with one's logic. Yet, a person still does it and considers it better than doing something for his own self, treating it as something sacred.

He (writer of the article) says that you are mistaken in saying that 'self-sacrifice' means preferring others over oneself. No, he gives preference to his 'self' than to his [other] 'self', because he has two types of 'self', viz. collective 'self' and individual 'self'. Now, it is the [former] self which has surfaced. It is still doing something for the sake of one's 'self' but not the individual 'self' but the collective 'self'. Morality, therefore, can also be explained within this framework. Nationalism, patriotism, self-sacrifices and other expressions of selflessness for the sake of community, nation or the collective are all explainable. These are not working for others; it is also [a form of] working for one's 'self' which is the collective 'self'.

The writer of the article has brought forth this discussion with the title 'Self-sacrifices' which I think is his own coinage[1] ...[2] He relinquishes his own collective 'self' and regards it as 'others' and gives preference to it over his own self. In a sense, he sacrifices his 'self'. He feels two types of 'self' within himself, viz. one is the individual 'self' which has 'I', 'self' and individuality, and there is another 'self' which has [the spirit of] the collective and society. Then he also does two types of works: works which are done by the social 'self' [and the works which are done by the individual 'self'.] Gradually, he would forget this social 'self'. It is like the allegory mentioned in the Qur'an that a person actually forgets God and [as a result] he forgets himself. He (writer of the article) says that man forgets his own collective 'self', and then he realizes that there is a series of virtues, thinking that his 'self' is limited to that individual 'self'. Later on, he will find an area for which his collective 'self' does something. He comes with the assumption that the said area is outside his self and it is metaphysical. There are many remarks along this line, but on the contrary, it acquires a mystical form:

1. It will be better of our colleagues could have an opportunity to find relevant books – more detailed ones – about Durkheim's theory and which also deals with this subject.
2. [It is an unrecorded part of the lecture.]

سالها دل طلب جام جم از ما می‌کرد　آنچه خود داشت ز بیگانه تمنّا می‌کرد

Search for the cup of Jamshīd (Divine knowledge) from me (*Zāhid* and '*Ābid*), years my heart made.
And for what it (the cup) possessed, from a stranger, entreaty made.[1]

He also says, "Sir, it is the same 'self' of yours; it is the same collective 'self' of yours; the only thing is that you have lost it. Since you have lost it, you were looking for it from others; from outside your own self." And this is 'self-alienation'; that is, a person forgets his 'self' and takes 'non-self' as his 'self' and that 'non-self' [as something metaphysical].

Now, of all the remarks and views the writer of the article has mentioned, he mentions this theory without many misgivings. He says, "Yes, of course, this view is also not devoid of flaws and for this reason, the followers of Durkheim improvised it (thereby implying that its improvised version has no more flaw). More or less, it is the view which this person himself also prefers and draws conclusion from it. As conclusion, he wants to say that according to the theory that "The origin of religion is ignorance," the inevitable conclusion is that religion shall wither away with the eradication of ignorance (because in the absence of cause, the effect will also cease to exist) and now, it is actually not so, it thus follows that this theory is false. And according to the theory which asserts that "The origin of religion is fear of the forces of nature," the moment man is no longer afraid of the forces of nature, religion is also expected to cease to exist. We see actually, however, that it is not so and rcligion continues to exist. So is the case of poverty, richness and class differences. We can also see that wherever class differences are eliminated and equality exists, religion also continues to exist. In those countries, conflicts continue to exist [between classes]; after

1. Ḥāfiẓ, *Ghazaliyyāt*, *ghazal* 143. [Trans.]

these counties have attained equality, as they say, it is still their concern to campaign against religion. Once again, you can see that day by day, the young ones' inclination to religion – even in the so-called Soviet Union – intensifies. If we choose this theory, however, it is not so; this is a principle which is also applicable to man; this is the very root of religion and for this reason, it will never be uprooted from human society. As such, this is only a theory for anyone who does not believe in religion as having a metaphysical and divine root, and at the same time, acknowledges that religion cannot also be extinguished. There is such a remark here.

This is also a baseless remark.

Refuting Durkheim's Theory

The fact of the matter is that there is no doubt or any dispute that the society is real unit and not a nominal one. The Qur'anic exegesis *Al-Mīzān* has discussed it to that extent many times in numerous places that society has its own unity and life, and since it has its own unity and life, it has its own common death, strength, weakness, destiny, and the like. In this thin booklet which I have recently published with the title *Qiyām wa Inqilāb-e Mahdī (A.S.) az Dīdgāh-e Falsafeh-ye Tārīkh* (*The Uprising and Revolution of the Mahdī (A.S.) from the Viewpoint of the Philosophy of History*), since the booklet was not that thick, while pointing to this discussion, in some parts I have cited the Qur'anic exegesis *Al-Mīzān* in the footnotes, and it is now necessary to refer to it. There are the following expressions in the Qur'an:

﴿ لِكُلِّ أُمَّةٍ أَجَلٌ إِذَا جَاءَ أَجَلُهُمْ فَلا يَسْتَأْخِرُونَ سَاعَةً وَلا يَسْتَقْدِمُونَ ﴾

> There is a time for every nation: when their time comes, they shall not defer it by a single hour nor shall they advance it. (10:49)

And basically, the Qur'an has thus decreed for every nation: "Nations were such and We let nations perish" and [according to the Qur'an,] there is no common destiny for all nations; if there is a pious minority within a nation, it shall not have effect on the condition of the nation – just as the opposite is also true. This is because a community or nation constitutes a single unit. [This fact confirms that society is a real unit and not a nominal unit.]

Up to this extent, the said theory is correct, but as to what kind of composition a society is, on the basis of the proposition we have discussed, we have arrived at the point that human society is a third type of composition; that is, it is not a kind of nominal composition (because it is actually a real composition) and not a kind of natural or chemical compositions, because in natural and chemical compositions the identity of parts has no independence at all; it is subsumed in the identity of the whole. The identity of the members of society, on the other hand, is not subsumed to that extent. [Moreover,] the theory of Durkheim and those who give primacy to the collective to such extent necessitates social determinism; that is, it necessitates that the individual should not have any willpower and identity of his own. In other words, when he feels, it should be this society that feels; when he desires, it should be this society that desires. And basically the individual should not have any independence in relation to the society. This is while although society is a fact and a kind of composition, individual independence to a certain extent remains, and thus, an individual can change his society. It is impossible for a subsumed 'part' to be able to modify and change [the state of the 'whole']. An individual can be able to swim against the tide of society. He can be able to intensify or slow down that advancement of society; he can bring it to a halt and change the course of history. This is the same fact that the human being has freedom and willpower. In contrast to social determinism, his freedom and independence remain to a great extent.

Human Being as Having a Multilayered 'Self'

It is such that the human being is not what this person says that human being really feels two types of 'self' within himself; that is, there is indeed two types of 'self', viz. individual self and collective self. Under the influence of society, the human being's 'self' takes form, grows, and acquires its own colour while keeping a sort of freedom and independence. In reality, however, human being cannot have two types of 'self' such that when I perform self-sacrifice, the 'I' is one identity within myself. When I am doing a literary work for my own self, another identity is doing so. Actually, there is a real duality in us. When we individually do something, we do so for our own selves; when we do something bad, commit injustices or do a literary work, we give preference to ourselves. The 'we' or 'I' is one 'self' in us that does the work. And when we render service to the society, perform self-sacrifice, do noble works, and worship, the 'we' or 'I' is another 'self' within us [that perform those works].

What remarks are these?! These are not issues which we could say that the gentlemen have proved in laboratories. They are discursive issues. In his innermost being, a person exactly feels that [as he does something bad,] he is the same person who does something good an hour later. These are different layers of a single entity, and not two separate personalities. This is quite different from having [different] layers of a single entity as it has. It is like a tree which has a trunk and branches – upper and lower branches; an upper part grows; so are lower and middle parts. Yet, these constitute only a single entity [called 'tree']. Yes, there is a difference between 'layers of a single entity' and 'two entities distinct from each other'. That which is correct and proper here [is that these I's are layers of a single entity and not entities distinct from one another].

The Qur'anic View

It is here that the human being could discern the profundity of logic of the Qur'an. Without [explicitly] dealing with these subjects,[1] the Qur'an talks about the 'commanding self' (*nafs al-ammārah*), the 'reproaching self' (*nafs al-lawwāmah*) and the 'tranquil soul' (*nafs al-muṭma'innah*).[2] Philosophers call this case 'unity in multiplicity and multiplicity in unity'. It is not true that human being has many distinct 'selves' such that the commanding self does one work; the reproaching self does another; and the tranquil soul does yet another work. It is not so. Sometimes, the human soul is in lower level and does something while in that lower level. There it is not under the control of reason; this is what we call the 'commanding self' (*nafs al-ammārah*). The same self opens its eyes in a higher level and becomes more circumspect. This is called the 'reproaching self' (*nafs al-lawwāmah*) which reproaches its own self. If they were two distinct entities, then 'reproaching one's self' has no meaning at all. It does something evil and later on, [it would condemn itself][3] It becomes the judge itself, the complainant as well as the plaintiff, and it issues a judgment against itself. This is the meaning of self-reckoning (*muḥasibat al-nafs*).

---

1. One would deal with any subject and in the end he would refer to the Qur'an and then realize that the Qur'an has already stated its view concerning it.
2. In Islamic mysticism (*'irfān*), *nafs al-ammārah*, the commanding self (the base self) is mentioned in the Qur'an (12:53), to be contrasted with *nafs al-lawwāmah*, the reproaching self (75:2), and finally, with *nafs al-mutma'innah*, the tranquil soul (89:27). [Trans.]
3. [This part was not recorded by the cassette recorder.]

﴿ لَا أُقْسِمُ بِيَوْمِ الْقِيَامَةِ ★ وَلَا أُقْسِمُ بِالنَّفْسِ اللَّوَّامَةِ ﴾

I swear by the Day of Resurrection! And I swear by the self-blaming soul! (75:1-2)

It is also mentioned alongside the Day of Resurrection that just as there is God who takes account on the Day of Resurrection, He has also endowed the human being with a level of his spirit and psyche that reproaches him even in this world.

﴿ يَا أَيَّتُهَا النَّفْسُ الْمُطْمَئِنَّةُ ★ ارْجِعِي إِلَىٰ رَبِّكِ ﴾

O soul at peace! Return to your Lord. (89:27-28)

As such, the human being is a single person and a single entity that climbs through this ladder. The commanding self is the reproaching self, and the reproaching self, in turn, is the same tranquil soul, but they are in different degrees. These degrees, in turn, are related to the extent of attention, awareness, consciousness, purity, the absence of veils (*ḥijāb*) [of moral vices and spiritual diseases], having stronger faith (*īmān*) and certainty (*yaqīn*), and the like. They are the same [self].

Summary

Therefore, this theory of Mr. Durkheim – which is a sociological theory and a psychological theory at the same time – is false. The human being does not have two identities which are independent and distinct from each other. There is one 'self' in him which singly performs all these varied things. Hence, this explanation that the human being has two types of 'self' and that one 'self' forgets himself and then attributes whatever he does to 'non-self' and 'other-than-self' which he regards as metaphysical, is not correct.

There are no such two types of 'self' which he tries to explain in that way.

Secondly, if it is really such, then more religious people must always come from those whom you call 'self-alienated'. That is, the more the individuals forget their social spirit within themselves, the more they are [socially] dead, and the more they are bereft of collective feeling, the more they are expected to be religious and religiously devoted, whereas the truth is the opposite. Collective feeling [of concern] is more alive in the individuals who are religious in the real sense of the word compared to others. Who had more sense of religiosity, the Commander of the Faithful ('Alī ibn Abī Ṭālib) (A.S.), or Mu'āwiyah? Who had more social concern, [Mu'āwiyah, or] the Commander of the Faithful (A.S.) who used to say, "If someone in one part of territory I govern is hungry, I also feel the same here." (Is there anything higher than this expression of empathy?!)

وحسبك داء ان تبيت ببطنةوحولك اكباد تحنّ الي القدّ

> It is enough for you to have a disease that you lie with your belly full While around you people may be badly yearning for dried leather.[1]

Yes, had the Commander of the Faithful (A.S.) who used to say that more social concern, or Mu'āwiyah? These individuals in whom this social concern has been alive to the utmost are religious ones, and not those who have forgotten their social 'self' and then treat themselves as mere individual 'self' and say that these (their

1. *Nahj al-Balāghah*, Fayḍ al-Islām Arrangement, Letter 45, 970. This letter was addressed to 'Uthmān ibn Ḥunayf al-Anṣārī who was Imām 'Alī's (A.S.) Governor of Baṣrah. [Trans.]

social 'self') belong to somewhere else. The individuals in whom these feelings are more alive are the same individuals who are more religious.

Moreover, in this final conclusion that this person tries to arrive at, he has attempted to give a sort of reply; that is, he wants to provide an explanation for this ultimate stronghold at the disposal of these anti-religious individuals – the last stronghold which is also about to be taken over. That is, they have been saying so far, thus: "Religion had gone; religious belief withered away; religion is about to go. Based on the way we see the world, religion is about to go. Science came and religion went away. Social justice came and religion departed." Little and little, they can see that all these criteria and indicators came out to be wrong. The way religion shows, it is not so; it lingers on. These gentlemen should know that it is not to go and exists. Now, they have come [and] given such an explanation: "No. religion is there; it remains and it cannot be obliterated [but it has no divine root]. The following is his (writer of the article's) last remark:

> "You may conclude from the foregoing [discussions] that ideology, in general, and religion, in particular, are among the basic manifestations of social life and those who think that with the advancement of man and his knowledge, they will wither away correctly understood neither the social structure nor the essence of ideology and religion."

They want to give such an explanation. They must be told that if this remark is correct, with the sophistication of Mr. Durkheim's sociology, religion is supposed to wither away because the implication of Durkheim's remarks is that belief in religion is traceable to a form of ignorance. So are the remarks of Feuerbach.

However, Feuerbach treats human being as an individual, saying that the human being has a set of good characters and another set of bad ones. Then, concerning the social, since he sees himself so much entangled with wicked character, he detaches and disconnects from his pure character, thinking of and supposing it to be outside himself and...[1]

1. [Unfortunately, the rest of Professor Muṭahharī's lecture has not been recorded.]

Chapter 11: The Qur'anic View on the Origin Of Religion

For some sessions, the discussion had been about the theories on the origin of man's inclination to religion or the origin of religion and religious belief presented by some [personalities] as religious sociology. In particular, by taking into account all the remarks of these gentlemen, certain points become clear. One is that whatever has been said is nothing but a series of hypotheses; that is, scientifically speaking, the maximum value of each of them is that of a hypothesis and not a theory which is a proven hypothesis. There is a difference between a hypothesis and a theory. There is a time when a person has an assumption regarding a certain thing; that, he considers something probable. This probability is presented as the initial assumption to be investigated we could know later whether proofs affirm it or not. It becomes a theory when proofs have affirmed it. Mere multiplicity and repetition of these hypotheses cannot be a justification for it to be named 'theory'. In addition, we have seen that none has ever mentioned any proof for his remark. One claims that the human being has an essential duality: an exalted and noble existence and a lowly existence. Gradually, he forgets about his lowly existence and he attributes to non-self whatever he has in his innermost being. We ask him, "What is the proof?"

It is nothing more than a mere 'hypothesis'. In fact, we have seen that proofs contradict it. Incidentally, one of these proofs which we always cite is this: why groups are the patrons of religion, or those who incline to it? Do people who are naturally and characteristically noble and honourable incline to religion? Or, do most of the noble and honourable people – those who have a sense of nobility – pay no attention to religion and do only those individuals who have forgotten their own nobility incline to religion? In actually, we can see that some have an objection – and an objection itself is a remark – that the religious devotees that you can see are so pure individuals and religion has not made them such pure. They had been pure and then they inclined to religion. If a person makes such an objection, he is near to acceptance compared to the one who says that the individuals who forget their purity, nobility and all [goodness] – for they lose these [virtues] – attribute nobilities to something else called 'God'. As such, notice the points and subtleties of the Qur'an. One question would be asked. Most would ask why the Qur'an, for instance, say:

﴿ الٓمٓ * ذَٰلِكَ الْكِتَابُ لَا رَيْبَ فِيهِ هُدًى لِّلْمُتَّقِينَ ﴾

> This is the Book; there is no doubt in it, a guidance to the God-wary. (2:2)

(And there are many similar verses in the Qur'an.) It is a guidance to the God-wary (*muttaqī*). They have such similar questions: here the assumption is that first of all, they are God-wary and then the Qur'an guides them and now the Qur'an makes God-wary those who are not. We also read in the blessed *Sūrat Yā Sīn*, thus:

﴿ يس ★ وَالْقُرْآنِ الْحَكِيمِ ★ إِنَّكَ لَمِنَ الْمُرْسَلِينَ ★ عَلَى صِرَاطٍ مُسْتَقِيمٍ ★ تَنْزِيلَ الْعَزِيزِ
الرَّحِيمِ ★ لِتُنْذِرَ قَوْمًا مَا أُنْذِرَ آبَاؤُهُمْ فَهُمْ غَافِلُونَ... ★ إِنَّمَا تُنْذِرُ مَنِ اتَّبَعَ الذِّكْرَ
وَخَشِيَ الرَّحْمَنَ بِالْغَيْبِ فَبَشِّرْهُ بِمَغْفِرَةٍ وَأَجْرٍ كَرِيمٍ ﴾

Yā Sīn! You are indeed one of the apostles, on a straight path. [It is a scripture] sent down gradually from the All-mighty, the All-merciful that you may warn a people whose fathers were not warned, so they are oblivious... You can only warn someone who follows the Reminder and fears the All-beneficent in secret; so give him the good news of forgiveness and a noble reward. (36:1-6, 11)

Intrinsic and Acquired Guidance

My point is the last verse.

This reply has been given – I think there is also a relevant topic in the exegesis *Al-Mīzān* – that the human beings have two types of guidance, viz. intrinsic guidance and so-called 'acquired' (*iktisābī*) guidance, and the Qur'an wants to state that so long as the light of intrinsic guidance of a person is not illuminated, acquired guidance has no benefit for him. This, in reality, is the same fact that unless a person preserves his intrinsic humanity, [the teachings of the prophets] will be of no benefit [for him]. That is, the teachings of the prophets are not beneficial for those who have changed and lost their [sense of] humanity (which is the exact opposite of what these people say), and experience and reality also show the same. For example, this is exactly how I understand *Surat al-Mā'ūn*:

﴿ أَرَأَيْتَ الَّذِي يُكَذِّبُ بِالدِّينِ ﴾

Did you see him who denies the Religion? (107:1)

Initially, it talks in a form of surprise thus: Can the human being be human and yet he denies the Religion?! It then goes into the details that he who goes beyond [the sense of] humanity denies the Religion:

﴿ فَذَٰلِكَ الَّذِي يَدُعُّ الْيَتِيمَ ﴾

That is the one who drives away the orphan. (107:2)

That is, this action is an acid test of humanity, and human nature dictates that a person is expected to be affectionate to the orphans.

﴿ وَلَا يَحُضُّ عَلَىٰ طَعَامِ الْمِسْكِينِ ﴾

And he does not urge the feeding of the needy. (107:3)

That is, he is a person who has no efforts in feeding the needy and giving nourishment to the hungry; he has no exhortation or encouragement [in this regard]; neither does he cooperate. In other words, he has initially lost his [sense of] humanity. A person who loses his humanity had naturally lost his 'Islam' beforehand; that is, he is no longer a natural person; he is a metamorphosed person.

We have again gone far from the subject. We wanted to point out that as you can see, their remarks are merely a series of hypotheses without any proof; in fact, they are hypotheses which are always contrary to the proofs. Perhaps, the most delusive of them all is this hypothesis of the Marxists that religion is an invention of the exploitative class. There is also no proof for this. Historical facts and current events totally negate it, and the proofs are all contrary to this.

Is Divine Revelation Rooted in the Human Beings?

Now, we would like to see the Qur'anic view on the origin and beginning of religion. Sometimes, we look at religion as something that comes from the prophets and presented to the people. It is known that its origin is Divine revelation (*waḥy*). Yet, does the Divine revelation which presents teachings as religious teachings, as well as [code of] morality and upbringing, [code of] laws and rules, and as a whole, the same Divine revelation which shows a Way for human thinking and action, have the same source and root for all human beings?

Not to mention the specific teachings of the Qur'an, it is not contrary to the nature of religion for a person to say that religion is only something which God has presented to mankind through the means of Divine revelation, but prior to this presentation, mankind has a sense of indifference toward religion and its opposite. We have said that in this case, mankind is like a wall or like a sheet of paper in a state of potentiality and possibility – in a sense, in a state of indifference. For this sheet of paper, there is the possibility of something to be written on it or nothing to be written on it; that is, there is an equal possibility for having written on it and none written on it. For this sheet of paper, there is an equal possibility for a verse of the Qur'an or something repugnant to the Qur'an to be inscribed in it. One may possibly say that on account of its nature, mankind has only a state of possibility and indifference with respect to religion. God just sent the prophets and they came in order to teach the Religion to mankind which is in a state of indifference toward it. If someone makes this remark, it cannot be said that he has denied religions. This is another notion.

Another theory, however, holds that what the prophets presented is not something with respect to which the human being has a feeling of indifference and apathy, but rather it is something which is embedded in his essence or nature. That is, to look for it, to search for it and to incline to it is embedded in man's nature or essence. In this case, the prophets are like a gardener who takes care of a flower or tree. In this flower or tree itself, there is already a potential or desire for a certain thing. If an apricot seed is planted on the ground, it is not such that the apricot seed is indifferent to become a date tree, an apricot tree or a cherry tree. It is up to the gardener to culture it to become an apricot, a date or a cherry!

There is also a natural disposition (*fiṭrah*) – in the sense of a demand – in the human being. The mission (*bi'thah*) of the prophets is a response to this demand which exists in the human being. In reality, that which the human being has been and will be searching for, on the basis of his nature, is exactly what the prophets have presented and present to him. This is exactly the meaning of *fiṭrah*.

The Famous Qur'anic Verse on *Fiṭrah*

Now, let us see whether there is a stipulation or an indication of *fiṭrah* in the Islamic teachings, or not. There is no doubt that the issue of *fiṭrah* has been widely discussed although the scholars (*'ulamā'*) might differ and not be unanimous in inferring the expression for *fiṭrah*. In any case, there is difference among the Muslims scholars – Sunnī and Shī'ah – in the principle there is such thing called *fiṭrah* - *fiṭrah* of religion, *fiṭrah* of Islam, *fiṭrah* of monotheism (*tawḥīd*), and many other names used for it. Now, I shall only point to some of them.

One of them is the same famous verse on *fiṭrah* which is in the blessed *Sūrat al-Rūm*:

﴿ فَأَقِمْ وَجْهَكَ لِلدِّينِ حَنِيفًا ﴾

> So set your heart on the religion as a people of pure faith. (30:30)

That is to say, "Be faithful [to the religion]; Be firm in following it; turn your attention to it purely while you are of pure faith (*ḥanīf*); while you are truth-inclined and truth-advocate."[1]

﴿ فِطْرَةَ اللهِ الَّتِي فَطَرَ النَّاسَ عَلَيْهَا ﴾

...the origination of Allah according to which He originated mankind. (30:30)

That is to say, "It is with you this Divine origination (which is the same pure faith). This Divine creation,[2] this religion, this special way in the creation of man through which God, the Exalted, has created all human beings.

﴿ لَا تَبْدِيلَ لِخَلْقِ اللهِ ﴾

There is no altering Allah's creation. (30:30)

It is inalterable. It is part of human nature. So long as the human being is in this world; so long as the human being is human; so long as he is to be born, he will still be born with this nature. That is, one cannot change the innate nature in the human beings and transform it into something else.

﴿ ذَٰلِكَ ٱلدِّينُ ٱلْقَيِّمُ ﴾

That is the upright religion. (30:30)

That is the upright religion – ultimately upright and straight.

With utmost clarity, this verse introduces religion as 'Allah's origination' (*fiṭrat Allāh*) to all people. We will discuss further if ever necessary.

---

1. We have said that perhaps the closest translation of the meaning of *ḥanīf* is 'truth-advocate'.
2. As we have said [earlier], *fiṭrah* means a special kind of creation (*khilqah*).

The Covenant Between God and Man in Sūrat Yā Sīn

Also, it is thus stated in the blessed *Sūrat Yā Sīn*:

> ﴿ أَلَمْ أَعْهَدْ إِلَيْكُمْ يَا بَنِي آدَمَ أَن لَّا تَعْبُدُوا الشَّيْطَانَ إِنَّهُ لَكُمْ عَدُوٌّ مُّبِينٌ ★ وَأَنْ اعْبُدُونِي هَذَا صِرَاطٌ مُّسْتَقِيمٌ ★ وَلَقَدْ أَضَلَّ مِنْكُمْ جِبِلًّا كَثِيرًا أَفَلَمْ تَكُونُوا تَعْقِلُونَ ﴾
> Did I not exhort you, O children of Adam, saying, 'Do not worship Satan. He is indeed your manifest enemy. Worship Me. That is a straight path'? Certainly he has led astray many of your generations. Did you not use to apply reason? (36:60-62)

It talks about a covenant and promise. "O children of Adam! (This does not address a person, two persons, a community or two communities.) Did I not make a covenant with you?" It says, "You and I concluded a covenant before and had an agreement that you will not worship Satan. Here, worship of Satan does not mean that we go to an altar and make an image of Satan. It rather means to follow Satan.

> ﴿ وَأَنْ اعْبُدُونِي ﴾
> And that you worship Me. (36:61)

That is to say, "We had a covenant that you will not worship Satan and that you worship Me."

> ﴿ هَذَا صِرَاطٌ مُّسْتَقِيمٌ ﴾
> That is a straight path. (36:61)

That is your straight path which will lead you to your perfection and felicity.

The Verse of Pre-Existence *(Āyat Al-Dharr)*

The other verse is the one which has become known as the Verse of Pre-existence (*āyat al-dharr*):

> ﴿ وَإِذْ أَخَذَ رَبُّكَ مِن بَنِي آدَمَ مِن ظُهُورِهِمْ ذُرِّيَّتَهُمْ وَأَشْهَدَهُمْ عَلَى أَنفُسِهِمْ أَلَسْتُ
> بِرَبِّكُمْ قَالُواْ بَلَى شَهِدْنَا أَن تَقُولُواْ يَوْمَ الْقِيَامَةِ إِنَّا كُنَّا عَنْ هَذَا غَافِلِينَ * أَوْ تَقُولُوا إِنَّمَا
> أَشْرَكَ آبَاؤُنَا مِنْ قَبْلُ وَكُنَّا ذُرِّيَّةً مِنْ بَعْدِهِمْ أَفَتُهْلِكُنَا بِمَا فَعَلَ الْمُبْطِلُونَ ﴾
>
> When your Lord took from the Children of Adam, from their loins, their descendants and made them bear witness over themselves, [He said to them,] 'Am I not your Lord?' They said, 'Yes indeed! We bear witness.' [This,] lest you should say on the Day of Resurrection, 'Indeed we were unaware of this,' or lest you should say, 'Our fathers ascribed partners [to Allah] before [us] and we were descendants after them. Will You then destroy us because of what the falsifiers have done? (7:172-173)

It is an amazing passage. Let us defer the elucidation of the verses. We shall discuss two or three subtopics and then we will elaborate a bit on the verses.

There are also other [similar] verses in the Qur'an, but perhaps they are not that explicit, although the explicitness of some of them is not less; for example, this verse:

> ﴿ أَفِي اللَّهِ شَكٌّ فَاطِرِ السَّمَاوَاتِ وَالْأَرْضِ ﴾
>
> Is there any doubt about Allah, the originator of the heavens and the earth?! (14:10)

That is, in the relationship between man and God,[1] the subject is such that there is doubt about it. It is not an issue like a discursive or theoretical one such that one would choose one theory and another person would choose another theory. Rather, if the issue is presented correctly, no one would doubt it. So, if someone has a doubt, it follows that the issue is [not presented] correctly. [For example,] one would cast a doubt about other-than-God and call it 'God', or he would not doubt but he would behave obstinately and ungratefully. We can also regard this verse as included in the verses of *fiṭrah.*

Presentation of the Divine Trust to Man

There is another verse which has more discussion; a verse which has mentioned the subject symbolically and figuratively:

> ﴿ إِنَّا عَرَضْنَا الأَمَانَةَ عَلَى السَّمَاوَاتِ وَالأَرْضِ وَالْجِبَالِ فَأَبَيْنَ أَنْ يَحْمِلْنَهَا وَأَشْفَقْنَ مِنْهَا وَحَمَلَهَا الإِنْسَانُ إِنَّهُ كَانَ ظَلُومًا جَهُولا ﴾
>
> Indeed We presented the Trust to the heavens and the earth and the mountains, but they refused to bear it, and were apprehensive of it; but man undertook it. Indeed he is most unfair and senseless. (33:72)

That is, "We have presented the Trust (but the Qur'an does not mention what this Trust is) to all creatures: the heavens, the earth and the mountains." It has specifically mentioned very huge creatures. In reality, it refers to all things. They all refused to accept this Trust. There was one creature who accepted to endure this Trust, and that is the human being. It then says that this human being is most unfair and senseless. There is a lot of discussion on this verse. Now, [there is a dispute] whether this verse is related to

---

1. Since the issue is about God, the doubter is the human being.

this issue of *fiṭrah* or not. I want to point it out up to that extent.

There are other verses in the Qur'an which are not that explicit, but of course, some exegetes (*mufassirūn*) have interpreted them in that way; for example, the verse which states, thus:

﴿ وَلَئِن سَأَلْتَهُم مَّنْ خَلَقَ السَّمَاوَاتِ وَالْأَرْضَ لَيَقُولُنَّ اللَّهُ ﴾

> If you ask them, 'Who created the heavens and the earth?' they will surely say, 'Allah'. (31:25)

This verse is interpreted in two ways. Some say that the Qur'an means that their belief in God being the Creator (*khāliq*) is perfect; that is, they recognize God as the Creator and do not regard the idols are creators or God's partners in creation. Their flaw is that although they recognize God as the Absolute Creator, in worship they treat other-than-God as partner of the Creator. If it is so, then this statement is the same known and common belief of the polytheists during the time of the Prophet (S). Others say, however, the Qur'an wants to say that due to their weak beliefs, they take partners of God even in being the Creator. Of course, this does not mean that they believe in the partner; in fact, they have no idea at all in this regard. But if you ask them whom they worship, definitely they will say that it is the Creator. Then, when you follow up, "Who is the Creator?" their intrinsic nature (*fiṭrah*) will answer, "It is God."

The Noble Messenger's (S) Saying

These verses are also mentioned but for the meantime, we are not concerned with these verses which elicit various interpretations. I shall quote to you three passages. One is a statement from the Noble Messenger (S); another one from the *Nahj al-Balāghah*; and the third one from *Ṣaḥīfah al-Sajjādiyyah.*[1] Of course, I shall quote them as examples, for regarding *fiṭrah* we have traditions and narrations far more than these. A statement which is narrated from the Noble Messenger (S) is this famous tradition:[2]

كُلُّ مَوْلُودٍ يُولَدُ عَلَىٰ ٱلْفِطْرَةِ فَأَبَوَاهُ يُهَوِّدَانِهِ أَوْ يُنَصِّرَانِهِ أَوْ يُمَجِّسَانِهِ.

> "Everyone born is born in the state of *fiṭrah*; it is their parents that make him a Jew, a Christian or a Magian."[3]

That is, everyone born is born in this world in the state of Divine origination; in the state of Islamic origination; it is his father and mother[4] who transform him. If they are Jews, they will make him a Jews; if they are Christians, they will make him a Christian; if they are Magians, they will make him a Magian; whatever group they belong, they will make him part of that group.

In the Sunnī corpus of *ḥadīth*, this tradition can be found in *Ṣaḥīḥ al-Bukhārī*[5] and in the Shī'ah [corpus of *ḥadīth*], it is in *Al-Kāfī*. Of course, I had read it before in *Biḥar [al-Anwār]*[6] but it can be said,

---

1. The book of fifty-seven prayers known as *Al-Ṣaḥīfah (al-Kāmilah) al-Sajjādiyyah*, which is one of the major Islamic manuals of supplications, was transmitted from Imām Zayn al-'Ābidīn as-Sajjād (A.S.), the fourth of the Twelve Imāms and the only son of Imām Ḥusayn to survive the massacre at Karbalā'. [Trans.]
2. This tradition has been more often narrated by the Sunnīs, although the Shī'ah have also narrated it. They have narrated it abundantly. In Sh'ī'ah [corpus of *ḥadīth*], I have not come across it in more than one instance.
3. *Ṣaḥīḥ al-Bukhārī*, "Kitāb al-Janā'iz," sections (*abwāb*) 80 and 93.
4. It is obvious that they have been mentioned as an example of external factors.
5. Ṣaḥīḥ al-Bukhārī is the leading title and one of the *Kutub al-Sittah* (six major Sunnī *ḥadīth* collections). [Trans.]
6. *Biḥar al-Anwār al-Jāmi'ah Li-Durar Akhbār al-A'immah al-Aṭhār* (or *Biḥār al-Anwār* for short): one of the Later Collections compiled by 'Allāmah al-Majlisī (Muḥammad Bāqir ibn Muḥammad Taqī) (d. 1110 AH/1698)

more or less, that the [pertinent] traditions which are narrated in *Biḥar [al-Anwār]* were taken from Sunnī [sources]. And there was a time when I thought that the Shīʿah have not narrated it in their reliable books because *Biḥar [al-Anwār]* which has narrated it has taken it from the book *Ghawālī al-La'ālī* by Ibn Abī Jumhūr al-Aḥsā'ī,[1] which is not that reliable source of *ḥadīth*. Later on, however, I have read in the exegesis *Al-Mīzān* which has quoted it from *Al-Kāfī*. Now, I cannot remember well if I have read it myself in *Al-Kāfī* but the exegesis *Al-Mīzān* quotes it under the commentary of the same verse:

﴿ فَأَقِمْ وَجْهَكَ لِلدِّينِ حَنِيفًا ﴾

> So set your heart on the religion as a people of pure faith. (30:30)

In the Sunnī narration, this tradition has an addendum. It is said that after [stating this statement], the Prophet (S) mentioned an allegory, which is an interesting one. He said, "Have you ever seen so far a sheep born out of its mother and whose ears are cut off?! Or, is it that a sheep will be born out of its mother with ears and later on, it is the human beings that would cut them off?" He likens the *fiṭrah* of Islam, which is consistent with the human nature or essence, to the intact ears, and that of other-than-Islam to the severed ears as an external factor would come to the scene and take a knife to cut off the sheep's ears. This is one tradition.

---

containing traditions and their annotations, historical subjects and commentaries on Qur'anic verses. [Trans.]

1. Muḥammad ibn ʿAlī al-Aḥsā'ī, known as Ibn Abī Jumhūr al-Aḥsā'ī (died 901 AH/1495-96): an orthodox Shīʿah scholar educated in Najaf (Iraq) and Jabal Āmil (Lebanon) who tried to integrate Sufism and Shīʿism. [Trans.]

Imām 'Alī's (A.S.) Saying

The one in *Nahj al-Balāghah* (Sermon 1) is as follows. After pointing out the creation of the universe and Ādam (A.S.), it is the turn of the issue of sending of the prophets, saying thus:

فَبَعَثَ فِيهِمْ رُسُلَهُ.

> "Then He sent to them (the people) His messengers."

وَوَاتَرَ إِلَيْهِمْ أَنْبِيَاءَهُ.

> "And he sent to them prophets one after the other."

That is, not only one prophet was sent; prophets were sent one after the other, and each of them came to confirm and affirm the previous ones. Why?

لِيَسْتَأْدُوهُمْ مِيثَاقَ فِطْرَتِهِ، وَيُذَكِّرُوهُمْ مَنْسِيَّ نِعْمَتِهِ، وَيَحْتَجُّوا عَلَيْهِمْ بِالتَّبْلِيغِ، وَيُثِيرُوا لَهُمْ دَفَائِنَ الْعُقُولِ.

> "...to get them to fulfill the pledges of His creation, to recall to them His bounties, to exhort them by preaching, to unveil before them the hidden virtues of wisdom."

It is said that God sent the prophets one after the other[1] to get them to fulfill the pledges in their nature; they came to tell human being, "O human being! In the depth of your natural disposition you made a pledge to your Lord. We have come so as for you to fulfill the pledge; that is, it does not begin with nothing. We have come, in a sense, to put to actuality that which already exists." It is the same when one day you come to get the pledge of some

1. Here the two views we have mentioned earlier are relevant. Did the prophets come to offer something to the people for the first time? Or, did they come to recall to the people the pledge they made in their nature?

individuals to do a certain thing and when they made the promise, you return back to ask them to fulfill it. The Commander of the Faithful (A.S.) says that the prophets have come to get the people to fulfill the pledges in their own natural disposition, and

وَيُذَكِّرُوهُمْ مَنْسِيَّ نِعْمَتِهِ.

"...and to recall to them His bounties."

That is to recall to the people the bounties of God which have been neglected and forgotten by them. (In other words, they have come as reminders and wake up callers.) They remind the people of something which they have become oblivious. That is, they have come to serve as reminder (*mudhakkir*) and not as teacher (*mu'allim*). As far as the people's natural dispositions are concerned, the prophet functions as 'reminder'.

وَيَحْتَجُّوا عَلَيْهِمْ بِالتَّبْلِيغِ

"...and to exhort them by preaching."

While reminding the people, exhorting them and conveying their prophethood to them, the prophets have also come to preach and argue with them. That is, they exhausted all arguments to the people, bringing them proofs, convincing them and leaving them no more excuse.

The next expression is the most profound of all:

وَيُثِيرُوا لَهُمْ دَفَائِنَ الْعُقُولِ.

"...to unveil before them the hidden virtues of wisdom."

Dafā'in means treasures and jewels. As you know, in ancient time treasures were buried on the ground. It was not because these would perish, for example, but rather to hide them from others.

Naturally, these would be hidden on the ground and no one would know that there were treasures there. One would pass by without knowing that there were treasures beneath the ground he was stepping in. The prophets came to inform the people that there are treasures in the depth of their soul; in the depth of their intellect. They came to dig on the ground and let the people know the treasures beneath – "We have had such treasures and we did not know!"

سالها دل طلب جام جم از ما می‌کرد   آنچه خود داشت ز بیگانه تمنّا می‌کرد
بی‌دلی در همه احوال خدا با او بود   او نمی‌دیدش و از دور خدایا می‌کرد

> Search for the cup of Jamshīd (Divine knowledge) from me (Ẓāhid and 'Abid), years my heart made.
> And for what it (the cup) possessed, from a stranger, entreaty made.
> One heart bereft (the lover of God), with him, in all states, is God:
> (But) he beheld him not, and from afar (the cry): 'For God's sake (be my helper)' made.[1]

It is for this reason that we come across with two types of verses in the Qur'an: outward (*āfāqī*) and inward (*anfusī*) verses. Outward verses refer to the verses about the things outside man's innermost being: the creation of other beings, the skies, the earth, the stars, the mountains, the plants, the animals, etc. Inward verses, meanwhile, refer to the verses about that which exists in man's innermost being. And the Qur'an gives more importance to the inward verses than to the outward verses, and the term *āfāq wa anfus* is also taken from the Qur'an which states, thus:

---

1. Ḥāfiẓ, *Ghazaliyyāt*, *ghazal* 143. [Trans.]

﴿ سَنُرِيهِمْ آيَاتِنَا فِي الآفَاقِ وَفِي أَنْفُسِهِمْ حَتَّى يَتَبَيَّنَ لَهُمْ أَنَّهُ الْحَقُّ ﴾

Soon We shall show them Our signs in the horizons and in their own souls until it becomes clear to them that He is the Real. (41:53)[1]

As we have said, *āfāq wa anfus* (horizons and souls) which became part of Muslim scholars' jargon [to mean 'outward and inward' or 'physical and spiritual'] is taken from the Qur'an.

Let us see to what extent [Islam] acknowledges the human being's primacy by affirming an intrinsic inward nature for him:

وَيُثِيرُوا لَهُمْ دَفَائِنَ الْعُقُولِ.

"...to unveil before them the hidden virtues of wisdom."

﴿ وَفِي الأَرْضِ آيَاتٌ لِلْمُوقِنِينَ * وَفِي أَنْفُسِكُمْ أَفَلا تُبْصِرُونَ ﴾

In the earth are signs for those who have conviction, and in your own souls [as well]. Will you not then perceive? (51:20-21)

This is also a statement from *Nahj al-Balāghah.*

Imām al-Sajjād's (A.S.) Saying

There is a statement in *Ṣaḥīfah al-Sajjādiyyah.* Incidentally, this statement is also in the first supplication of *Ṣaḥīfah al-Sajjādiyyah.* It is a supplication which begins with praise and eulogy to God and its entirety is a supplication of praises and eulogy. In the initial part of the supplication, there is this statement:

ابْتَدَعَ بِقُدْرَتِهِ الْخَلْقَ ابْتِدَاعاً.

"He originated the creatures through His power with

1. Or 'until it becomes clear to them that it [i.e. the Qur'an, or Islam] (or he) [i.e. the Apostle] is the truth.' [Q. Trans.]

an origination."

We have said that *ibdāʿ* (origination) means creating something on the basis of no imitation or duplication. We have said that the human being is also a kind of creator in this own realm and to the extent of his power, but his creatorship – although we call it 'origination' – is based on a pattern (in nature or creation). God, the Exalted, however, who is the Creator of the universe, had no precedent in that He would create something from a sketch.

وَاخْتَرَعَهُمْ عَلَى مَشِيَّتِهِ اخْتِرَاعاً.

"And He devised them in accordance with His will with a devising."

Ikhtirāʿ (to devise) also gives the meaning of *ibdāʿ*; that is, God is the [sole] Deviser, just as, for example, a certain person initially originated – as we say – voice recording. The succeeding persons could not be considered 'originators' no matter what they will do.

ثُمَّ سَلَكَ بِهِمْ طَرِيقَ إِرَادَتِهِ، وَبَعَثَهُمْ فِي سَبِيلِ مَحَبَّتِهِ.

"Then He made them walk[1] on the path of His desire, and He sent them out on the way of His love."

Basing on the succeeding indication, it means that through the path of creation, He desires (and not in the path of what He has desired). In the path which He desires, He put them and made them walk. The next statement made the point clearer:

"And He sent them out on the way of His love."

(It is a very amazing statement.) That is, all these motions and movements of creation – whether they know it or not – are

1. *Salaka* means to walk or make a stride. When *salaka* is mentioned with *bi* (*bā' al-taʿdiyyah*), it means 'to let someone walk'.

basically along the path of God's love. On the issue of love (*'ishq*), we have engaged in some discussions. [We have said that] even the one who looks for other-than-God, his main motivation is searching for God. He is mistaken in the application. Now, the word *khāliq* (creator) which was mentioned in the beginning of this statement – "He originated the creatures through His power with an origination" – may possibly means absolute creation and origination which naturally includes that of the human being. In this case, the statement means that all facets of existence move along the path of God's love. The plant which moves has nothing except His love. The stone, which moves through what we call the 'force of attraction,' is in reality nothing except that it searches for the essence of the Real and that His love is embedded in his being. Then verses such as the following shall acquire more general very broad scope of meaning:

﴿ وَإِن مِّن شَيْءٍ إِلاَّ يُسَبِّحُ بِحَمْدَهِ وَلَكِن لاَّ تَفْقَهُونَ تَسْبِيحَهُمْ ﴾

> There is not a thing but celebrates His praise, but you do not understand their glorification. (17:44)

﴿ أَفَغَيْرَ دِينِ اللهِ يَبْغُونَ وَلَهُ أَسْلَمَ مَنْ فِي السَّمَاوَاتِ وَالأَرْضِ ﴾

> Do they, then, seek a religion other than Allah's, while to Him submit whosoever there is in the heavens and the earth? (3:83)

﴿ وَلِلهِ يَسْجُدُ مَنْ فِي السَّمَاوَاتِ وَالأَرْضِ طَوْعًا وَكَرْهًا ﴾

> "To Allah prostrates whoever there is in the heavens and the earth, willingly or unwillingly."(13:15)

(Or, "...whatever there is in the heavens and the earth" can be found in numerous other verses.)

﴿ سَبَّحَ لِلَّهِ مَا فِي السَّمَاوَاتِ وَمَا فِي الْأَرْضِ وَهُوَ الْعَزِيزُ الْحَكِيمُ ﴾

> Whatever there is in the heavens glorifies Allah and whatever there is in the earth. (59:1, 61:1)

That is, the Qur'an gives us an amazingly broad worldview. Mystic poets have said many things in this regard, such as those famous poems by, apparently, Niẓāmī:[1]

خبر داری که سیاحان افلاک   چرا گردند گرد مرکز خاک
چه می‌خواهند از این منزل بریدن   که می جویند از این محمل کشیدن
در این محرابگه معبودشان کیست   از این آمد شدن مقصودشان چیست

Are you aware of those who travel in the heavens?
Do you know why do they roam around the earth?
They have detached from this abode and want to unload this burden.
But do you know whom they are seeking?
In this earth which is also their locus of worship and altar, do you know their Object of worship?
Do you know their goal in this coming and leaving this world?[2]

He then says:

همه هستند سرگردان چو پرگار   پدید آرنده خود را طلبکار

All are wanderers like a compass,
Searching for the One that originated them.[3]

---

1. Niẓām al-Dīn Abū Muḥammad Ilyās ibn Yūsuf ibn Zakkī, better known as Nizāmī Ganjawī (1141 – 1209): considered the greatest romantic epic poet in Persian literature and best known for his five long narrative poems, the *Khamsah* or *Panj Ganj* (*Five Treasures*). [Trans.]
2. Nizāmī, *Panj Ganj*, Khosrow and Shīrīn, part 3. [Trans.]
3. *Ibid.* [Trans.]

[He discloses] the same truth. Also, the popular poem in the famous *ghazal*[1] of Ḥāfiẓ commences with this couplet:

ما در این در نه پی حشمت و جاه آمده‌ایم
از بد حادثه اینجا به پناه آمده‌ایم

Not in pursuit of pomp and of pageant, to this door (of the murshid) we have come:
For shelter from ill-fortune, here we have come.[2]

He then says:

رهرو منزل عشقیم ز سر حدّ عدم   تا به اقلیم وجود اینهمه راه آمده‌ایم

Wayfarers of love's stage are we: and from the limits of non-existence.
Up to the climes of existence, all this way we have come.[3]

The secret behind the creation is love. (It is a very elegant *ghazal*.)

آبرو می‌رود ای ابر خطاشوی ببار   که به دیوان عمل نامه سیاه آمده‌ایم

O cloud, sin-cleansing! Honour goeth; (mercy) rain:
For in the court of action (as opposed to theory) black of book, we have come.[4]

Ḥāfiẓ has many [poems] about this subject. It is not just one or two. I shall recite a *ghazal* from him which is a bit clearer [in

1. *Ghazal* is a lyric form of Persian poetry, with rhyme in the first two and in even numbered lines, and allowing various metric forms. With respect to content, it usually does not express the linear development of an idea, but rather its couplets express variations on an idea or mood. [Trans.]
2. Ḥāfiẓ, *Ghazaliyyāt*, *ghazal* 366. [Trans.]
3. *Ibid.* [Trans.]
4. *Ibid.* [Trans.]

meaning]:

روشن از پرتوی رویت نظری نیست که نیست
منّت خاک درت بر بصری نیست که نیست
ناظر روی تو صاحبنظران‌اند آری
سرّ گیسوی تو در هیچ سری نیست که نیست

(O true beloved!) From the ray of Thy face, luminous a glance is not, that is not:[1]
The favour (of collyrium) of the dust of Thy door, on an eye is not, that is not.[2]
Those possessed of sight (the prophets who, with the inward eye, behold the real beauty of God), are the spectator of Thy face. Yes:
The desire of Thy tress, in any, a desire is not, that is not.[3]

The experts are those who see you and know that they see, while others are those who see and they themselves do not know that they can see.

مصلحت نیست که از پرده برون افتد راز
ورنه در مجلس رندان خبری نیست که نیست

No good counsel is it that the mystery should fall out of the screen.
And, if not, in the assembly of profligates, a piece of news (of both worlds) is not that is not.[4]

1. That is to say that he is nobody, not even a denier. His glance at the ray of the Beloved's face is not clear, yet he does not know or understand it.
2. It emphasizes the same point with a different expression.
3. Ḥāfiẓ, *Ghazaliyyāt*, *ghazal* 73. [Trans.]
4. *Ibid.* [Trans.]

Ḥājjī Sabziwārī,[1] author of the treatise *[Sharḥ] al-Manẓūmah*,[2] is a sage, philosopher, mystic, and an extremely pious man with good composure. His fame pertains to his knowledge, but his status in the field of action is higher than that of his knowledge. He also used to compose poetry, both in Arabic and Fārsī. Of course, he is not a first-class poet but he has elegant poems anyway. Some of his poems are indeed excellent. He has welcomed this *ghazal* of Ḥāfiẓ. One or two poems in it could, more or less, be at par with those of Ḥāfiẓ, and these have also become very popular. He recites, thus:

شورش عشق تو در هیچ سری نیست که نیست
منظر روی تو زیب نظری نیست که نیست

The uproar of Your love is not in anyone's head that is not.
A glance of You is not a sight's beauty that is not.

He utters the same words of Ḥāfiẓ with the following expression:

نیست یک مرغ دلی کش نفکندی به قفس
تیر بیداد تو تا پر به پری نیست که نیست
نه همین از غم او سینه ما صد چاک است
داغ او لاله صفت بر جگری نیست که نیست

A bird of the heart is not that which is not taken out of

1. Ḥājj Mullā Hādī Sabziwārī (1797-1878): a famous Iranian philosopher, mystic theologian and poet noted for disseminating and clarifying the doctrines of Mullā Ṣadrā, and who wrote some fifty works of prose and poetry in both Arabic and Persian. [Trans.]

2. Written in Arabic and completed in around 1845, *Sharḥ al-Manẓūmah* (*A Treatise on Logic in Verse*) likewise known as *Ghurar al-Farā'id*, one of Sabziwārī's more notable works with numerous later commentaries, is a versified summary and commentary of the transcendence philosophy of Mullā Ṣadrā. [Trans.]

the cage.
The shooting pain of your injustice not full is not that is not.
It is not that out of your grief our breasts are a hundred times torn.
His mark is not tulip-like on a liver that is not.

The *ghazal*'s distich of his most popular poem is as follows:

موسیای نیست که دعوی انا الحق شنود
ورنه این زمزمه اندر شجری نیست که نیست
چشم ما دیده خفّاش بود ورنه تو را
پرتو حسن به دیوار و دری نیست که نیست
گوش اسرار شنو نیست و گرنه «اسرار»
برش از عالم معنا خبری نیست که نیست

He is not Moses that could hear the cry of 'I am the Truth!'
And if not, this is not a murmur in the tree (bush) that is not.[1]
Our eyes saw the bat, otherwise, you.
It is not a ray of beauty in the wall and door that is not.
He listens not to the Secrets (*asrār*), otherwise to *Asrār*.[2]
He is not aware of the noumental world that is not.

At any rate, this passage in *Ṣaḥīfah al-Sajjādiyyah* is also extraordinarily amazing, instructive and meaningful. Now, if we take the meaning of absolute creation for *khalq* (origination) in the

1. It alludes to the occasion of the beginning of prophethood of Prophet Mūsā (Moses) (A.S.) by receiving Divine revelation through the burning bush granted with the power of speech by God in the sacred valley of Ṭuwā. See Qur'an 20:12 and 79:16. [Trans.]
2. 'Asrār' is Sabziwārī's pseudonym. *Asrār* (*Secrets*) is also the title of a collection of his poetry. [Trans.]

statement "He originated the creatures through His power with an origination," then [these statements] constitute a general philosophy for the entire creation which includes the human being, and if we consider *khalq* to refer exclusively to the human beings, then obviously it still includes the human beings. These are among the things that I would like to highlight as an example – concepts which can be found in Islamic sources.

Intuitive and Sensory Natural Disposition

Now, I shall initially mention a subject and then I shall embark on elucidating the verses (the Verse of *Fiṭrah* and Verse of Pre-existence).

Regarding man's natural disposition (*fiṭrah*), we might have two types of *fiṭrah* which are not contradictory but rather complement each other. One is the intuitive (*adrākī*) natural disposition while the other is sensory (*iḥsāsī*) natural disposition. (*Iḥsās* is meant in the same way when we pluralize and call it *iḥsāsāt* (senses or emotion).) Intuitive natural disposition means that religion or monotheism in particular – which we will discuss under the verse '...the origination of Allah according to which He originated mankind' (30:30) – is intuitively or mentally intrinsic for the human being. That is, it is an idea which the human mind intrinsically accepts and in accepting it, he is in no need of a lesson, teacher and school. [And in general,] whatever we call intuitively 'intrinsic' means that it needs no proof, it is basically self-evident and it is one of the propositions whose proofs, if ever needed, are embedded in them.

قضايا قياساتها معها

> "[They are] propositions whose analogies are with them."

Since its proof is always attached to itself, again there is no need for a teacher to teach it to a person in school. This is what we call 'intrinsic perception' (*adrāk-e fiṭrī*) which is related to the realm of the mind, perception and intellect. Now, I shall cite another example of it from the corpus of *ḥadīth*.

There is a tradition mentioned in *Tafsīr al-Ṣāfī*,[1] which is narrated from Imām al-'Askarī (A.S.). It is a very elaborate tradition. Although its chain of transmission (*sanad*) is not so reliable (*mu'tabar*), its content is something which, Shaykh al-Anṣārī says, shows indications of its authenticity. It is so interesting as well. It is under this verse:

﴿ وَمِنْهُمْ أُمِّيُّونَ لَا يَعْلَمُونَ الْكِتَابَ إِلَّا أَمَانِيَّ ﴾

> Among them are the illiterate who know nothing of the Book except hearsay. (2:78)

The Qur'an condemns a bunch of ignorant Jews. That is, apart from condemning [the likes of] Aḥbār[2] and his cohorts, it says, "Among them are the illiterate who know nothing of the Book except hearsay." A group of them is also an illiterate people who know nothing of their Torah except a set of wishes and imaginations (such as the Muslim masses [with respect to the

1. *Al-Ṣāfī fī Tafsīr Kalām Allāh al-Wāfī* (*The Purity in the Exegesis of the Sufficient Word of Allah*), better known as *Tafsīr al-Ṣāfī* (*The Pure Exegesis*) is an exegesis of the Qur'an written by Muḥsin Fayḍ Kāshānī (died 1680), an Iranian Muslim poet, philosopher and *muḥaddith* (*ḥadīth* scholar). [Trans.]
2. Perhaps, it alludes to the likes of Ka'ab al-Aḥbār (full name: Abū Iṣḥaq Ka'ab ibn Matī' al-Humyarī al-Aḥbār) (died 32 AH) who was a prominent Jewish rabbi from Yemen who converted to Islam during the caliphate of 'Umar ibn al-Khaṭṭāb, and narrated many *Isrā'iliyyāt* (the body of narratives originating from Jewish and Christian traditions, rather than from other well-accepted sources that quote Prophet Muḥammad (S)). [Trans.]

Qur'an]). They just know that there is the Torah, but if we ask them about its content, they know nothing. Perhaps, there are certain things, which they think, could be found in the Torah but these are not there, and there are things which could be found in the Torah but they think these are not there. They are so uninformed. The tradition is as follows:

Someone asked Imām al-Ṣādiq (A.S.) about the fault of the illiterate masses. The Qur'an itself acknowledges that they are ignorant and illiterate people. Whatever they know is what the learned among them have taught. All the blame, therefore, should be shouldered by the learned ones. The common people have no faults of their own. They are supposed to be excused in the eyes of God. Why does the Qur'an condemn them? [In reply,] the Imām (A.S.) had an elaborate discussion. In one of the monthly lectures that I had in that association approximately 15 years ago,[1] I had cited many parts of this tradition. There the Imām (A.S.) made a very excellent discussion, dividing the men of learning into what they are and what they are not, describing the wicked scholars and the righteous scholars, and asserting that the evil deeds of scholars are more harmful to Islam than the army of Yazīd ibn Mu'āwiyah to Ḥusayn ibn 'Alī (A.S.), etc.

The discussion touched on the common people. The Imām (A.S.) said, "No. It is not so. There are things which they do not need to understand such that we could say that since they have not studied, they are excused. On some issues, the common people are excused – issues which they must have learned and they have learned them because others hindered them from learning so. Naturally, they are excused. There are other issues, however, which require no

1. [The transcript of] this lecture has been published in the book *Dah Guftār* (*Ten Discourses*) with the title *Aṣl-e Ijtihād dar Islam* (The Principle of *Ijtihād* in Islam).]

learning [to understand them]. Since they are intrinsic pieces of knowledge, the human heart could inevitably understand them." The Imām (A.S.) then cited an example and what an excellent example it was! He (A.S.) said that the Jewish populace would saw that they instructed them to observe God-wariness (*taqwā*) and purity of intention, not to practice usury (*ribā*), and not to eat forbidden foods, but they themselves would not act upon their own instructions. In fact, they would do the opposite, and the common people openly saw these things. Then the Imām (A.S.) said:

وَقَدْ اضطرّوا بمعارف قلوبهم.

That is to say, under necessity and compulsion, man's heart could understand it for being an intrinsic piece of knowledge that if somebody commanded something and was doing the opposite, his words could not be trusted words and he must be rejected. It requires no more learning in any university that if the people see a scholar urging them to be God-conscious, yet he is not God-conscious himself, they should not follow him. This needs no more going to any university or school. Everyone's natural disposition could understand to that extent.

We call these as 'primary intrinsic perceptions' which a person could naturally understand to that extent even if no one teaches them.

One type of *fiṭrah*, therefore, is 'intrinsic natural disposition'. In this context, we say "Religion is intrinsic" or "Monotheism is intrinsic". That is, it is based on intrinsic perception. The second [type] is sensory natural disposition. That is, attention to God and even attention to the religious commands are [in such way that] the human emotion draws him toward God and religion. Two points are involved here. Sometimes we say that a person intrinsically knows God, and at other times we say that intrinsically he is inclined and attracted to God.

Now, we have to see meaning of whatever is mentioned in the Qur'an, *Nahj al-Balāghah*, *Ṣaḥīfah al-Sajjādiyyah*, and sayings of the pure Imāms (A.S.) regarding the intrinsic nature of religion, in general, and monotheism (*tawḥīd*), in particular. Does it mean that religion and monotheism are intrinsic from the perspective of intuitive natural disposition in the sense that there is an intrinsic perception in man? Or, does it mean that these are intrinsic inclination and inherent attraction for him? Or, does it mean both? In the next session when, God willing, we will discuss some verses and elaborate them further, perhaps, inevitably we will touch on these statements again. We will deal with this subject, "Religion in general, or monotheism in particular which is one of the principles of religion, is intrinsic." Does it mean that religion or monotheism is an intrinsic perception in the human being, or is it an intrinsic feeling and inclination in him?[1]

---

1. [As can be deduced from the words of Professor Muṭahharī, the discussion on *fiṭrah* – especially the discussion on [pertinent] verses of the Qur'an – was supposed to be continued, but apparently the lecture series has ended here and the said sessions were not held anymore there.]

Bibliograghy

The Holy Qur'an.

'Abd al-Laṭīf ibn Muḥammad al-Khaṭīb, *Matn Alfiyyat Ibn Mālik,* (Kuwait: Maktabat Dār al-'Arūbah Li'n-Nashr wa't-Tawzī', 2006).

'Alī Qulī Qarā'ī', *The Qur'an with a Phrase-by-Phrase English Translation,* (London: Islamic College for Advanced Studies, 2004).

'Alī Rabbānī Gulpāygānī', *Discursive Theology* (Makati City, Philippines: Al-Mustafa International College, 2013).

Bertrand Russell, *Human Society in Ethics and Society,* (London: George Allen & Unwin, 1954).

Ibn Abi Al-Jumhūr 'Iḥsā 'ī, *Ghawālī al-La'ālī,* (Qum: Sayyid al-Shohadā, 1405 A.H.).

Ilyās ibn Yūsuf Nizāmī, *Panj Ganj,* Khusrow and Shīrīn, (Tehran: Mu'assisah Farhangī Kitāb-e Khūb, 1391 S.A.H.).

Imām 'Alī, *Nahj al-Balāghah,* trans. 'Ali Raza, (Qum: Foundation of Islamic Cultural Propagation in the World, 1995).

Imām 'Alī, *Nahj al-Balāghah,* trans. Fayḍ al-Islām, (Tehran: Ḥeydarī, d).

Imām Khomeinī, *Ṣaḥīfeh-ye Imām: An Anthology of Imām Khomeinī's Speeches, Messages, Interviews, Religious Decrees, Permissions, and Letters,* volumes 1-22 (Tehran: The Institute for Compilation and Publication of Imām Khomeinī's Works, 2007).

Jalāl al-Dīn Muḥammad Mawlāwī, *The Mathnawī of Jalālu'ddīn Rūmī,* edited by. Reynold A. Nicholson, (Tehran: Soad Publisher, 2002).

Mubārak Ibn Muḥammad Ibn al-'Athīr, *Al-Nihāyah,* (Qum: 'Īsmā'īliyān Publications, 1367 S.A.H.).

Muḥammad Bāqir Majlisī, *Biḥār al-Anwār,* (Tehran: Dār Kutub al-Islāmiyyah, 1362 S.A.H).

Muḥammad ibn Ismā'īl Al-Bukhārī, *Al-Ṣaḥīḥ* (Bierut: Dār al-Fikr, 1401 A.H.).

Muḥammad ibn Ya'qūb Kulaynī, *Al-Kāfī*, (Tehran: Dār Kutub al-Islāmiyyah, 1362 S.A.H).

Muḥammad Riḍā Al-Muẓaffar, *Al-Manṭiq*, (Qum: Daftar Tablīghāt Islāmī, 1392 A.H.).

Muḥammad Shams al-Dīn Ḥāfiẓ, *The Dīwān of Ḥāfiẓ* (Tehran: Aban Book, 2005).

Murtaḍā Muṭahharī, *Fiṭrat* (Tehran: Ṣadrā Publications, 1385 S.A.H).

Robert Edward Egner, *Bertrand Russell's Best* (*Barguzīdeh-ye Afkār-e Russell*), (Tehran: Shirkat-e Sahāmī Intishār, 1350 S.A.H).

Ṣadr al-Dīn Muḥammad Shīrāzī, *Al-Ḥikmat al-Muta'āliyah fī al-Asfār al-'Aqlīyyat al-Arba'ah* (Tehran: Dār al-Ma'ārif al-Islāmiyyah, 1378 A.H).

Shaykh 'Abbās Qumī, *Safīnat al-Biḥār*, (Tehran: Farāhānī, 1363 S.A.H).

Shaykh 'Abbās Qummī, *Nafas al-Mahmūm*, (Qum: Dalīl-e Mā, 1389 S.A.H).

Shaykh Muṣliḥ al-Dīn Sa'dī, *Kulliyāt Sa'dī*, ed. Muḥammad 'Alī Furūghī, (Tehran: Muḥammad Ḥasan'Ilmī, d).

Shaykh Muṣliḥ al-Dīn Sa'dī, *Gulistān of Sa'dī*, (Tehran: Peyk-e Farhang, 1998).

Shaykh Muṣliḥ al-Dīn Sa'dī, *The Būstān of Sa'dī*, (Tehran: Peyk-e Farhang, 2004).

Shaykh Ṣadūq, *'Ilal al-Sharāyi'*, (Qum: Al-Sharīf al-Raḍī, 1379 S.A.H).

Index

Abū Dharr al-Ghiffārī, 187
Abū Rayḥān, 68
American, 87, 88, 106, 115
Ancient Greece, 93
Aristotle, 43, 44
Asia, 56
Balkh, 66

Bergson, Henri-Louis, 189
Biḥār al-Anwār, 21, 25, 174, 224
biology, 129
British, 45, 69, 89
Būstān, 1, 56

capitalism, 111, 112
Carrel, Alexis, 41
China, 159
Christianity, 23, 24, 148, 156, 159, 185
Comte, Auguste, 151, 152, 153, 166
constitution, 31, 33, 34, 35, 44, 45, 55, 163

Dah Guftār (*Ten Discourses*), 239
dialectic, 141
dialectical materialism, 54
Du'ā' Kumayl, 178

Egypt, 56, 114, 159
empiricist, 89
Europe, 93, 132, 140, 146
existentialism, Faculty of Law, Farīmān, 131

Feuerbach, Ludwig Andreas von,
France, 141, 142, 147, 149, 210, 211
France, 4
Freud, Sigmund, 87, 88, 116

general relativity, 116
Germany, 44, 45, 94, 115, 141, 184, 189
Ghazālī, Imām Muḥammad Ḥamīd, 175
Gulistān, 1, 56, 95

Ḥāfiẓ, Khwājah Shams al-Dīn Muḥammad, 1, 75, 170, 203, 228, 233, 234, 235
heart (qalb), 15, 43, 71, 76, 105, 157, 167, 174, 177, 178, 179, 203, 218, 225, 228, 235, 240
Hegel, Georg Wilhelm Friedrich, 49, 132, 141, 142, 146
Hume, David, 45
Ḥusayn ibn 'Alī, Imām al-Shahīd ('a), 169

ibn Sīnā, 66

Iḥyā-ye Tafakkur-e Islām (The Revival of Islamic Thought), 6
Imām Khomeinī, 4, 5, 9
India, 56, 200
individualism (individualist), 13, 14, 61, 63, 69, 70, 71, 85, 96, 152, 181, 193, 195, 196, 197, 199, 201, 202, 205, 206, 209, 211
Iran (Iranian), 6, 66, 83, 113, 114, 124, 125, 139, 191
Iraq, 225
Iṣfahān, 73
Islamic Revolution, 5, 9, 139

Ja'far ibn Muḥammad, Imām al-Ṣādiq ('a), 22, 239
James, William, 87, 88, 189
Judaism (Jew), 24, 148, 159, 184

Kant, Immanuel. See , See , See , See , See , See , See , See , See

Laylā al-'Āmirī, 81, 82, 98, 100
Locke, John, 45
London, 1, 7, 156
Majnūn al-'Āmirī, 81, 82, 83, 98, 99
Marxism (Marxist), 45, 50, 101, 112, 130, 132, 134, 182, 185, 190
Mashhad, 4, 73
materialism (materialist), 54, 94, 95
mathematical rules, 114, 116
metaphysics (metaphysician), 66
Mu'āwiyah ibn Abī Sufyān, 168, 209, 239
Muṭahharī, 1, 2, 4, 5, 6, 8, 9, 45, 118, 140, 142, 166, 181, 211, 241

Nahj al-Balāghah, 1, 18, 142, 168, 209, 223, 226, 229, 241
Najaf, 225
Nāṣir al-Dīn Shāh Qājar, 125

Paris, 4
Pharaoh, 112, 185
philosophers, 44, 45, 46, 66, 68, 85, 86, 88, 101, 108, 119, 126, 141, 144, 155, 160, 163, 197
physics, 66, 115, 189
Plato, 43, 45, 53, 77
polytheism (shirk), 172
Prophet Ādam (Adam) ('a), 23, 101, 148, 161, 220, 221
Prophet Ibrāhīm (Abraham) ('a), 24
Prophet Mūsā (Moses) (*'a*), 24, 236
psychoanalysis, 80, 85, 87psychology ('ilm al-nafs), 55, 67

Qum, 1, 2, 4, 6, 8, 73, 139
Qummī, Shaykh 'Abbās, 21, 169
Quraysh, 20

rationalism (rationalist), 94
Religion and the Mind, 88
Rūmī, Jalāl al-Dīn Muḥammad, 1, 76, 86, 96, 98, 109, 144, 145, 154
Russell, Bertrand, 89, 155, 156, 157, 189

Sa'dī, 1
Sa'dī, Muṣliḥ ibn 'Abd Allāh, 56, 95, 170, 175, 177
Sabziwārī, Ḥājj Mullā Hādī, 235, 236
Ṣadr al-Muta'ālihīn, Muhammad ibn Ibrāhīm (Mullah Ṣadrā), 75
Safīnat al-Baḥār, 21
Shāh 'Abbās, 73
Shī'ah, 6, 96, 97, 139, 218, 224, 225
Shushtarī, 172
socialism, 129, 141
Socrates, 43, 47, 48, 70, 115, 117
Soviet Union (Soviets), 204
Spencer, Herbert, 151, 152

spirituality, 129, 135
Suhrawardī, Shaykh Yaḥyā (Shaykh al-Ishrāq), 56, 66
Suhrawardī, Shaykh Yaḥyā (Shaykh al-Ishrāq), 66
Sunnah, 10
Sunnī, 96, 97, 218, 224, 225
Switzerland (Swiss), 115

Tehran, 1, 2, 4, 5, 6, 8, 82, 125, 139, 142, 172
Torah, 148, 187, 238
Ṭūsī, Khwājah Naṣīr al-Dīn Muḥammad, 81, 125

Uṣūl-e Falsafeh wa Rawish-e Realism (The Principles of Philosophy and the Method of Realism), 45

wisdom (ḥikmah), 65, 115, 117, 169, 226, 227, 229

www.ingramcontent.com/pod-product-compliance
Lightning Source LLC
Chambersburg PA
CBHW021431080526
44588CB00009B/498
9781922583208